GEORG FORSTER

THE MAX KADE RESEARCH INSTITUTE SERIES:
GERMANS BEYOND EUROPE

Series Editor *Founding Editor*
Daniel Purdy   A. Gregg Roeber

The Max Kade Research Institute Series is an outlet for scholarship that examines the history and culture of German-speaking communities in America and across the globe from the early modern period to the present. Books in this series examine the movements of the German-speaking diaspora as influenced by forces such as migration, colonization, war, research, religious missions, or trade. This series explores the historical and cultural depictions of the international networks that connect these communities, as well as linguistic relations between German and other languages within European global networks.

This series is a project of the Max Kade Research Institute located on Penn State's campus. It was founded in 1993 thanks to a grant from the Max Kade Foundation, New York.

Georg Forster

German Cosmopolitan

TODD KONTJE

The Pennsylvania State University Press
University Park, Pennsylvania

Library of Congress Cataloging-in-Publication Data

Names: Kontje, Todd Curtis, 1954– author.
Title: Georg Forster : German cosmopolitan / Todd Kontje.
Other titles: Max Kade German-American Research Institute series.
Description: University Park, Pennsylvania : The Pennsylvania State University Press, [2022] | Series: The Max Kade Research Institute series : Germans beyond Europe | Includes bibliographical references and index.
Summary: "Examines the life and work of writer and political activist Georg Forster (1754–1794), a participant in Captain Cook's second voyage and one of the leading figures in the Mainz Republic"— Provided by publisher.
Identifiers: LCCN 2022006302 | ISBN 9780271093260 (hardback) | ISBN 9780271093277 (paper)
Subjects: LCSH: Forster, Georg, 1754–1794—Criticism and interpretation. | Forster, Georg, 1754–1794—Travel—Pacific Area. | Forster, Georg, 1754–1794—Travel—Rhine River. | Travelers' writings, German—18th century—History and criticism. | Mainz (Rhineland-Palatinate, Germany)—History—18th century.
Classification: LCC PT1865.F15 Z76 2022 | DDC 838/.609—dc23/eng/20220419
LC record available at https://lccn.loc.gov/2022006302

Copyright © 2022 Todd Kontje
All rights reserved
Printed in the United States of America
Published by The Pennsylvania State University Press,
University Park, PA 16802-1003

The Pennsylvania State University Press is a member of the Association of University Presses.

It is the policy of The Pennsylvania State University Press to use acid-free paper. Publications on uncoated stock satisfy the minimum requirements of American National Standard for Information Sciences—Permanence of Paper for Printed Library Material, ANSI Z39.48–1992.

CONTENTS

Acknowledgments (vii)

    Introduction (1)
1. What Is an Author? (24)
2. A Voyage Round the World (43)
3. Race, History, and German Classicism (83)
4. Views of the Lower Rhine (113)
5. Revolution in Mainz: Liberation or Conquest? (143)

    Conclusion: A Different Kind of Classic (171)

Notes (175)
Bibliography (185)
Index (195)

ACKNOWLEDGMENTS

I would like to thank the Academic Senate Research Grant Committee of the University of California, San Diego, for funding a trip to Germany in September 2019, which included visits to Weimar, the German Literary Archive in Marbach, and the permanent exhibit on "Georg Forster und die Wörlitzer Südseesammlung" in Dessau-Wörlitz.

I am grateful for the permission to reuse some of the material from my article "Decentering Germany's Classical Center: Colonial Critique and Weimar Classicism" that appeared in *German Quarterly* 93 (2020): 221–36.

I thank Kathryn Bourque Yahner and Daniel Leonhard Purdy for their interest in my work, and the production team at Penn State University Press for transforming my manuscript into a book. Finally, I would like to acknowledge the exceptionally detailed and thoughtful comments from the two anonymous readers for the press. As always, my greatest debt is to my family.

Georg Forster (ca. 1782), anonymous silhouette. Reproduced with the permission of SLUB Dresden / Deutsche Fotothek / photographer unknown.

Introduction

When twenty-year-old Georg Forster returned to Europe in the summer of 1775, he was already famous. Forster had sailed around the world with Captain Cook, drifted among icebergs off the coast of Antarctica, and spent time on Tahiti, the island that inspired European fantasies of tropical paradise. For most Europeans, for whom travel across even short distances was difficult, dangerous, and prohibitively expensive, Forster was the equivalent of an astronaut who had walked on the moon or returned from a voyage to Mars. For the rest of his life—which was cut short by the hardships he endured along his journey—Georg Forster remained a celebrity.[1] Shortly after returning to London, Forster and his father were granted an audience with King George III, and a few days later they presented the queen with exotic animals from their voyage.[2] In January 1777, Forster became one of the youngest scientists ever elected to the Royal Society; later that year, Forster met with the comte de Buffon, Louis-Antoine de Bougainville, and Benjamin Franklin in Paris. "I was horribly fêted," wrote Forster with some embarrassment after attending a large dinner party in his honor among high society in Vienna, where he was toasted with a poem in his honor.[3] The next day, Emperor Joseph II spoke to Forster in private; two months later, Forster dined with the king of Poland. Goethe sought him out on more than one occasion. Forster visited with Wieland and Herder in Weimar and corresponded with Schiller and Kant. In the days before photography, people did not always recognize celebrities, and there are accounts of Forster surprising a young man in Düsseldorf who happened to be speaking about a certain Forster who had made a journey around the world. When Forster identified himself as the person in question, the man was taken aback: "You should have seen his astonishment and joy!"[4]

Forster's fall from favor was as abrupt as his ascent to fame. In 1793, he become one of the leaders of the Mainz Republic, a short-lived attempt to establish a revolutionary democracy on German soil. Forster renounced his ties to Germany and declared his allegiance to France before setting off to Paris to seek recognition for the new republic. His speech before the National Assembly achieved the desired goal, but he won a Pyrrhic victory. Prussian troops quickly crushed the Mainz Republic, and Forster was left alone in Paris, where he was increasingly disturbed by the rising toll of the revolutionary tribunals. Abandoned by his wife and mortally ill, Forster struggled on for several months before he died in Paris at the age of thirty-nine. Within a year of his death, Goethe and Schiller mocked the revolutionary idealist in their satiric "Xenia," setting the tone for generations of Germans who could not forgive Forster for his betrayal of the nation.[5] There were a few exceptions: Friedrich Schlegel praised Forster for his prose style and personal integrity, liberal literary historian Georg Gottfried Gervinus commended Forster's turn from literature to politics as an admirable example for a nation of disengaged subjects, and Alexander von Humboldt remained loyal to his friend long after he had become unfashionable. For the most part, however, Forster was forgotten. There was no nineteenth-century critical edition of his works, no scholarly biography, not even a statue erected in his honor or a street named after him.[6]

Forster's revolutionary politics were primarily to blame for his eclipsed fame, and those same politics have swung the pendulum back in his favor in the twentieth and twenty-first centuries. The German Democratic Republic embraced Forster as a "socialist figurehead": one of the few "good Germans" who embraced revolutionary democracy and thus anticipated the antifascist agenda of the communist state.[7] More recent postcolonial critics have rediscovered Forster's polemics against Christoph Meiners, a racist anthropologist admired by the Nazis, and celebrated him as a cosmopolitan humanist in an age of European imperialism.[8] The sense remains, however, that Georg Forster is a writer more often referenced than read by contemporary critics. In his prize-winning study of Germany's contributions to the theory of world literature, for instance, B. Venkat Mani correctly highlights Forster's role in the transmission of ancient

Indian literature to Germany with his translation of the Sanskrit play *Sakuntala*. In the same paragraph, however, Mani makes a series of inaccurate statements: Forster was not "a young German migrant... who had been living in England since the age of seven" when he encountered Jones's work. Forster arrived in England for the first time in early October 1766, when he was eleven years old, and left in the fall of 1778, a dozen years before he discovered Sir William Jones's English rendering of *Sakuntala* during a brief visit to London in the early summer of 1790 (not 1791, as Mani incorrectly states). "Georg had published the journals of his father," Mani continues, "first in English as *A Voyage Towards the South Pole and Round the World* (1777), and then in German as *Reise um die Welt* (1778–80)."[9] Here again, imprecisions abound: Forster drew on his father's journals, but the travelogue is his own work and its title in English is *A Voyage Round the World in His Britannic Majesty's Sloop, Resolution*. *A Voyage Towards the South Pole* was written by Captain Cook.

These minor inaccuracies do not detract from Mani's monumental achievement in tracing the history of Germany's engagement with world literature over the past two hundred years. I cite them here only to highlight the clouds of obscurity that continue to shroud the figure of Georg Forster. Unlike Goethe, Forster was not a creative writer and thus left no body of poetry or prose for posterity. Nor was Forster a systematic thinker to rival a philosopher such as Immanuel Kant. He preferred empirical observation to theoretical speculation, and his work was dispersed into a series of essays rather than a single magnum opus. While Goethe had the steady support of Duke Karl August of Weimar throughout his lengthy career, Forster had to struggle to stay financially afloat as he moved from one job to the next, which, coupled with his failing health, made it difficult to find time for sustained productivity. Those who sought to tarnish Forster's reputation did not hesitate to stoop to personal slander. While Goethe appeared to subsequent generations as a robustly heterosexual man with a list of lovers cataloged by hagiographers and memorized by schoolboys, Forster was remembered as the cuckolded husband who was willing to share his wife with another man. When he first arrived in Weimar, Herder described him somewhat condescendingly as "a good-hearted, learned little man" (ein gutherziges, gelehrtes Männchen) who had been visibly weakened by his voyage with Cook.[10] There was gossip in Kassel about Forster's suspiciously affectionate friendship with Samuel Thomas

Soemmerring, and students in Göttingen were convinced he was gay.[11] The sense of indeterminacy surrounding Forster's sexuality may well have been a projection of those determined to disparage his character, but it coincides with his chameleon-like tendency to resist national and linguistic categories in a way that made him difficult to enshrine in the literary canon.

While Forster's cultural capital seemed exhausted by the end of the nineteenth century, Goethe's value continued to rise. He too had become famous at an early age, first with the publication of *Götz von Berlichingen*, a Shakespearean drama of tragic heroism that inspired a generation of German writers, and then—while Forster was sailing the South Pacific— *The Sorrows of Young Werther*, a sensational novel about a suicidal young man that captured the imagination of an entire continent. Almost overnight, the young lawyer from Frankfurt am Main became a European celebrity, a star who had "it," which Joseph Roach defines as "a certain quality, easy to perceive but hard to define, possessed by abnormally interesting people."[12] For the rest of his life, *Werther* would be Goethe's calling card and his curse, his claim to fame and the work that fixed him in the public eye as a twentysomething man of feeling, decades after he had moved on to other roles and different styles.

Forster's fame was of a different sort. Goethe had written a novel that his admirers had read, multiple times in the case of fans such as Karl Philipp Moritz and Napoleon Bonaparte. In fact, the fictitious editor of Goethe's novel encourages the sort of intensive rereading that had previously been reserved for religious texts: "And you, good soul, who feels the same urge as he, take comfort from his sufferings and let this book be your friend if, due to fate or personal responsibility, you can find no closer one."[13] Forster, in contrast, was initially more famous for what he had done rather than for what he had written. The emperors, kings, and lesser mortals who sought him out wanted to hear firsthand about what he had seen and to experience the aura of the man who had been to the far side of the world. In Vanessa Agnew's words, "travel conferred symbolic capital."[14] As the son of an independently wealthy patrician who had married into one of the most prominent families in Frankfurt, Goethe would have enjoyed a certain amount of social prestige even if he had not written *Werther*, but Forster was a nobody, the son of an itinerant Lutheran pastor who had decided to pursue a career in science. Thus his celebrity status signaled a new phase in the history of fame. As noted by Joseph A. Boone and Nancy J. Vickers, "The pursuit of fame ... forms a constant throughout history," but the eighteenth century "created a form of celebrity that is recognizable to this day."[15] Leo Braudy writes of the "democratization of fame" during this period in his comprehensive study of the topic from ancient times to recent years.[16] The Tudor and Stuart monarchs of early modern England carefully managed their public image, but it was only in the eighteenth century that a person of humbler origins could shine on the public stage. Also new during this period was the active role that the audience played in defining the celebrity. Rousseau set the standard. The man who did more than anyone else to establish the paradigm of romantic individualism was also a celebrity of the first order. His fervent fan base corresponded with him on intimate terms, even though in most cases they had never met the man.[17] Rousseau experienced this adulation as a decidedly mixed blessing. As Braudy puts it, Rousseau "deserves a special place [in the history of fame] because of the extreme contrast between his urge to be recognized and his urge to retreat." The "shy star" who achieved unprecedented fame became an increasingly paranoid recluse in his final years.[18]

Forster did not suffer from Rousseau's paranoia, but he did sometimes tire of his fame. Everyone wanted to hear the same story: Goethe "asked me about the peoples of the South Pacific, whose simplicity delighted him."[19] While visiting Berlin in the spring of 1779, Forster grew impatient with his command performances for the local public. "During the five weeks I ate lunch or dinner in at least 50 or 60 different homes and every time I had to crank out the same story, listen and respond to the same questions—in short, I had to kill time for a thousand idle people."[20] At other times, however, Forster resented the fact that a man with his experiences should be reduced to a penurious scholar in provincial Germany. When he landed his first job as a professor in Kassel, Forster reported to his publisher, Johann Spener, that his starting salary would be quite modest: "and basically it doesn't matter that you have sailed around the world; *that alone* makes you no more valuable."[21] Six months later, Forster was overcome with frustration at the injustice of it all: "Let me think: I am Buffon's translator, ... I correspond with princes and am writing a foundational textbook about natural history. I sail around the world and arrive in Kassel to teach twelve-year-old snotty brats [Rozlöffeln] how to spell in their own language."[22]

A GERMAN COSMOPOLITAN

Three years after Forster's death, Schlegel published an essay in which he gave an overview of Forster's works and praised him as "a genuine cosmopolitan of German origins" (ein echter Weltbürger, deutscher Herkunft).[23] Goethe had recently lamented the fact that Germany had no "classical national authors," although, against the critical comments of a "literary rabble-rouser," he went on to defend what German writers had achieved despite adverse conditions.[24] Schlegel also takes up the topic of literary classicism, only to reject it—at least in its traditional understanding of works that survive the test of time. "Most people cannot even think about the *classical* without colossal size, massive weight, and a lifespan of eons," he writes sarcastically. "But I would prefer to have the dubious and ominous attribute of immortality completely removed from our concept of the classical. I hope that Forster's works are soon so far surpassed that they become superfluous and no longer good enough for us, that we can justifiably make them *antiques!*"[25] Schlegel appreciates Forster's work because it is of the moment and thus to be superseded by works of the next moment and the one after that; they are the antithesis of classics frozen in timeless monumentality. "In this regard one could well say: heaven preserve us from eternal works."[26]

The following study thinks through the implications of Schlegel's paradoxical claim that Forster is "a genuine cosmopolitan of German origins." A cosmopolitan or *Weltbürger* thinks in global terms, whereas someone of German origins is defined by national boundaries. Schlegel's formulation avoids direct contradiction by suggesting a progression in time: Forster begins as a German and becomes a cosmopolitan. Yet Forster was never German in any simple sense of the term (he was the polyglot son of an Anglophile father who was born in today's Poland and died in Paris as a self-proclaimed French citizen), nor, conversely, did he ever completely abandon his sense of belonging to German culture, even as he espoused cosmopolitan ideals. We might therefore think more accurately about the relationship between the national and the cosmopolitan as an ongoing, unresolved tension that not only provides insight into Forster's life and works but also reflects the preoccupations of his contemporary Europeans, who confronted political revolution at home and were increasingly affected by global exploration and transnational exchange. As a participant in Captain Cook's second voyage and one of the leading figures in the Mainz Republic, Forster was a cosmopolitan thinker who had traveled the world and a political activist in a revolutionary age.

Georg Forster lived in what Ottmar Ette has termed the "*second phase* of accelerated globalization."[27] In the first phase, driven primarily by explorers and entrepreneurs such as Christopher Columbus, Ferdinand Magellan, and Vasco da Gama, "Europe came into possession of enormous riches" from its overseas colonies. The second phase "extends from the middle of the 18th century to the beginning of the 19th, and is modeled perhaps most clearly by the voyages of Bougainville, Cook, or Laperouse."[28] The expeditions combined scientific research in the spirit of the Enlightenment with the pragmatic search for potentially lucrative colonies. Spain and Portugal spearheaded the first phase of globalization; now, England and France took the lead in an increasingly complex network of world trade.

For many years, Western historians cast the increasing European engagement with the world in a heroic light, an "Age of Discovery" that coincided with the Renaissance emergence of humanist thought out of medieval darkness. As the decolonial movement gathered steam in the postwar period, however, writers such as Frantz Fanon and Edward Said began to question the cost of this triumphalist narrative. Drawing on the work of Michel Foucault, Theodor Adorno, and Max Horkheimer, postcolonial critics linked the increase of knowledge to the exercise of power. Writing in 1989, for instance, Robert Young notes that the leading figures of contemporary French thought "were all either born in Algeria or personally involved in the events of the war," and thus he concludes that if "'so-called poststructuralism' is the product of a single historical moment, then that moment is probably not May 1968 but rather the Algerian War of Independence."[29] Young goes on to link the ideals of European humanism to the practice of European colonialism: "Every time a literary critic claims a universal ethical, moral, or emotional instance in a piece of English literature, he or she colludes in the violence of the colonial legacy in which the European value or truth is defined as the universal one."[30] In his view, the conceptual decentering characteristic of poststructuralist thought is also an act of decolonizing the ethnocentrism intrinsic to Western logocentrism: "If one had to answer, therefore, the general question of what is deconstruction a deconstruction of, the answer would be, of the concept, the authority, and assumed primacy of, the category of 'the West.'"[31] Rosi Braidotti comes to similar conclusions in her study *The Posthuman*: "Humanism historically developed into a civilizational model, which shaped a certain idea of Europe as coinciding with the universalizing powers of self-reflexive reason."[32] As a result, she declares at the outset that she is "none too fond of Humanism or of the idea of the human which it implicitly upholds . . . with its Eurocentric core and imperial tendencies."[33] Both authors are quick to insist that by attacking a particular version of Western humanism they are not assaulting humankind. "To criticize humanism in this context therefore does not mean that you do not like human beings and have no ethics," writes Young, "but rather the reverse. It questions the use of the human as an explanatory category that purports to provide a rational understanding of 'man'—an assumed universal predicated on the exclusion and marginalization of his Others, such as 'woman' or 'the native.'"[34] Likewise, Braidotti states that although she is "inclined towards anti-humanism," she affirms the "basic principles of social justice, the respect for human decency and diversity, the rejection of false universalism; the affirmation of the positivity of difference; the principles of academic freedom, anti-racism, openness to others and conviviality," and she insists "that these ideals are perfectly compatible with the best humanist values."[35]

Critics have been quick to denounce the equation of the Enlightenment with instrumental reason as simplistic, illogical, and dangerous.[36] Of course, "reason and knowledge may be implicated in structures of power," concedes Russell Berman. "It is hard to argue with the obvious."[37] To suggest, however, "that all knowledge is power" and that "that power is something sinister and oppressive" nevertheless seems "presumptuous and rather condescending," according to Suzanne Marchand. "Of course, knowledge can be used in this way, but knowledge as understanding can also lead to appreciation, dialogue, self-critique, perspectival reorientation, and personal and cultural enrichment."[38] The blanket denunciation of the Enlightenment, moreover, proceeds from an act of critical bad faith. "To condemn a collaboration between Enlightenment and empire can only indicate that one has accepted the critical terms of Enlightenment thought," writes Berman.[39] Dipesh Chakrabarty intervenes at precisely this point, acknowledging the "unavoidable—and in a sense indispensable—universal and secular vision of the human" that emerged in the European Enlightenment, while at the same time observing that "the European colonizer of the nineteenth century both preached this Enlightenment humanism at the colonized and at the same time denied it in practice."[40] We reject humanist universalism at our peril, according to this view, because we need its ideals in the pursuit of justice, but we also know that those ideals have often served to subjugate those they purport to liberate.

These theorists write as if the European imperialists of prior centuries were blind to the contradictions that seem clear today, and yet at least some of those who participated in or reflected on the "second phase of globalization" were quite aware of the violence and self-interest behind Europe's civilizing mission. "In the late eighteenth century, a number of prominent European political thinkers attacked imperialism," writes Sankar Muthu, "not only defending non-European peoples against the injustices of European imperial rule, as some earlier modern thinkers had done, but also challenging the idea that Europeans had any right to subjugate, colonize, and 'civilize' the rest of the world."[41] "We debauch their morals," confided Cook to his journal as his ships prepared to leave New Zealand; "we interduce among them wants and perhaps diseases which they never before knew.... If any one denies the truth of this assertion let him tell me what the Natives of the whole extent of America have gained by the commerce they have had with Europeans."[42] To be sure, we must balance such misgivings against other passages in which Cook reflects with pride on his accomplishments, but there are moments when he empathizes with indigenous peoples: "We attempt to land in a peaceable manner, if this succeeds its well, if not we land nevertheless and mentain the footing we thus got by the Superiority of our fire arms, in what other light can they than at first look upon us but as invaders of their Country."[43] Cook answers his rhetorical question by suggesting that, over time, he and his crew will be able to "convince them of their mistake," but the previous passage suggests that he has his doubts about the beneficial impact of this invasion into alien lands.

Georg Forster and his father dined every day with Cook on their three-year voyage, and it would be surprising if they did not from time to time weigh the potential costs against the assumed benefits of their mission for the peoples they encountered. Even if Cook kept his concerns to himself, Forster's account of the voyage reveals a similar combination of self-righteousness and self-doubt. In deference to the sort of mixed feelings that we find in such explorers as Cook and Forster, Sankar Muthu begins his study "with the presumption that we should diversify our understanding of Enlightenment thought."[44] By "diversify" in this context Muthu means that we should take into account the range of opinion among European thinkers regarding their efforts to explore and colonize the non-European world, but we might also consider the diversity of national perspectives within Europe during this period. It is one thing to acknowledge, as Ottmar Ette does, that England and France took the lead during this phase of accelerated globalization, but something different to use those nations as a synecdoche for Europe as a whole. In her study of *The Intimacies of Four Continents*, for instance, Lisa Lowe places European liberalism in the context of the colonization of the Americas, the transatlantic African slave trade, and the distribution of Chinese "coolies" across the British Empire. Her work continues the effort on the part of previous critics to show how modern historians, philosophers, and sociologists "have more often treated liberalism's abstract promises of human freedom, rational progress, and social equality apart from the global conditions on which they depended."[45] In making the argument, however, England becomes one of the continents sharing intimacies beneath the sheets of the world's four-post bed.

We find a similar slippage from the nation to the continent in Chenxi Tang's study of *The Geographic Imagination of Modernity*. He argues that the perceived acceleration of temporal change in the late eighteenth century brought with it a corresponding transformation of social space. Tang singles out two developments that were of particular importance in creating a new sense of human culture's embeddedness in physical geography. "First, the geographic imagination was essentially a European imagination, asserting discursive authority over the earth in parallel to the asymmetrical power relations between Europe and the rest of the planet. Second, the geographic imagination was intertwined with a restructuring of the spatial order of the European continent around 1800, when the idea of nation was joined with that of territorial sovereignty to bring into being the modern nation-state."[46] Tang's study focuses almost exclusively on German contributions to the modern geographic imagination, and yet Germany was not a modern nation-state during the romantic era, nor would it be for decades to come. If Tang is correct in his assertion that the formation of the European nation-state was the necessary precondition for the emergence of the modern geographic imagination, how could the Germans have played such a central role in the articulation of the latter when they lacked the former? They had "the idea of nation" but not "territorial sovereignty," which would seem at the very least to complicate their role in the European imagination of global geography.

The Germans were not entirely innocent of the European efforts to explore the world and exploit its resources.[47] In 1669, for instance, Johann Becher encouraged the count of Hanau-Münzenberg "to establish a German coastal colony between the Amazon and the Orinoco" as part of a larger effort to revitalize the economy of the Holy Roman Empire in the wake of the Thirty Years' War, but the venture only "swallowed vast sums of money before the count's relative deposed him and the project collapsed."[48] Susan Buck-Morss reminds us that Johann Wilhelm von Archenholz kept Germans abreast of current events in the Caribbean by devoting more than one hundred pages of his journal, *Minerva*, to the successful Haitian slave rebellion in 1804–5, and Birgit Tautz notes that Hamburg was a center of transatlantic commerce and that some of its merchants were engaged in the slave trade.[49] For the most part, however, German residents in the old Reich were not directly involved in Europe's colonial projects around 1800. Forster and his father joined an expedition sponsored by the king of England; Adelbert von Chamisso sailed with a mission backed by the czar of Russia, and Georg Forster almost did the same, eagerly agreeing to join a Russian expedition destined to last at least four years that was canceled at the last minute. Alexander von Humboldt financed his own expedition to the Americas and exhausted his family wealth by funding the publication of a series of lavishly produced volumes about his discoveries.

Although the Germans played a peripheral role in this phase of European imperialism, they were acutely interested in the discoveries of others. The rapidly expanding reading public had an insatiable appetite for travelogues, and Georg Forster profited from the expanding market. In fact, I would argue that for a number of reasons, Forster was the single most important individual involved in the globalization of German thought in the late eighteenth century. First, he had sailed around the world and written a bilingual, thousand-page account of his voyage that was well received in both the English- and German-speaking worlds. Second,

Forster continued to publish essays about related topics in the fields of botany, history, anthropology, and ethnology in the years after his return from the South Seas. Third, he was a prolific translator and book reviewer who specialized in travel literature, and fourth, he served as a personal mentor to the young Alexander von Humboldt, who accompanied Forster on his journey from Mainz to the Netherlands, England, and France. Humboldt has garnered extensive critical and popular attention of late as a cosmopolitan German who was critical of imperialism, rejected slavery, supported democracy, and pioneered an understanding of nature as a series of interconnected ecosystems. What is not often realized is the extent to which Forster led the way in each of these areas, which is why Humboldt repeatedly acknowledged Forster's influence in publications ranging from his popular *Views of Nature* (*Ansichten der Natur*; the title is a homage to Forster's *Ansichten vom Niederrhein*) to his magisterial late work, *Cosmos*.

THE *SATTELZEIT*: BETWEEN EMPIRES AND NATION-STATES

Forster's other claim to fame—or notoriety in the eyes of conservative German nationalists—was his leading role in the Mainz Republic. Why did Forster become a revolutionary when the majority of Germans did not? Is there any link between Forster's two careers, one as a scientist-explorer and the other as a political activist? Jürgen Goldstein finds the connection in Forster's understanding of political revolution as a manifestation of natural violence.[50] Confounding those who claim that the revolution was an outgrowth of enlightened reason, Goldstein claims that Forster viewed it as an irrational eruption of natural forces. What Goldstein says is not wrong; there are passages in Forster's letters and essays to support this view. I would suggest, however, that the way in which Forster articulates his political views arises out of two conflicting understandings of government in the transitional era that Reinhart Koselleck has dubbed the *Sattelzeit* (literally "saddle age").

Koselleck's concept serves as a useful alternative to the hagiographic "Age of Goethe" when seeking to characterize the complexities and contradictions of the revolutionary era in a German context. In his introduction to a multivolume work of conceptual history (*Begriffsgeschichte*), Koselleck introduces the term to refer to a transitional era that falls in a metaphorical hollow, like the seat of a saddle, between the cantle of the premodern past and the pommel of modernity. Concepts that slide down into the seat take on double meanings: "Looking to the past, they refer to social and political circumstances that we can no longer understand without critical commentary; looking forward and turned toward us, they have taken on meanings that can certainly be explained, but which also appear to be immediately comprehensible."[51] The term *revolution*, for instance, which we understand today as a violent upheaval that produces something radically new, originally meant a literal return, a circling back, to an older state of affairs.[52] The terms *empire* and *nation* display a similar fluidity around 1800 that is easily forgotten today. We think of empires as aggressive states that seek to expand their influence and economic power by conquering new lands. In keeping with this idea, the Holy Roman Empire was originally established through violent territorial acquisitions led by Charlemagne in the eighth century, but over time it evolved into a political organization composed of a bewildering array of kingdoms, duchies, bishoprics, city-states, and free imperial knights (Reichsritter), all subject to the ultimate authority of the emperor, but also exercising considerable local autonomy. Class-specific privileges and ancient traditions governed a society in which allegiances were multiple and overlapping, power rested in the hands of a hereditary aristocracy, and political borders were porous. Conquering new lands mattered less than maintaining the delicate balance of power between the disparate components of the existing Reich.[53]

While England, France, Portugal, and Spain jockeyed for control of vast lands in the Americas, subjects in the smaller segments of the Holy Roman Empire witnessed the rise of Prussia under the leadership of King Frederick II ("the Great") and the strengthening of the Austrian monarchy under Joseph II. Two tendencies distinguished these territorial states from the old Reich: the move to establish centralized governments that imposed uniform laws on the diverse subjects of the realm, and the effort to expand the boundaries of the state whenever possible. Frederick's bold acquisition of Silesia in 1740 triggered Austrian desires for revenge and marked the beginning of an era scarred by power struggles for the control of Bavaria, the Netherlands, and Poland. At the same time, Joseph and Frederick were products of the Enlightenment, and both instituted progressive reforms within their realms. In a program known as Josephism or Josephinism, the Austrian monarch sought to curb the power of the Catholic church, reform education, liberalize censorship, and organize poverty relief.[54] Joseph encouraged mass literacy and religious tolerance, eased restrictions on Jews and the persecution of witchcraft, reformed criminal law, and abolished torture.[55] While these social policies anticipate those of liberal democracies, both Austria and Prussia remained monarchies in which the enlightened rulers retained absolute authority, at least in theory, although in practice their power to control every aspect of life in their sprawling territories was inevitably limited.

The two rulers' attitudes toward governance marked a radical break from traditions in the Holy Roman Empire. "Frederick insisted upon the primacy of the state as an abstract structure quite separate from his own person," explains Christopher Clark. Despite the cult of personality built up around him, Frederick the Great styled himself as a model civil servant who subordinated the person of "the monarch to the political and social order he represented."[56] Joseph also developed "a fanatical cult of the impersonal, unified state, strongly armed against its enemies, under a single absolute sovereign."[57] In place of a loose assemblage of semiautonomous principalities, each bound in loyalty to a local lord and following traditional customs under the aegis of a supreme but distant emperor, Frederick and Joseph sought to standardize society and centralize government in accordance with universal principles. In the process, as disapproving contemporaries saw it, they turned the living organism of the state into a lifeless machine.

Looking back in 1793 at the reigns of the two enlightened monarchs, Johann Gottfried Herder found himself torn between conflicting emotions. He praises the young Frederick as a philosopher-king and admirer of Voltaire but regrets that as he grew older, the "evil politics" of "Europe's system of states" compelled him to become rigid and harsh in ways that ran contrary to his nature.[58] "My quiet admiration for the great man grows almost every year," Herder confesses, and yet that esteem is tinged with sadness: "At the time of the Seven Years' War it almost rises to tragic sympathy."[59] Turning to Joseph II, Herder recalls how his ascent to the throne inspired unprecedented hope, and he cites Klopstock's effusive poem of praise for the new emperor. No one worked harder than Joseph II, no one sought to accomplish more, and yet he achieved little. "In the end, the unfortunate man could not say 'I came, I saw, I *conquered*!' He could barely say 'I came, I saw, and I *wanted*! [to get things done]'" (Ich kam, ich sah, ich *wollte!*).⁶⁰ Herder praises Joseph's crusades against superstition, intolerance, and censorship but criticizes his suppression of the Bohemian Deists and subsequent tendency to tar all his enemies with the same brush. He also questions Joseph's imposition of a single legal codex on the many different peoples within his realm in a way that overrode local customs. Still worse was Joseph's attempt to establish German as the official language of his multilingual realm. If God tolerates multilingualism, Herder concludes, then so should rulers.

Standardization, enforced uniformity, the misguided elevation of the local and particular to a forcibly imposed universal law are anathema to Herder and at the heart of his resistance to the modern territorial state. Already in *Another Philosophy of History*, Herder rails against mechanisms that drain the life out of nature. The invention of the printing press, compass, and modern firearms transformed valiant knights into faceless pawns: "The army has become a hired machine, devoid of thought, power, or will, that *one man* directs *in his head*: a mere marionette of motion, a live wall that is said to throw bullets and catch bullets."⁶¹ Herder goes on to castigate the arrogance of the Enlightenment's pretensions toward universal validity and to mock the image of a monolingual continent: "All the rulers of Europe are speaking French already, and soon we will *all* be doing so. And then—state of bliss!—the golden age shall be upon us again 'when *all the world* will have *one tongue* and *language* and there shall be *one flock* and *one shepherd*.' National characters, where have you gone?"⁶²

Against the leveling tendencies of the modern state, Herder prefers federations that preserve local traditions.⁶³ Subjects suffer under despotic rulers, but they flourish in lands where the states remain small. Ancient Greece, for instance, was an assemblage of kingdoms and city-states that were conducive to the production of a free and flourishing culture.⁶⁴ Herder acknowledges the violence of their wars, harsh treatment of conquered enemies, and proclivity for same-sex relationships that he finds alienating, and yet he voices highest praise for a nation that was divided by geography yet united in culture. The ancient Hebrews serve as another positive example of a people that managed to combine unity with diversity in a productive fashion.⁶⁵ While Herder can be sharply critical of his contemporary Jews, he venerated ancient Israel, contrasting the authentic culture of the Old Testament patriarchs with the corruption of modern times. In his study of *The Spirit of Hebrew Poetry*, written in Weimar shortly before he embarked on the decade-long project of *Ideas Concerning the Philosophy of History for Humanity*, Herder praises Moses for his ability to unite the twelve tribes of Israel in a way that allowed each to retain "its autonomous property, the right to its own customs and courts, and even the freedom to conduct its own wars."[66] The ancient Romans, in contrast, violently eradicated local cultures before attempting to conquer the world, as Herder argues in his *Ideas*: "When Rome set off on its heroic path, Italy was covered with a multitude of minor peoples, each of which lived according to its own laws and character. Some were more enlightened than others, but all were lively, diligent, and prosperous."[67] When Rome fell, "Italy reverted to its natural condition of the most manifold diversity."[68] As at home, so abroad: the Romans' mad desire for conquest (*Eroberungswut*)[69] led them far beyond Italy in the effort to control the world, only to corrupt it in the end: "Foreign peoples were subject to customs that they did not know; they were introduced to vices and their consequences that they had never heard of before," until in the end there was nothing left of the native cultures.[70]

While Herder and others reflected on the tensions between local traditions and enlightened absolutism within the German lands of the Holy Roman Empire, a new form of the nation-state arose in neighboring France. The Revolution replaced vertical hierarchies with lateral bonds between brothers, declared universal human rights, and redrew the map to replace a patchwork quilt of local governances with a rational network of departments subject to the central authority of Paris in a state with firmly drawn borders.[71] Very quickly, however, the French sought to export their revolution, either by proclaiming the good news of its egalitarian ideals or by sending its armies into neighboring territories. As Krishnan Kumar describes it, "the archetypal nation-state" began acting like an empire. "Whereas the Ottomans and the Habsburgs and even the British would accept and even promote difference, for the French it seemed inconceivable that, once exposed to French culture, everyone would not wish to share in that culture to the fullest extent possible, to become, in a word, French."[72] Yet those Germans on the receiving end of the revolutionary armies might be excused if they were not always seduced by "the image of French missionaries bringing liberty and equality to the stygian darkness of feudal despotism," for they experienced "an incursion of these unpaid, unfed, undisciplined hordes" not as "liberation, but 'an invasion of barbarians, with the sole object of pillaging and looting.'"[73] Many Germans preferred traditional liberties to universal human rights, local self-governance to state control. They responded to the Revolution, in other words, as subjects of a centuries-old empire and not as citizens of a modern nation-state intent on expanding a new sort of imperial power.

Within this historical context, Forster is typically viewed as the exception to the German norm. Against a flock of disenfranchised and disengaged German subjects content or resigned to dwell in the ruins of a moribund Reich, he stands out as a political activist who risked his life to import French virtues onto German soil. As I argue in the following pages, this point of view needs correction on multiple fronts. First, the Holy Roman Empire was by no means as frail as its critics have assumed. If not perhaps in perfect health, it nevertheless survived throughout the eighteenth century and continued to adapt to changing times, as Joachim Whaley and others have argued.[74] "Far from being the gale which blew away the desiccated feudal leaves," writes Timothy Blanning with typical flair, "the French Revolution is better likened to a chain-saw, which felled an ancient, gnarled, but still flourishing oak."[75] Second, while Forster does differ from his German contemporaries in his willingness to commit to the revolutionary cause, his reflections on the Revolution move within the parameters of the political thought of his time, as he weighs the advantages of universal rights against the appeal of regional traditions. Third, Forster's nuanced response to intra-European conflict coincides with his ambivalent assessment of the European engagement with the non-European world. In both cases, he witnessed the clash between the local and the universal, the one and the many. In his study of Herder, Forster's closest intellectual ally, John Noyes explores "the struggle at the heart of Enlightenment Europe to describe common human development in a way that will not fall prey to those claims to universality that were—even then—understood to be in league with European imperialist interests."[76] As someone who had spent his formative years sailing with Captain Cook and his final months in the border zone between Germany's old Reich and the new French nation, Forster was uniquely positioned to perceive the parallels between intra- and extra-European imperialism. As a result, we cannot reduce his response to the French Revolution and European imperialism to a clear moral opposition—the French Revolution is "good" and European imperialism is "bad." Forster thinks dialectically, weighing the pros and cons of each side of the equation. The revolution sweeps away feudal injustice but creates new forms of territorial aggression and domestic tyranny, while expeditions undertaken in the name of the Enlightenment can cause unintended collateral damage.

Finally, Forster's marginal role in both movements not only afforded him a liminal position from which he could retain a degree of critical detachment while engaged in ongoing events—either as a "supernumerary" aboard the *Resolution* or as a German exiled in France—but it also allowed him to envision a cosmopolitan alternative to European imperialism. The Holy Roman Empire was universal as well as local; at once secular and sacred, the Empire was the political manifestation of God's rule on earth, of a Christendom that sought salvation for all those born in sin. As Benedict Anderson observes in *Imagined Communities*, nations delimit, drawing sharp boundaries between themselves and their neighbors, whereas the Holy Roman Empire (in theory, of course) could expand to embrace the entire world.[77] This Christian universalism informs the secular German cosmopolitanism that we find in Forster and subsequent German thinkers. While other European nation-states seek to colonize lands through violent conquest, the Germans envision themselves as the center of a peaceful network of international exchange. In his preface to his translation of the Indian play *Sakuntala* and other essays that I examine herein, Forster plays a leading and hitherto unacknowledged role in this paradoxical vision of a German cosmopolitanism.

CHAPTER OVERVIEW

I begin with reflections on the understanding of language and the meaning of authorship in Forster's work. In place of a "discourse network" circa 1800, in which men channeled their mother's voice to write works of literary genius,[78] polyglot Forster ran a translation workshop that served as a medium for international exchange. He did so reluctantly, dreaming of a time when he could devote himself entirely to his own work, but that time never came. Instead, he remained torn between literary ideals inspired by the aesthetics of genius and a literary practice based on the manufacture, sale, and circulation of literary products. The tension in Forster's work raises larger questions about the German institution of literature around

1800. At a time when the literary market split along gendered lines between a few male authors of genius and a larger group of scribblers, Forster straddled the divide, writing demanding essays that engaged with the leading thinkers of the day but also running a translation factory that employed women who helped him churn out pages for popular consumption. While Yasemin Yildiz writes of the "monolingual paradigm" that emerged as German matured into a literary language,[79] Forster was at home in multiple tongues and made his living switching between them. As communities imagined discrete identities expressed and molded by national literatures, Forster fostered international literary exchanges that gave birth to the cosmopolitan concept of world literature.

Forster's first major travelogue, *A Voyage Round the World*, takes center stage in the second chapter. In a country that was largely excluded from the exploration and colonization of non-European cultures, Forster was one of the few who had traveled around the world and written about his experiences. In doing so, he expanded German horizons by encouraging readers to reconsider their location in the world, their relation to global cultures, and the place of human beings on the planet. Forster fluctuates between a wholehearted endorsement of the expedition as an outgrowth of the European Enlightenment and moments of critical reflection in which he observes the detrimental effects of the civilizing mission on distant peoples, pondering the shortcomings of his society. In addition to the anthropological observations prompted by his travels, Forster engaged in the beginnings of ecological thought. Captain Cook brought not only scientists on his voyages to catalogue new species of indigenous plants and animals but also European livestock and seeds that he thought would benefit remote cultures. Observing these attempts to export European flora and fauna to the Pacific islands, as well as the crew's eagerness to slaughter indigenous birds, seals, and other marine wildlife, prompts occasional reflections on Forster's part about the relation between humans and the environment that inspired the work of his young admirer Alexander von Humboldt. Together, they were among the first to think through the consequences of the Anthropocene, the period in earth's history in which humans have left an indelible scar on the face of the natural environment and begun to question their status as the uncontested lords of the earth.

I turn to the interrelated topics of racial difference, human history, and German neoclassicism in chapter 3. In the decade and a half between his return to England and his participation in the Mainz Republic, Forster led a peripatetic life that involved teaching for a few years at a small college in Kassel, an appointment at the distant University of Vilnius in today's Lithuania, and his final regular job as a university librarian in Mainz. His teaching duties and never-ending translation projects and book reviews made it impossible for him to complete a major book, but he did write a series of essays that build on the themes of his first travelogue and engage with the ideas of others. While feeling isolated in Vilnius, Forster jumped at the chance to reenter the conversation among European intellectuals by intervening in debates about human racial distinctions. He responded to Kant's reflections on race and went on to denounce the racist theories of Christoph Meiners in essays that combine righteous indignation, paternalistic condescension, and philosophical pessimism. Forster's reflections on what he viewed as primitive cultures arose in tandem with his veneration of classical antiquity, which in turn prompted thoughts about the course of human history. Northern Europeans occupied an ambivalent place in this narrative: on the one hand, they seemed the impoverished heirs to the rich cultural past, whose idealized image served as an implicit critique of current European conditions, but on the other, they had the potential to rejuvenate the spirit of antiquity in a new age of modern humanism. This diachronic narrative that traced the course of human history from classical antiquity to northern Europe was in turn mapped onto a synchronic opposition between European civilization and global primitivism. While this Eurocentric narrative of universal history could be used to legitimate world conquest and settler colonialism, Forster envisions a cosmopolitan alternative in which the Germans, largely excluded from active participation in European imperialism, took pride of place as the benevolent center of cultural exchange, an idea that would resonate in the work of Novalis, Schiller, Goethe, and Thomas Mann.

In the spring of 1790, Forster set off on his second great journey or, more precisely, the journey that inspired his second great travelogue, *Views of the Lower Rhine*, which I discuss in chapter 4. Forster had been invited to join a new expedition around the world, this time sponsored by the Russian government, but an unexpected war between Russia and the Ottoman Empire scuttled those plans. Instead, he accepted a position as the university librarian in Mainz, but a combination of professional interest, marital discord, and irrepressible wanderlust inspired him to travel with Alexander von Humboldt, then only twenty-one years old, down the Rhine to the Netherlands, across the English Channel to London, and back to Mainz via revolutionary Paris. The journey was conceived from the outset as source material for a new travelogue, and each night, Forster would record his impressions of the day's events in notes and letters. As soon as he returned to Mainz, he began to revise these records and negotiate with potential publishers.

In comparison with *Voyage Round the World*, *Views* covers more familiar territory. If the immediate appeal of *Voyage* was to inform domestic readers about distant worlds, *Views* seeks to make the familiar strange by observing local customs with critical distance and reflecting on the causes of political conflicts. The timing of the journey was propitious, as it coincided with the first anniversary of the French Revolution and gave Forster and Humboldt a firsthand look at European cities at a time of unprecedented historical change. Forster never completed the third volume of his travelogue, which was intended to provide descriptions of the final stages of the journey in England and France. The existing narrative focuses exclusively on the regions of the lower Rhine, which include the northwest corner of today's Germany, parts of Belgium, and the Netherlands. Visits to Cologne, Aachen, Liège, and Brussels gave Forster the opportunity for a microanalysis of political conflicts that spurred broader reflections on revolutionary change. By focusing on individual cities, Forster moves beyond the consideration of "the" Revolution as a unique event in one European nation to explore the ambiguities of political struggles during the *Sattelzeit*, which often combined enlightened reform, conservative restoration, and radical revolution in complex and contradictory ways. The efforts of Prussia and Austria to impose their will on distant regions of the old Reich awakened memories of early modern European history, when the Spanish sought to control the same provinces. Forster depicts present-day events, but he draws on knowledge of past occurrences that feature prominently in Goethe's *Egmont* and Schiller's *Don Carlos*. Together, these authors reveal that imperialism was not just a global affair between Europeans and their overseas colonies, but it also involved conflicts closer to home.

While Forster worked to complete *Views of the Lower Rhine*, despite the constant interruptions caused by his busy translation schedule and frequent bouts of debilitating illness, political events continued to unfold at an accelerating rate in revolutionary France. Matters came to a head in the summer of 1792. While a coalition of Prussia and Austrian forces joined with French emigres and smaller German states in an effort to invade France and restore the monarchy, French armies moved in the opposite direction, as they sought to expand their influence along their eastern border from the Netherlands to Switzerland. The First Coalition's advance into France soon stalled on the plains outside the town of Valmy, and Goethe, who accompanied the expedition as the contemporary equivalent of an embedded war correspondent, recorded the increasingly dire conditions as the defeated army slogged its way back toward Germany. Meanwhile, French troops under the leadership of General Custine pushed east, capturing Frankfurt and entering Mainz in late October. Within weeks a German Jacobin Club took shape, in which Forster played a leading role. The Mainz Republic was formed, representing—depending on one's political perspective—either the admirable exception to Germany's resistance to revolutionary change, or a renegade band of traitors to the German fatherland.

My purpose in the fifth chapter of this study is neither to praise nor to scold Forster for his role in the revolution but rather to view his participation in light of his earlier ideas. He was sharply critical of Germany's old regime and supported progressive reforms, but his enthusiasm was tempered by concern about the forceful imposition of alien ideas onto indigenous peoples. Forster's reflections on the revolution, both during the short-lived Mainz Republic and while spending his final months in France, explore a double concern: He embraces the Revolution as the political manifestation of the philosophical Enlightenment and yet recoils at the violence perpetrated in its name, and he welcomes the French armies as liberators in Mainz, but grows increasingly uncomfortable as liberation turns to occupation and occupation then becomes conquest. While Forster never wished for a return to the pre-Revolutionary past, he articulates what Adorno and Horkheimer will term the dialectic of Enlightenment, as he witnesses the evolution of a newly democratic nation into an aggressive empire.

This book is not a biography, although it is informed by previous studies of Forster's short but eventful life. I focus primarily on the interrelated themes in Forster's oeuvre outlined previously, including questions of authorship, empire, history, race, and revolution, but because his work engages with that of his contemporaries, I occasionally digress to explore treatments of the same topics in the work of Herder, Goethe, Schiller, and others. Forster was a dialogical thinker, the antithesis of a solitary visionary, and his contributions gain contour when considered in relation to the thought of others. In doing so, moreover, we see that Forster was not an anomalous outsider in the Age of Goethe, a world traveler and political revolutionary among a nation of reactionary provincials, but rather a writer who experienced many of the same conflicts and explored similar ideas. This is not to say that he should be immortalized as a classic in the sense derided by Friedrich Schlegel. Instead of erecting a colossal memorial to Georg Forster that rivals Tischbein's iconic image of Goethe in the Campagne, we might better use his works as ways to think about the Age of Goethe differently: as multilingual, malleable, and mobile, both local and cosmopolitan, dynamic and decentered.

CHAPTER 1

What Is an Author?

Forster was born in a part of today's Poland just outside the city of Gdansk. His father, Johann Reinhold Forster, traced the family lineage back to George Forster, an Englishman of Scottish descent, who had immigrated to the region around Danzig in the wake of the seventeenth-century civil war. "So we are almost English, at least not German," Johann Forster later maintained, adding (in English), "though a man be born in a Stable he is not a horse."[1] In honor of his ancestor, Johann Forster had his eldest son baptized as Johann *George* Adam Forster, not Georg, and he preferred to call him by the English version of his second name.[2] "I will be, until I croak [bis ich verrecke], the same George Forster, whom you embraced for the last time in London on the 29th of August," Forster declared in an early letter to his editor, Johann Spener.[3] But a few years later, when he was pondering his prospects for marriage, Forster's name had changed: "I often found girls who wanted me,—but they only wanted the professor and not *Georg*."[4] Forster signed *A Voyage Round the World* as George Forster, and he continued to use the English spelling of his name for the first German edition of this travelogue, as he did for his second travelogue, *Views of the Lower Rhine*. Forster's first volume of collected essays, *Short Works* (*Kleine Schriften*, 1789), in contrast, identifies the author as Georg rather than George Forster, as does the memorial plaque on his former home in Mainz.[5]

Forster left home with his father at the age of ten for an extended journey to the interior of Russia. Rather than returning to his mother and younger siblings, Georg sailed with his father directly from St. Petersburg to England, as the former Lutheran minister had decided to begin a new career as a scientist and thought he would have more opportunities in the British capital. When the younger Forster returned to London after his voyage with Cook, he confessed that he was "certainly enthusiastic for all things German," but not to the point that he would look down on other nations.[6] In his early letters, Forster often refers to his German heritage in terms of ironic stereotypes. He tells Spener that he was happy to receive his letter but quickly qualifies the nature of his delight: "Not the happiness of an Englishman! [Nicht, the happiness eines Engländers!]—No, something more ecstatic, which an English friend never feels, . . . I am in that regard still a German."[7] "In my thoughts I am an emotional *German*" ([ich] bin in Gedanken ein *Deutscher* und schwärme), he wrote a few months later to his friend Friedrich Adolf Vollpracht, a German theology student living in London.[8] In his first letter to his future father-in-law, Professor Christian Gottlob Heyne of the University of Göttingen, Forster strikes a more serious tone, perhaps in part for diplomatic reasons. Forster had been named a corresponding member of the Göttingen Academy of Sciences and Heyne, as its secretary, had presumably been delegated to convey the good news. "I am proud of the honor that Your Honor has shown me in this way," responded Forster. "For despite the fact that I live here as if banished from my fatherland, my spirit is still too genuinely German for it not to be delighted to be held in some respect by one of Germany's worthiest men."[9]

Feeling German in spirit is not the same as pledging allegiance to a particular government, however, and years later, when he became increasingly involved in revolutionary politics in Mainz, Forster bristled at the offer of a loan from his new publisher, Christian Friedrich Voss, on the condition that he remain "a good Prussian" at a time when the Prussian government was pursuing antirevolutionary policies. He insists that he was never a Prussian subject, having been born just outside Danzig in a region that was under Polish control until long after he left town,[10] and adds that he has also lived in England, Kassel, Vilnius, and Mainz. "Wherever I was, I tried to be a good citizen," he continues, without, however, feeling any particular loyalty to the local government. "*Ubi bene ibi patria* has to be the scholar's motto; he also remains a free man when from time to time he has to live isolated in lands that do not have a free constitution." If being a good Prussian means living in peace, "then I am a good Prussian, just as I am a good Turk, Russian, Chinese, Moroccan, etc.," but if they are asking me to deny my democratic principles, "then they are demanding something for which I would deserve to be hanged from the nearest lantern post."[11] Two months before he died, Forster defined himself "as a human being, a citizen of the world, a European, a German, and a Frenchman" (als Mensch, als Weltbürger, als Europäer, als Deutscher, als Franke).[12]

Forster's malleable sense of national identity carried over into his remarkable facility for languages. His family spoke German at home during his first years on the outskirts of Danzig, but the boy must have heard Polish on the streets. Forster enjoyed some of his only formal schooling for a few months in St. Petersburg, where he learned Russian, French, and some Latin. The linguistically precocious adolescent published his first work when he was twelve, a translation of a Russian history text into English.[13] Shortly before embarking on his voyage with Cook, Forster translated Louis-Antoine de Bougainville's *Voyage autour du monde* into English; he would later translate the English description of Cook's final voyage into German, together with William Bligh's account of the mutiny on the *Bounty*.[14] During a two-year stint at the University of Vilnius, Forster learned to speak Polish with the locals, while communicating with his colleagues in French and delivering lectures in Latin. Forster played such a prominent role in the revolutionary government in Mainz at least in part because he spoke fluent French and could mediate between the occupying forces and local residents. The same facility enabled him to deliver the speech to the National Assembly that brought about the incorporation of Mainz into the French Republic, but in the following weeks in Paris, he also spent time speaking English with Mary Wollstonecraft and Thomas Paine. He even found three "worthy Poles" who were "very fond of him" and with whom he could practice his rudimentary Polish.[15] In his final days in France, Forster planned to learn Persian; he died in a Parisian garret still dreaming of a journey to India.[16] Forster summarized his linguistic abilities in a letter to a potential employer as follows: "I know enough Latin to meet expectations for a scholar today.... I can speak and write fluently in German, French, and English. I can read and understand Dutch, Italian, Spanish, Portuguese, and Swedish. I have some knowledge of Polish and elementary Russian."[17] Forster neglected to mention that he had also learned some Tahitian and a smattering of other Polynesian dialects on his travels to the South Pacific.

MULTILINGUALISM AND THE MOTHER TONGUE

Forster's peripatetic life, shifting political allegiances, and extraordinary linguistic abilities challenge assumptions about the monolingual nationalism said to emerge in the late eighteenth century. In *Beyond the Mother Tongue*, Yasemin Yildiz questions the common belief that individuals and cultures "possess one 'true' language only, their 'mother tongue,' and through this possession [they are] organically linked to an exclusive, clearly demarcated ethnicity, culture, and nation."[18] She examines what she terms the "postmonolingual condition" typical of many writers today, who may have grown up speaking one language but publish their literary works in another, or bi- or trilingual authors for whom the very concept of "the mother tongue" seems inappropriate. In writing about such authors as Yoko Tawada, Emine Sevgi Özdamar, and Feridun Zaimoğlu, Yildiz joins with critics who explore literatures that emerge in bilingual and bicultural border zones and solidarities forged through strategic alliances rather than common origins or national identities.[19] From a minoritizing point of view, multilingual authors reinforce the monolingual norm; they are the exceptions to the rule, the losers in a game of musical chairs left standing while the majority settles into discrete and stable seats.[20] From a universalizing perspective, however, the marginalized outsiders defy the widespread assumption that the mother tongue is as natural as mother's milk. "The native speaker is in fact an imaginary construct," writes Claire Kramsch, "a canonically literate monolingual middle-class member of a largely fictional national community whose citizens share a belief in a common history and a common destiny."[21]

In some ways, today's multilingual authors represent something new. Their literature emerges at a time of unprecedented mobility and migration, and in tandem with a shift in theoretical discourse from a focus on the universally human or nationally specific to hybrid forms and impure mixtures. As Yildiz stresses, the very term *postmonolingual* has "a temporal dimension: it signifies the period since the emergence of monolingualism as a dominant paradigm, which first occurred in late eighteenth-century Europe." Although multilingualism has become increasingly common among today's writers, they work within the lingering presupposition of a monolingual norm. Yildiz goes on to explain that the monolingual paradigm "spread only gradually and unevenly across different contexts and not at all to others," so her term has to be applied flexibly in specific social and historical situations.[22] Nevertheless, eighteenth-century Europe remains the point of departure for a study that divides the postmonolingual present from the monolingual past.

A new valorization of the mother tongue did in fact arise in late-eighteenth- and early-nineteenth-century Germany.[23] In his prize-winning *Treatise on the Origin of Language,* Johann Gottfried Herder stresses the importance of language learning in childhood development. "The weak child—who is considered immature for a good reason—does it not have to acquire language? For it is with language that it enjoys its mother's milk and its father's intellect." Herder goes on to assert that "our mother tongue was simultaneously the first world we saw, the first sensation we felt, and first activity and pleasure we enjoyed!"[24] Friedrich Schleiermacher bases his discussion of the relative merits of a "domesticating" versus a "foreignizing" approach to literary translation on the premise that, with the rare exception of truly bilingual individuals, most people are so deeply rooted in their native language that adequate translation is almost impossible.[25] Jacob Grimm describes the multivolume dictionary that he and his brother began to publish in 1854 as a service to the German *Muttersprache* and a gift to the German people,[26] and patriotic appeals to preserve the purity of the mother tongue play a central role in Fichte's *Addresses to the German Nation.* Thomas Bonfiglio has traced the history of an increasingly dangerous ethnolinguistic nationalism that linked the mother tongue to racial characteristics, which eventually fueled myths of Aryan supremacy and sparked outbursts of anti-Semitic violence.[27]

Given the deadly association of the native speaker with isolationism, ethnocentrism, and racist nationalism, the current desire to move beyond the mother tongue is understandable and commendable when considering contemporary cultural production. In tracing the origins of the ideology to predominantly German writers around 1800, however, we should be careful not to impose a teleology onto the past that leads directly from the first manifestations of linguistic nationalism to the genocidal policies of the Third Reich, nor should we confuse earlier idealizations of the native speaker with the multilingual reality against which they were conceived. Latin, for instance, remained a stubborn presence well into the nineteenth century, as Jürgen Leonhardt observes in his history of that language. "It is understandable that scholars would be more interested in the waxing of literatures in the vernacular than in the waning of Latin," he concedes, and yet he cautions against the cultural amnesia that accompanies the narrative of vernacular triumph.[28] The birth of the vernacular did not cause the death of Latin; for over a millennium, multilingualism was the norm, much as it is becoming the norm again today, although English has taken the place of Latin as the global lingua franca, just as French served that purpose for Europeans in the past. Ancient Greek, Sanskrit, and classical Chinese have functioned as what Leonhardt terms *world languages* in other times and places.[29] All of the major German writers around 1800 were multilingual, some remarkably so, and the German literary language of the time was an artificial construct for publication purposes, not the spontaneous expression of the mother tongue. "Almost no one spoke this supra-regional language at the time," comments the editor to a critical edition of Goethe's poetry. "We can imagine the conversations between Goethe, who was from Frankfurt, the East Prussian Herder, the Swabian Wieland, and the members of the Thuringian court as quite Babylonian." When Goethe prepared his first edition of collected works, he had to revise his texts to remove Frankfurt regionalisms. Goethe's early verse, which is generally viewed as *Erlebnislyrik*, lyric poetry that arose from direct personal experience, first appeared in print in a version that was modified to meet the expectations of the new reading public. "The new publication form required a kind of translation into the supra-regional norm of printing and taste."[30] As Michel Foucault reminded us decades ago, authors are made, not born—the product of selective editing, the conferring of copyrights, and the granting of social status.[31] Rather than viewing the Age of Goethe as the period that produced a limited number of literary works that captured the spontaneous expression of creative genius in the mother tongue, we might view it instead as a period of textual excess, a time, as Andrew Piper puts it, "when there were suddenly too many books,"[32] a surplus from which relatively few authors were selected and marketed as the voice of the nation even as the winds of transnational exchange disseminated the pages of literary production.

Georg Forster plays a pivotal role in the history of late eighteenth-century German literature. On the one hand, he was a famous individual who published original works under his own name, but on the other, he was an indefatigable translator, reviewer of travelogues, and supervisor of a translation workshop. While Goethe consolidated his public persona by publishing ever-expanding editions of his collected works, Forster's multifaceted literary production worked as a centrifugal force that undercut "the twin nineteenth-century aesthetic ideals of personality and totality" that supported "the spiritual edifice on which rested the new *Kulturnation*."[33] As Andrew Piper observes, however, Goethe's late poetic practice tends to unravel the fabric of personal and national cohesiveness that the collected works sought to sustain. In his exploration of the various prequels, sequels, editions, and revisions of *Wilhelm Meister's Travels*, for instance, Piper shows how Goethe disrupts the sense of a single genius-authored text and places it in the context of dynamic literary networks.[34] Forster, conversely, yearns for the financial independence that would allow him to escape the rat race of the translation industry and devote his time to his own oeuvre. Taken together, the authors expose the appearance of two seemingly contradictory tendencies in German literature around 1800: the one moves to restrain language to the mother tongue and consolidate the national literature, while the other unleashes multilingualism and spurs the dissemination of world literature.

BORN TRANSLATED: FORSTER'S *VOYAGE ROUND THE WORLD*

We get a sense of the tension between these tendencies in the publication history of Forster's *Voyage Round the World*, which both established his reputation as an original author and began his career as a prolific translator. The participation in Cook's voyage that launched Forster's fame was more of an accident than a carefully conceived plan. Johann Reinhold Forster was enlisted as a last-minute replacement for Joseph Banks, the famous naturalist who had accompanied Cook on his first voyage to Tahiti. As a condition for his participation in Cook's next voyage, Banks had demanded modifications to the *Resolution* to meet the needs of his extensive entourage—which was to have included a painter, three draftsmen, "two secretaries, six servants, and for entertainment, two horn players"[35]— but when the ship became unseaworthy as a result of the reconfigured superstructure, Cook insisted that it be restored to its initial condition. Banks flew into a rage and quit the mission, whereupon Cook replaced him with Forster.[36] The aspiring scientist eagerly accepted the offer, with the understanding that he would be allowed to bring along his son. The Forsters purchased supplies in London and traveled by land to Plymouth.

There they found the two ships that would undertake the voyage: Cook commanded the *Resolution* and Tobias Furneaux was the captain of the *Adventure*. The ships set sail on July 13, 1772.

Georg Forster's authorship of *Voyage Round the World* and its German counterpart was equally serendipitous.[37] When he returned from his travels in the summer of 1775, he had no idea that he would soon be enlisted in the task of writing a bilingual travelogue. Johann Reinhold Forster believed from the beginning of the voyage that he had been granted the official rights to the description of the journey, but Cook soon made it clear that he intended to publish his own account of his second expedition. Cook had been outraged to discover that his journals from his first voyage had been spruced up for public consumption by a certain Dr. John Hawkesworth, who had been commissioned by Lord Sandwich "to 'write the voyage'— that is, to take Cook's journal and put it into a form suitable for the reading of the polite world." Cook was "surprised beyond measure; worse, he was 'mortified' . . . because he did not recognise himself" in the ghost-written narrative.[38] He was therefore determined this time to take the project into his own hands. The awkward question of Johann Forster's claim to the potentially lucrative narrative remained, however. At first it seemed possible that they might undertake a joint project, with Cook focused on seamanship and Forster on science, or perhaps they could produce two separate volumes divided along the same lines. Before final approval was granted, however, Johann Forster was required to submit a writing sample, which, to his infinite displeasure, was deemed in need of significant stylistic revision. The elder Forster stubbornly refused to edit his prose and the admiralty declared that he would have no part in the official publication. At this point, Johann Forster enlisted his son to write a rival travelogue. Georg worked tirelessly on the project from the summer of 1776 until it was published on April 13, 1777, six weeks before Cook's narrative appeared.[39]

Despite winning the race toward publication and receiving positive reviews, Forster's *Voyage Round the World* was soon eclipsed in sales by Cook's *Voyage Towards the South Pole and Round the World* (1777), in part because Cook had sole access to the expensive engravings that illustrated his text. While Georg Forster struggled in vain for years on behalf of his father to recuperate financial losses incurred in the wake of the voyage from the British Admiralty, the immediate strategy to bolster sales of his

Voyage was to publish it in translation. Plans for a French version fell through, but the Forsters were able to engage a German writer, Rudolf Erich Raspe, to translate it into German. Raspe, best known as the author of *The Surprising Adventures of Baron Munchausen* (1785), was on the lam in London after having been accused of selling precious items for his own profit from his patron's private collection in Kassel. He made a good start on the translation but was soon distracted, so Georg stepped in and took over the project, which was published in two volumes in Berlin as *Reise um die Welt* in 1778–80.[40] With its nearly simultaneous release in both English and German, Forster's *Voyage Round the World* anticipates the many books today that "do not appear at first only in a single language," as Rebecca Walkowitz observes, but rather "simultaneously or nearly simultaneously in multiple languages. They start as world literature."[41]

Georg—or George, as he was known at the time—Forster's authorship of the bilingual travelogue has been questioned since it first appeared.[42] Johann Reinhold Forster had assumed that he would be the author and had kept a journal for this purpose during the voyage. When he was denied the right to publish his version of the narrative, some assumed that he simply avoided the proscription by publishing his work under his son's name (thus reversing his usual practice of publishing Georg's translations under his own name). Georg Forster's age cast further doubt on his authorship. In 1778, the astronomer on the voyage, William Wales, published a booklet in which he furiously challenged the veracity of Forster's *Voyage*. Exactly what motivated him to write his screed is not entirely clear, but personal animosity toward Johann Reinhold Forster certainly played a role; the abrasive elder Forster had a talent for infuriating almost everyone he met. Wales begins his polemic by insisting that "notwithstanding Mr. George Forster's name stands both in the title-page and at the end of the preface, and the Doctor, his father, appears but in the second or third person, there can be but little doubt that he had the principal hand in it." As further proof, Wales notes that "the whole book is written with so much arrogance, self-consequence, and asperity, . . . that I cannot suppose it to be the production of a young man scarcely twenty years of age."[43] Clearly dumbfounded by the vehemence of the attack and anxious to clear his good name, Georg Forster responded in detail to Wales's various accusations, while insisting that "every line of the work in question, is most undoubtedly drawn up by myself, according to my own circumscribed ideas. The manner and the turn of the expressions, is likewise entirely my own." Forster admits only that a reader at the press checked the grammar and style "to smooth the rugged dialect of one who is not a native," while maintaining "that my father's manner of expressing himself, and mine, are widely different, and that we also frequently differ in matters of opinion, which are hitherto undecided."[44] As the editors of the modern edition of *Voyage Round the World* summarize, Georg Forster based his narrative on the facts in his father's journal, but the actual writing is his own, supplemented by his memory of events not recorded in Johann Reinhold's notes and sometimes adding lyric passages about nature's beauty or original interpretations of Polynesian society.[45]

What of Forster's role in the German-language version of the work? In Klaus Harpprecht's view, Forster's translation of his English travelogue into German gave him the opportunity to relearn his mother tongue, but with the advantage of avoiding the baroque formality of the chancellery style typical among German writers of his day.[46] Forster's account of how he came to translate the *Voyage* suggests a different interpretation. Clearly exasperated by Raspe's procrastination, Forster explains in a letter to his publisher, Spener, that he finally had to take matters into his own hands, "which I would have preferred not to do, because it is always better to have a single author."[47] Forster goes on to explain that he did his best to imitate Raspe's style and expresses confidence that Spener will clean up any stylistic loose ends. Although Forster makes a self-deprecating reference to his "*bad English German*" (*böses englisches Deutsch*),[48] just as he had excused "the rugged dialect" of his nonnative English, his letter, written in fluent German, does not give the impression that he has forgotten his mother tongue. Quite the contrary, in fact: he has the ability not only to write in his own voice in the letter but also to mimic the style of his translator in the travelogue. Rather than describing Forster as someone who had become alienated from the monolingual source of his linguistic facility, we might think of him as a linguistic switchboard or coding device capable of alternating between languages and stylistic registers in a way that renders distinctions between original and imitation, the mother tongue and other tongues, irrelevant.[49]

BETWEEN HACKWORK AND GENIUS

In a world awash with books, Forster facilitated the circulation of new products across national borders and the translation of texts between languages.[50] While hard at work on his bilingual travelogue, Forster also sought to keep abreast of cultural developments in both countries. During the first months after his return from his voyage with Cook, Forster urged Spener to send him the latest works from Germany and in turn provided detailed reports about theatrical performances in London. Forster's role as a translator and cultural mediator continued during his most productive years as a university librarian in Mainz between 1788 and 1793. His official duty in Mainz was to catalogue the library's holdings and oversee the acquisition of new books. His initial impression was not good: "Currently, a large percentage of the books are lying on the dirty floor and are being consumed by dust; no one has swept in several years, no books have been dusted, and there is no workroom and no filing cabinet."[51] The estimated holdings of the library turned out to be vastly exaggerated, and the majority of the works were either from antiquity or theological in nature. "By these calculations, the value of this library for the use of teachers and students is virtually nil," concluded Forster bitterly, "although it could still count as a raree show [Raritätenkasten]."[52] Forster soon realized that plans to build a new library would fall through, and that efforts to acquire modern literature would be in vain: "The barbarism is worse than you think. People from whom you would expect a completely different opinion responded to the idea [of buying new books] in these words: 'Let them just read all the old books first.' When people talk like *that*, I probably have no option but to keep quiet and wait."[53]

Forster's duties as university librarian only took up about three or four hours a day, so he had time for his other literary endeavors.[54] Chief among these were his own works, which included the first volume of his collected essays, a series of new articles on a wide range of topics, and his second travelogue, *Views of the Lower Rhine*, which he began almost immediately after returning from his trip. Unfortunately, other demands often made it impossible for Forster to keep his focus on his primary task. Forster reviewed books for his father-in-law's literary journal at a breakneck pace: he wrote twenty-four reviews for the *Göttinger Gelehrte Anzeigen* in 1788, thirty-three in 1789, and continued at this rate in subsequent years.[55] In addition, Forster wrote detailed annual overviews of English literature and art for Wilhelm von Archenholz's *Annalen der Britischen Geschichte*. Translation projects took up more time. Forster specialized in the literary travelogues that were flooding the European markets, some of which he translated himself, others of which he delegated to coworkers who provided rough drafts that he edited and furnished with prefaces.[56] All of these projects required regular correspondence with journal editors (Heyne and Schiller) and book publishers (Spener and Voss).

Despite his generally poor health and repeated bouts of serious illness, Foster was a diligent man who rose before dawn and wrote until he was exhausted, but the work never ended and he never got ahead. On a typical day, he would start translating at five in the morning, browse through the latest journals while eating, and then get back to work. "For the rest of the day I sit like a galley slave chained to my pen, in part to translate, in part to work on my travelogue, which I can only write when I am in the mood."[57] His correspondence voices a litany of complaints about the unsustainable demands of the literary profession. "No thought disgusts me more about my current literary existence than my dependence on book dealers, good weather, good digestion, and an unclouded imagination," lamented Forster in the fall of 1789 in a letter to Friedrich Heinrich Jacobi, the author and early friend of Goethe who had been one of the first to welcome Forster to Germany when he arrived from London.[58] Two years later, Forster's situation had not improved. "Throughout the entire year I have worked incessantly with iron discipline and great mental stress. My strength is exhausted, my body is incapable of any more effort, my mind is dulled, and I have the dreariest prospects for the winter and the coming year."[59] "If only I could get away for a year," Forster exclaims on multiple occasions, but he knows that will never happen. Unlike Goethe, who enjoyed nearly two years of rest and recuperation in Italy, Forster had no friends in high places and no family fortune, like most of his fellow writers. Goethe was exceptionally talented but also exceptionally fortunate in a financial situation that allowed him the leisure to pursue his personal rebirth at his patron's expense.

Translation soon became the bane of Forster's existence. He longs to find the financial stability that he will never attain "by means of eternal translation"[60] and travels to England in part because he hopes that the king will finally reimburse him and his father for the costs of their journey with Cook: "My wish was just to extricate myself from the translator yoke and make enough so that I would be able to tinker with my own works in peace for a few years."[61] The problem, as Forster's reference to his "own works" (eignen Arbeiten) in this passage makes clear, is not just that he has too many irons in the fire and cannot keep pace with his demanding translation schedule but that the translation gets in the way of his proper work. In drawing a clear distinction between his job and his calling, Forster judges his own work by the standards of genius and denigrates his day labor as mere hackwork. "Then for whom are we writing, my dear Jacobi? Not for the multitude, but for the few that understand us."[62] "The way I write, which pleases a few thinking men, is not popular," he writes a year later, disdainfully distancing himself from those "scribblers" (Schmierer) who get rich from their books.[63] Unfortunately, esoteric works written for the fortunate few do not pay the bills: "Because I get paid 2 Pistoles for a sheet of translation that I can complete *in one day*—that's how great the reading mania [Lesewut] of our public is—and you probably won't notice that I worked on my little essay for *three entire weeks*." Financial logic compels Forster to keep translating, but he pays a bitter price for his labor. "But you have to consider that translating adds nothing to one's reputation, nor to one's pleasure, nor to one's intellectual stimulation, which one's own works *can* do; thus, you do have to distinguish between work for money and work for honor."[64] He concludes to his regret that he belongs "to the writers' guild, . . . that is, because I have to deliver products for money."[65]

It would be easy enough to take Forster at his word and view his plight as symptomatic of many a would-be genius forced to work for filthy lucre, but it is also possible to suspend judgment and look more closely at the kind of writing Forster felt compelled to produce. He leaves us with a literary world divided between mere writers and poetic geniuses, *Schriftsteller* and *Dichter*; subsequent generations of literary historians would simply ignore the labor of the former and concentrate on the productions of a few great men. As Christa Bürger shows in her work on the institution of German literature, the bifurcation of the literary market around 1800 fell along gendered lines, with Goethe, Schiller, and a handful of male companions producing classical works of genius. Female "dilettantes" admired the work of the masters while producing their own middlebrow fiction and toiling in the fields of literary translation.[66] Martha

Woodmansee has suggested that the relative unpopularity of demanding literature could be used as a marketing ploy: while "extensive" readers consumed and disposed of popular novels like so many facial tissues, the new classics required the sort of intensive rereading formerly reserved for religious texts.[67] Christine Touaillon's pioneering analysis of the German *Frauenroman* and the foundational studies of second-wave feminists sought to recuperate the work of some of Germany's forgotten women writers, while more recent digitization projects have rendered hitherto rare copies of ephemeral fiction accessible to an unlimited audience.[68] Given that there are simply too many books for any one individual to read, as Franco Moretti is quick to remind us,[69] the question remains: Do we simply add a limited number of women writers to the canon (and, if so, on what basis do we make our choice?), or do we undertake a more thoroughgoing revision of literary categories? As Andrew Piper has observed in his discussion of Sophie Mereau, another prolific translator in the Age of Goethe, critics often expand the canon by taking "a historically contingent notion of authorship and [applying] it to new categories of authors in order to make room for those new authors," rather than rethinking our understanding of authorship itself.[70]

What kind of an author was Georg Forster, then? How might we characterize his work? It was international rather than national, multilingual rather than monolingual, and more interested in European and even global networks than individual works of art. As Christine Haug has argued in her study of Forster and his publishers, Forster was a product of the Enlightenment who was intent on overcoming communicative boundaries and disseminating ideas. He preferred publishing houses that had connections abroad, and Spener made calculated use of Forster's fame for his plans to establish an international publishing house.[71] Spener had particularly good contacts with London publishers, and Forster later played a leading role in bringing news of the latest English literature to Germany. Improved postal services facilitated the movement of letters and books that was essential to Forster's literary practice. As the university librarian in Mainz, Forster was able to send letters at no cost, which was of vital importance to his work at a time when postage was expensive and delivery services unreliable.[72] The location of Mainz on the Rhine, in close proximity to Frankfurt, and in the border zone between Germany and France, also positioned Forster well for his role as an intercultural mediator.

Forster's translation practice was collaborative, as he and his coworkers manufactured products for the literary market rather than creating inspired works of individual genius. Both literally and figuratively, his writing was gendered female rather than male, in that he employed women to produce rough drafts of translations that he corrected, edited, and introduced for the reading public, and in the broader sense that the works were collectively produced rather than sole authored. In this regard, Forster's translations emerged from a fundamentally different sort of "discourse network" than the one described by Friedrich Kittler. In his view, German mothers around 1800 taught their sons how to read through the phonetic method: they read aloud so that their boys could learn how to decipher the signs that comprised the written text. The mother's voice served as the source of meaning, a plenitude that the young men transcribed into the written text. Paradigmatic for this process is E. T. A. Hoffmann's story of *The Golden Pot*, in which the protagonist translates an otherwise indecipherable text in a hallucinatory state while listening to the dictation of a female voice.[73] The mother or lover is at once elevated into the inspirational medium that enables poetic creativity and denigrated into the muse who cannot contribute to the male world of writing.

Forster had no time to wait for inspiration in his translation workshop in Mainz, and he was more than willing to hire women to help churn out the pages of translated travelogues. His favorite collaborator was Meta Forkel-Liebeskind, the unconventional wife of the music director at the University of Göttingen, who had published an epistolary novel, *Maria*, before moving to Mainz to work with Forster. She translated quickly, if sometimes inaccurately, and got along well with Forster, who once jokingly identified her as his stepdaughter when she accompanied him on a journey to Karlsruhe.[74] She also shared his political views and was eventually imprisoned, together with Caroline Böhmer-Schelling, for several months when apprehended by German authorities as they tried to escape from Mainz in March 1793.[75] In the years preceding the Mainz Revolution, however, Meta joined with Caroline and Therese Forster in a lively social circle centered on the Forster home: "Teatime between six and nine o'clock in the evening was considered an institution in Mainz, to which the closest friends, guests of high intellectual quality who were passing through town, and also often enterprising young people were invited."[76] The Forster home was a place where the translators could unwind after a day of hard labor:

"In the evenings we used to display the completed pages like victory trophies," wrote Meta Forkel to their publisher, going on to express her unbridled admiration for Forster's preface to their latest translation.[77] As this anecdote suggests, gender hierarchies did not completely disappear in Forster's literary workshop: he made the final revisions to the translations and prepared the works for publication. Meta Forkel's description nevertheless indicates that they worked as a team to provide new material for the literary marketplace.

When it came time to sell his wares, Forster was not shy about driving a hard bargain. Immediately after returning from his travels to the Netherlands, England, and France, Forster approached Spener with the idea that he planned to turn the letters and notes written during the journey into a new travelogue. Forster assures Spener that he has the right of first refusal but goes on to make a series of demands, specifying the precise title of the as-yet-unwritten work, the typeface and book format, when the first volume should appear, how many desk copies he should receive, and how much he should be paid.[78] Perhaps put off by Forster's brusque demands, Spener did not respond, so Forster wrote to him again a month later, still assuring him that he would be his first choice as publisher, but casually noting that he was also in correspondence with no less than six other potential publishers.[79] Three days later, Forster wrote to a new prospective publisher for *Views of the Lower Rhine*, Christian Friedrich Voss. The immediate occasion for the letter was to clear up a misunderstanding: Forster had promised to provide a condensed translation of two works for Spener before he learned that his father was already translating the same works for Voss. "Collisions [Collisionen] are unfortunately inevitable in today's German book market," explained Forster, and thus it is unfortunate but not surprising that from time to time "an unpleasant collision arises between father and son that some readers may find irritating." Normally he would feel compelled to step back when he learned that someone else was already at work on the same translation project, "but, ever since German intellectuals have had to work for their daily bread, you can't expect that from anyone."[80] Voss had apparently suggested that such conflicts of interest might be avoided if both Forster and his father worked for him, but Forster responds that Spener is an old friend whom he is reluctant to leave, although he adds in the next breath that Spener has his quirks and that he does work with other publishers from time to time. In this spirit,

Forster closes his long letter with reference to his own forthcoming travelogue, now claiming that seven different publishers are competing for the rights. Two months later, Forster reported to Spener that he had decided to publish *Views of the Lower Rhine* with Voss.[81] The decision not only ended the longest professional association of Forster's career but also jeopardized one of his oldest friendships. The following spring, he made one last attempt at salvaging his relationship with his former publisher, but he also made it clear that their professional differences remained irresolvable: "For the price—I use the term in its broadest sense here—for which I work, you do not want my wares; I therefore grant them to a businessman who pays me."[82] The attempt at partial reconciliation failed; Spener never wrote to Forster again.

Forster is engaged in the business of what Benedict Anderson terms *print-capitalism*, which he argues "laid the basis for national consciousnesses" by creating "unified fields of exchange and communication below Latin and above the spoken vernaculars," giving "a new fixity to language," and establishing "languages-of-power of a kind different from the older administrative vernaculars."[83] Translations play an ambivalent role in this process. On the one hand, there is no reason why a work in translation could not have the same consolidating effect on the language as a work originally written in that language. While the translators were of course fluent in both languages, their readers were not, so for them, reading a work that had been translated into German was no different from reading one that was originally written in German, at least regarding the tendency of the printed word to stabilize and standardize the language. On the other hand, however, the very fact that the book was translated reminded readers that it was not part of the national culture but a product of international exchange, while the subject matter of a translated travelogue deflected readers' attention away from the confines of national borders and took them on imaginary journeys around the world.

In contrast to the aesthetics of genius, in which works of literature serve as the focus of disinterested contemplation, Forster crafts products that he sells on the literary marketplace. While the new understanding of *Literature* constricts the meaning of the term to individual works of creative fiction produced by solitary geniuses, Forster works with a more capacious concept of *literature*, which comprises just about anything that appears on the literary market. His annual histories of English literature do mention some works of literature in the narrow sense of the term, but they also survey the latest contributions to history, politics, theology, travel, geography, mineralogy, epidemiology, and the abolitionist movement.

If we return to Andrew Piper's suggestion that we should rethink our understanding of authorship around 1800, we find that Forster both supports and complicates this notion. He supports it in the sense that I have described previously: in a world overwhelmed by a surfeit of books, Forster works to speed their circulation, to move texts beyond borders rather than to consolidate discrete national identities, to switch between languages rather than create works that arise organically from the depths of national consciousness, to drive hard bargains for a literary product rather than to create timeless treasures for repeated rereading. These practices are in line with Piper's claims that we should challenge the notion of the romantic artist as an "isolated, hermetic genius" (10), shift our focus from "the problem of textual ownership" to "geographical displacement and authorial displacement" (15), think of "the author not only as a towering singularity but also as a member or embodiment of a corporate or communal entity" (15), and of books as part of dynamic networks, "mobile, evolving, collectively generated webs of writing" (25).

On the other hand, Forster ascribes to the aesthetics of genius that his literary practice would seem to refute. In the same letters to his prospective publishers in which he unabashedly negotiates the terms for his literary productions, he also insists on absolute control over the completed project. "Let my authorial dignity (Autorwürde) be my responsibility!" Forster would be happy to have Spener publish his work, but only if he takes it on Forster's terms: "You must not demand that I revise, correct, cross out, etc."[84] In what turned out to be his final letter to Spener, Forster oscillates between protestations of friendship and accusations that Spener had consistently underpaid him and found his translations in need of stylistic revision in ways that disrespected his authority and violated the integrity of his literary works. Forster's repeated laments about being shackled to the soul-crushing labor of translation, which prevented him from concentrating on his own work, arise from the same concept of genius that draws a neat distinction between wage labor (*Brotarbeit*) and inspired creativity. Nor was this dilemma unique to Georg Forster. Goethe, who epitomized the idea of romantic genius and whose collected works solidified his status as a national icon, was also not above demanding top dollar for his creative productions. *Hermann und Dorothea*, the work of his classical period that resonated most deeply with the nineteenth-century reading public, was released both for a general audience and in a limited luxury edition, and Goethe received an extraordinary honorarium from his publisher for his work.[85] Goethe was shielded by the patronage of Duke Karl August from the vagaries of the literary market in ways that Forster and most of his contemporaries were not, but even he was not immune to the mundane realities of professional authorship.

The aesthetics of genius, the monolingual paradigm, and imagined national communities arose in tandem with "the bibliographical diversity that was characteristic of the romantic age."[86] Travelogues turned readers' attention from local concerns to distant horizons, and translations sped the international circulation of literary commodities, even as national literatures were beginning to concentrate authority in the hands of a few writers deemed capable of distilling the spirit of the nation into works of genius in the mother tongue. The tension that pulls Forster between the desire to focus exclusively on his own creations and the financial need to translate and review the books of others runs through the center of literary production in the Age of Goethe. On one extreme we find a poet like Friedrich Hölderlin, whose visionary works became increasingly esoteric and inaccessible to all but the most devoted readers, and on the other, we see writers such as Ludwig Tieck and E. T. A. Hoffmann, whose fiction might be said to arise out of, rather than in opposition to, popular taste. Women writers of the period fall across the same spectrum, ranging from Karoline von Günderrode's poetic fragments to the many novels of Therese Forster-Huber, whose career was just beginning as her first husband's life was coming to an end. Rather than recuperating a limited number of Forster's works to show that he was a literary genius on par with the best of his contemporaries, or using his prodigious talent as a translator as an example of a different kind of transnational authorship, we might better view him as both of the above—a writer who embodied the dual demands of genius and the marketplace in the German institution of literature around 1800.

CHAPTER 2

A Voyage Round the World

In late March 1775, Captain Cook sailed for home. He had been searching for the better part of three years for the great Southern Continent, and although he had long since suspected that it did not exist—or, if it did, that it lay so far south as to be uninhabitable—he was punctilious in fulfillment of his duty and reluctant to abandon his mission. Conditions on board ship had become increasingly dire, however, and even Cook conceded that they could not continue indefinitely. The remains of the meat that had been placed into barrels before the start of the voyage had decomposed into a barely edible gelatinous brine, and it was only a matter of time before scurvy claimed the lives of captain and crew. Thus Cook gave the order to turn to the north, with plans to put in for provisions and repairs at the Cape of Good Hope before resuming the final journey to England.

The decision released long-suppressed hopes and fears among the men. "Our voyage had now lasted twenty-seven months after leaving the Cape of Good Hope," recalled Georg Forster in *A Voyage Round the World*, "since which time we had not touched at any European port, and lived chiefly upon salt provisions."[1] Their first renewed contact with Europeans came off the coast of South Africa. The captain of a Dutch Indiaman invited the officers on board for what he considered a simple meal of roast goose and quail, but to the famished explorers it might as well have been manna from heaven. "On relating how long they had been absent from any European settlement, how long they had lived upon salt-beef, and how oft they had regaled themselves with seals, albatrosses, and pinguins, the captain and his mates dropt their knives and forks, and in pure pity to the strangers, resigned all pretensions to their dinner" (654). The prospect of relief from the physical hardships of the voyage triggered a surge of mental anguish. When the Dutch ship first came into view, men crowded the rails to stare with an eagerness that offered "the strongest proof of that universal longing for an intercourse with Europeans, which, though hitherto silent, now broke out into loud and fervent wishes" (653). In our era of instant global communication, it is difficult to imagine how utterly isolated from all contact with their homes these men had been, and their concerns about what they might learn now were correspondingly great. "All those who had left behind them relations and parents, were apprehensive that they had lost some of the number during their absence; and it was more than probable, that this interval of time would have dissolved many valuable connections, diminished the number of our friends, and robbed us of the comforts which we used to find in their society" (653). When the men finally came ashore, they consumed the news as eagerly as fresh food and drink: "We passed our time very agreeably, and assiduously collected, from heaps of old gazettes, the history of those years, during which we had been banished, as it were, from all the world" (657).

Forster's account of his three-year journey around the world with Captain Cook soon captured the attention of a wide reading public, and it can still be read with interest today. Unlike Alexander von Humboldt's equally fascinating but obsessively digressive *Personal Narrative of a Journey to the Equinoctial Regions of the New Continent*—which was published in three substantial volumes over the course of more than a decade and yet describes less than half of his five-year expedition to the Americas[2]—or his father's thematically organized *Observations Made During a Voyage Round the World*, Forster's *Voyage* tells a satisfying story, beginning with preparations for departure and ending with a triumphant return.[3] Along the way, Cook and his crew are exposed to constant physical danger and psychological stress. They encounter radically alien cultures that had rarely, if ever, had contact with Europeans, catalogue countless new species, and endure bitter cold and burning heat as they circumnavigate the globe. And yet, *A Voyage Round the World* aspires to be more than just another travelogue packed with adventures in exotic lands. In his preface to the work, Forster explains that his father was originally engaged to write "a philosophical history of the voyage, free from prejudice and vulgar error, where human nature should be represented without any adherence to fallacious systems, and upon the principles of general philanthropy; in short, an account written upon a plan which the learned world had not hitherto seen executed" (5–6).[4]

The gripping narrative serves as the vehicle for philosophical reflections on the nature of humankind and the course of human history. Georg Forster left Europe—"banished, as it were, from all the world"—for three formative years but inevitably carried European thought with him as he traveled "round the world." The double meaning of "the world" in Forster's text—as that which is both familiar and unfamiliar, European and non-European, canny (*heimlich*) and uncanny (*unheimlich*)—underscores a fundamental tension between Eurocentrism and cosmopolitanism that reproduces in modulated form the dual concepts of authorship explored in the previous chapter. There we found Forster torn between the aesthetics of genius and the demands of the translator's workshop: on the one hand, he was drawn to a model of writing linked to the consolidation of identity, the stabilization of the vernacular, and the construction of the national culture; on the other, he engaged in the business of translation that reduced the writer to a medium of exchange but also enabled the international circulation of books and ideas. Depending on his mood and perspective, Forster sees himself either as a translating machine, a drone condemned to Sisyphean labors, or as a cosmopolitan intellectual who produces world literature that transcends national provincialism. The underlying tension between the one and the many now carries over into the relationship between Europe and the world. Did European explorers bring light to the darkness of primitive societies or impose a monochrome uniformity onto polychrome diversity? Could they learn to appreciate difference without falling into a cultural relativism that excused even egregious violations of human rights? Was there room for self-criticism in the triumphant narrative of European progress?

The isolation of the ship on a voyage that oscillated between protracted exposure to the elements and occasional encounters with alien peoples gave Forster ample opportunity to ponder these questions. Although he was only seventeen when he left England with Cook and twenty-one when he completed his account of the voyage, Forster was a precocious intellectual whose erudition belied his years. As Ludwig Uhlig has shown, Forster was influenced by the work of writers associated with the Scottish Enlightenment, including Adam Ferguson's *Essay on the History of Civil*

Society (1767), John Millar's *Observations Concerning the Distinction of Ranks in Society* (1771), and Henry Home's (Lord Kames) *Six Sketches of the History of Man* (1774).[5] He also immersed himself in the latest works of German literature immediately after his return to London, where he was particularly moved by Goethe's *Sorrows of Young Werther*. The works of these authors, in turn, form part of a larger shift in European thought since the Renaissance toward a focus on this world rather than the next, inspiring voyages that broadened European horizons and intensified interactions with the non-European world.

I begin this chapter with a look at essays Forster wrote in the decade after the expedition to establish a conceptual framework for his "philosophical history of the voyage" before turning to a close reading of *A Voyage Round the World*. Three broad tendencies become clear when reading through Forster's travelogues, essays, and letters. Forster remained in the first instance a representative of the European Enlightenment, with faith in the powers of reason and the possibility of progress. He was also a nascent romantic, who recorded not only the facts of his travels but also the emotions they inspired. Finally, a deep strain of pessimism runs through Forster's work, not just in his final days in Paris but already in passages of his *Voyage*. To claim, as Jürgen Goldstein does, that Forster gradually shed his Eurocentric views in the course of the voyage, is only partially accurate.[6] Russell Berman's contrast between Cook, the colonialist who instrumentalizes reason, and Forster, the empathetic observer who reveals the emancipatory potential of the Enlightenment, oversimplifies this as well.[7] Forster certainly raises questions about European claims to cultural superiority and weighs the benefits of the voyage against its detrimental potential, but he never completely abandons his faith in human reason or his Eurocentric perspective.[8] *A Voyage Round the World* marks the beginning of Forster's lifelong effort to expand knowledge and dispel prejudice even as he ponders the limits of reason and the transience of human progress.

NATURE AS A WHOLE

In a lecture delivered in Kassel during the academic year of 1782–83, Forster offered his students "A Look into Nature as a Whole" (Ein Blick in das Ganze der Natur). He begins by lamenting the splintering of modern science into a series of subdivisions. Specialists work within their narrow fields, but they forget "that they only advance human happiness" when they connect their research with other lines of inquiry."[9] Before focusing more closely on the topic of the course (zoology), therefore, Forster steps back to provide a larger perspective. He explains that God reveals himself in nature, and that creation and destruction are two parts of a greater whole. "Nature did not grant immortality to any of the fragile bodies it assembles. The material of which they are composed is in constant motion" (8:87). Humans perceive destruction and renewal, death and new life, on an individual basis, but the being (Wesen) behind nature sees the whole: "It sees in this destruction and renewal—in all these alternations and sequences—it sees nothing but permanence and continuance" (8:90). And what is the point of this "procreation and reproduction of beings that incessantly destroy and renew themselves, that always stage the same drama, and neither increase nor decrease the population of nature?" (8:91). Forster answers that this has been the nature of nature ever since the "world machine" (Weltmaschine) was first set in motion. Everything changes, but the system remains the same: "The machine remains in place; all of its parts are moveable" (8:92).

Forster's description of nature as a living, constantly changing, interconnected whole reflects thoughts expressed in Goethe's *Werther* and anticipates similar ideas in the work of other contemporary authors. While Forster was delivering his lecture in Kassel, for instance, Herder was writing the first volume of his *Ideas*, which begins by placing humankind in the grand cosmic perspective of a dynamically evolving universe. Alexander von Humboldt would go on to think of nature in terms of interconnected ecosystems rather than discrete species and distinct geographical formations, while Goethe would later grant Faust insight into the life force that drives the perpetual motion of "form in transformation" (Gestaltung, Umgestaltung) in the physical world.[10] These German writers tap into a longer philosophical tradition associated with Spinoza, Heraclitus, and Lucretius. Like the Renaissance humanists before them, they turned away from spiritual concerns to concentrate on life on earth in the time we have. Stephen Greenblatt has revitalized interest in the Renaissance by focusing on the rediscovery of Lucretius's *De rerum natura* (On the nature of things) as a central event in the rise of this new mentality. For centuries, medieval theologians sought to repress the Roman writer's life-affirming philosophy, espousing "a hatred of pleasure-seeking and a vision of God's providential rage."[11] As a result, "the pursuit of pain triumphed over the pursuit of pleasure."[12] With the advent of a new era, however, that mentality began to change. In Lucretius, scholars and artists discovered a vision of a world in constant flux, with no creator and no grand plan, a world in which humans do not reign supreme and for whom God does not reserve a place in heaven. The here and now is all we have, and for that reason it should be cherished and embraced, "for we are a small part of a vast process of world-making that Lucretius celebrated as essentially erotic."[13]

Where do humans stand in relation to nature? They are part of nature, Forster explains, but a very special part: "God made only him capable of being a beholder of His works, a witness to His wonders. The divine spark that lives in man allows him to partake in these secrets" (8:86–87). Nature, which would seem to be a self-contained whole, would in fact not be complete without the human subject who perceives it. In pondering nature, humans raise themselves toward the divine: "By contemplating and measuring nature, the atrium of the throne of divine splendor, he lifts himself step by step to the inner seat of omnipotence and omnipresence" (8:87). This reciprocal relationship between humans and nature lies at the heart of what Chenxi Tang terms "the geographical imagination of modernity." In an incisive reading of Goethe's "On the Lake" (Auf dem See), a short poem composed while or immediately after he spent a morning on Lake Zurich on June 15, 1775 (as Forster was in the final weeks of his three-year voyage), Tang shows how Goethe expresses a new understanding of nature in relation to the human subject. Nature "is no longer conceived in terms of universal order," as in the work of Albrecht von Haller, "but as a dynamic process driven by a hidden, internal productive force. No natural element in the landscape stands alone. Every one of them is engaged in interactions with others."[14] Instead of depicting a particular lake or specific locale, as in the case of Klopstock's "Lake Zurich" (Der Zürchersee) or Haller's "The Alps" (Die Alpen), Goethe creates a generalized landscape that serves "as a symbol of the whole of nature." "Now," continues Tang, "the symbol always requires an interpreting subject who glimpses the idea in the appearance, intuits the general in the particular." Thus, even though the subject is not explicitly mentioned in the poem's final stanza, with its images of interactive nature, it is implicitly there. "The landscape constitutes itself as a symbol of nature through the viewing of the subject, the subject constitutes himself through viewing the landscape as signifying the totality of nature, and the totality of nature constitutes itself in the moment when the subject interprets the landscape to be a symbol of it."[15] Goethe's "On the Lake" thus offers a small but important example of the modern geographic imagination that conceives of nature as a dynamically unfolding process in a symbiotic relation with the perceiving subject. Schelling would go on to base his philosophy of nature (*Naturphilosophie*) on the idea that nature comes to self-consciousness in the human subject.[16]

For Forster, the passive perception of nature is not enough; humans must play an active role in cultivating nature and changing it for the better. A persistent critique of Rousseau's nostalgic yearning for the lost or perhaps only hypothetical state of nature informs Forster's work, in keeping with ideas expressed by the writers of the Scottish Enlightenment.[17] In his *Essay on the History of Civil Society*, for instance, Adam Ferguson insists that human nature is the same everywhere. "In the condition of the savage, as well as in that of the citizen, are many proofs of human invention; and in either is not any permanent station, but a mere stage through which this travelling being is destined to pass."[18] All humans are inherently capable of growth, and the process of development never stops. To speak of the "state of nature" as a primeval, static condition that is fundamentally different from what humans have become makes no sense: "If we are asked therefore, Where the state of nature is to be found? we may answer, It is here; and it matters not whether we are understood to speak in the island of Great Britain, at the Cape of Good Hope, or the Straits of Magellan."[19] In this spirit, Forster begins a short essay on "New Holland [Australia] and the British Colony in Botany Bay" with a programmatic statement of his point of view. Any impartial observer will admit that humans who use their minds are more in tune with their natural talents than those who are content to satisfy mere sensual desires and blind impulses, he maintains. Those who believe that there is a "contradiction between nature and culture" are mistaken. "The capacity for thought, with all of its consequences, is as intrinsic to our nature as the impulse to eat and procreate."[20]

It follows that humans fulfill their God-given destiny by shaping and improving the natural world. Georg's father makes just this argument in *Observations*. "Where man the lord of the creation on this globe, has never attempted any change on it, there nature seems only [to] thrive; for in reality it languishes," asserts Johann Reinhold Forster. "How beautiful, how improved, how useful does nature become by the industry of man!"[21] In improving nature, moreover, humankind improves itself: "This therefore shews evidently, that mankind, in a pastoral state, could never attain to that degree of improvement and happiness, to which agriculture, and the cultivation of vegetables, will easily and soon lead them."[22] Georg Forster makes the same argument in "Nature as a Whole": "Made to worship the Creator, he rules over all creations; as a vassal of heaven and king of the earth, he ennobles, populates, and enriches nature: he compels the living creatures to orderliness, submissiveness, and harmony; he beautifies nature; he cultivates, expands, and refines her" (8:94). Nature is not self-sufficient after all; "she" must be improved by human labor: "Is she not beautiful, this cultivated nature [diese gebaute Natur]! How human care has adorned her in such a sparkling, splendid way!" (8:95).

What is true of humans in relation to nature is also true of different human cultures in relation to one another. We are all God's children, but that does not mean we are all at the same stage of development. "The Laplander, the Patagonian, the Hottentot, the European, the American, and the Negro all stem from the same father, to be sure, but, as brothers, they are far from being equal" (8:88). Some cultures are more advanced than others, and it is inevitable, indeed, natural in the sense described previously, that more developed cultures would want to expand their territory. "The progress of culture is therefore in the interest of humanity, and populating the entire earth with civilized inhabitants is the great goal that we see before us and is worth our effort to attain."[23] Australia, for instance, offers great opportunity as a vast new continent whose aboriginal inhabitants will pose no problem for British settlement. "The few miserable people who wander around the shores in scattered groups with no permanent homes pose no danger to the settlers, nor do they have anything to fear from them."[24] In fact, by colonizing Australia, the British may well be doing the indigenous peoples a favor. Forster explains that the Aborigines, like all peoples, have embarked on the path to culture, which will eventually lead "to intellectual *maturity* (Besonnenheit), and hence to sociability."[25] They have barely started their journey, however, and progress is so slow that millennia may pass before they reach their goal. Perhaps the contact with a more advanced civilization will speed them on their way: "And who knows what sort of fortunate influence the example of European settlers might have even on these uneducated but not barbaric natives?"[26]

COOK, THE DISCOVERER

This unabashed celebration of European cultural superiority and the civilizing mission informs the essay of which Forster was most proud, "Cook, the Discover"—or at least that would seem to be the case at first glance. In the summer of 1786, while living and teaching in Vilnius, Forster began to translate Cook's three-volume description of his final voyage. At first, Forster planned to farm the job out to his brother-in-law, but his efforts were so hopelessly inept that Forster took over the translation and added an extensive critical commentary.[27] "A translation will never make an author famous," wrote Forster to his friend Georg Christoph Lichtenberg, a physicist and author of the satirical *Sudelbücher* (scrapbooks), who had befriended Forster in Göttingen, "but such an important book deserves a careful translation."[28] A few months later, Forster mentioned in a letter to Herder that he was planning to write an introduction to the volume,[29] and in April he could report that he was finished. His primary purpose in writing the introductory essay was not to produce a panegyric, Forster explained, although Cook certainly deserved one; "the only thing that I really enjoyed about the work was that it gave me a chance to express my own philosophy."[30]

"Cook, the Discoverer" falls into three main sections. The first describes each of Cook's three voyages and situates his accomplishments in the context of European exploration since Columbus. The second describes life on board ship in fascinating detail and the crew's encounters with indigenous peoples, while the third summarizes Cook's major contributions to the understanding of the world. Forster's tone hovers between appreciation and hagiography. Half the world was still unknown before Cook first set sail, yet little of significance remained to be discovered by the time he met his premature death. Drawing on personal experience, Forster describes the captain as a man in complete control of his ship and full of concern for his crew. He cared for his men like a father, convincing them by his good example to eat the sauerkraut that supposedly staved off scurvy[31] and, when possible, avoiding the corporeal punishment endemic to the British Navy. "Cook punished rarely and reluctantly, never without an urgent cause and always with moderation" (5:249). Cook was exceptionally kind to the indigenous peoples he encountered, Forster maintains, and they in turn venerated him as a god. Received wisdom held that fresh pork could not be salted in the tropics and that it was impossible to get fresh water from frozen seawater, that there was a great Southern Continent and an easy Northwest Passage from England to China, but Cook set prejudice aside and discovered the truth through empirical experience. Like Columbus and a handful of other explorers before him, Cook had the curiosity that characterizes the true discoverer. When the Spanish crossed the Pacific from Manilla to Mexico, they followed the exact same course for two centuries and passed by the Hawaiian Islands in ignorance, whereas Cook enlightened the world with his relentless inquisitiveness. In the body of his essay, Forster displays no doubt in Cook's personal righteousness or the legitimacy of his voyages. He contrasts Asia, whose indolent inhabitants have failed to progress beyond a rudimentary level of culture and actively resist foreign influence, with Australia, which is so thinly populated that it seems perfectly suited for European settlement. Forster imagines a future in which even Asia will be roused from its torpor and cease its resistance "to all the achievements of the Enlightenment." Then we would look back at "Cook's epoch of discovery as the point in time when a new, purposeful development of the human race and its powers began" and European wisdom triumphed over Asiatic obstinacy (5:292). Entranced by his own vision of the future, Forster ends his essay with a vision of Cook being borne aloft on eagles' wings to take his place among the Olympian gods. If then he were to cast an eye on the earth below, he would see a grateful people erecting monuments in his memory and bewailing his loss.

Forster's essay contributes enthusiastically to "the intellectual mythologization of Cook as the humane embodiment of the Enlightenment."[32] In his withering critique of "European mythmaking in the Pacific," Gananath Obeyesekere challenges the self-congratulatory willingness on the part of many Europeans to believe in reports that the Hawaiians venerated Cook as a god; he also disparages those who celebrate Cook as the good colonialist who brought the benefits of British civilization to the rest of the world. While Forster insists that Cook treated his men with exceptional kindness, Obeyesekere claims that Cook was even more tyrannical than the notorious William Bligh.[33] Forster's final image of

Cook ascending into the heavens may have been influenced by a play produced in London shortly after the news of Cook's death reached the city, which in turn inspired several paintings, "the most interesting being a depiction of the allegorical trio of Cook, Britannia, and Fame hovering in the clouds above a view of Kealakekua Bay where Cook was killed."[34] The inclusion of Britannia implies a contrast between violent Spanish conquistadors and the enlightened English that Germans found equally flattering when imagining their future colonial endeavors. Forster imports this exculpatory vision of British imperialism in the hope that it will motivate young Germans to carry on the work that Cook began. "German youth! You too read Cook's unforgettable, action-packed story of discovery. Speak! Were you not educated, enlightened, inspired to reflect . . . and filled with thankfulness and admiration for the discoverer?" (5:297).

Forster's essay would thus seem to fit into Susanne Zantop's reading of Germany's precolonial past, with its insistence on present innocence and anticipation of a future empire. Zantop views precolonial German literature as the mental training ground for imperial reality. "Imaginary colonialism anticipated actual imperialism, words, actions. In the end, reality just caught up with the imagination."[35] Fantasies of future glory assuaged fears of current belatedness: "No, Germany had not come too late—there was still territory to be had; no, Germans were not incompetent colonizers . . . and no, Germans had no share in colonial guilt."[36] Forster underscored his hopes for enlightened German leadership by dedicating his essay to Emperor Joseph II, with whom he had had an audience in Vienna on his way to his professorship in Vilnius, and the emperor gave Forster an expensive diamond ring in return.[37] Given his clear statement of satisfaction with this essay in the previously cited letter, there is no reason to doubt that Forster meant what he wrote in his assessment of Captain Cook: that he admired the man and respected his accomplishments. If we look at the introduction to "Cook, the Discoverer," however, a more complicated picture of Forster's philosophy emerges.

Forster was acutely aware of the anti-imperial tradition in European thought and addresses it directly in the opening pages of "Cook, the Discoverer." He announces his plan to erect a monument to the man and his accomplishments, but first, he considers "the moral value of the discoveries" (5:193). What if "the eloquent man" (Rousseau) was right when he identified "science" as "the source of all human misery"? The evidence points in his favor: "Who could seriously deny the damage that is inextricably linked to the development of various abilities in humans?" But did we have a choice? "However, if you concede this inextricability, we still cannot prove that the education of the human race could have taken a different path than it actually did; and until you prove this, there is no point in calling us back into the forests" (5:193). In his *Discourse on the Origins of Inequality*, Rousseau argues similarly that the inherently human desire to improve our lot removes us from nature and makes us unhappy, but then he laments the existence of that impulse and wishes—understandably but inconsistently—that humans had been made differently. Forster, in contrast, accepts the fact that the human desire for progress contains the seeds of its own destruction and extends it to a general principle of nature: "Just as every growth presupposes destruction and ends in destruction again, so too the development of one capacity entails the repression of another" (5:194–95). What is true of nature is also true of culture: progress and destruction are intimately entwined. "The first wars, even those of savages, contain the seeds of culture; for, as the conqueror enjoys his victory, his needs increase. Luxury, art, and science, the children of *one* birth, wed one another and bring a new brood—monsters and geniuses—into the world." There is no point in complaining, for it is "only by means of this incessant change" that "everything exists." Time marches on, "without listening to the lamentation of the hypochondriac," who wishes that the world was made differently and holds the human race to an unrealistic standard.

With these general principles in place, Forster turns to the specific question regarding the ethics of European exploration. "Our sophists know how to determine with a disgusting display of arithmetic precision how many drops of Negro sweat go into an ounce of sugar," he sneers; they weigh the discovery of new cures against the spread of new diseases like a businessman balancing his ledger, but they fail to address the fundamental question: "Can they stop up the source of evil without causing the source of good to dry up at the same time?" The Greeks were at least consistent with their myth of a box that, when opened by the curious Pandora, unleashed misery onto the world, even though the moral of their story is depressing, "a bleak lesson!" (5:198). Who would not prefer the image of a benevolent nature that makes steady progress toward the good? Who does not hope for the return of the Golden Age? "This harmless hope, a philosopher's stone of our century, at least deserves no mockery, as long as it remains the goal that is held aloft to keep so many forces in motion for the needs of the *present* moment and inspires everyone to strive for that degree of perfection in their career *that they are capable of attaining*" (5:199). After mocking the naivete of people who criticize the collateral damage caused by those who seek to discover new worlds, Forster reintroduces the desire for unmitigated progress as a relatively harmless deception that encourages individuals to strive for realistic goals. In Kantian terms, Forster transforms the literal belief in human progress into a regulative ideal, a useful illusion. We act as if it were true: "That way, at least, no punishment could be less harmful and at the same time more beneficial than the images that the mind uses to lead us to a real goal." Against this standard we must measure "the benefit of the discoverer for the present and the future" (5:200). We will never realize complete perfection; the search for the same may cause suffering for some, and the voyages of discovery, like all human endeavors, are ultimately futile, in that whatever they achieve in the short run will inevitably be subsumed into a new cycle of procreative destruction. Striving to advance the human race through voyages of discovery is nevertheless a worthy undertaking that uses ideals as inspiration for the provisional accomplishment of lesser goals.

In pondering the relationship between human discord and the potential for progress, Forster shares the concerns of his contemporaries. In his "Idea for a Universal History with a Cosmopolitan Intent" (1784), Kant argues that conflict contributes to human development. Individuals suffer and tension between cultures is inevitable, in his view, but strife is the motor that drives us forward. Schiller will take issue with Kant's thesis in the sixth letter of his treatise *On the Aesthetic Education of Man* (1795). He acknowledges that "there was no other way of developing the manifold capacities of Man than by placing them in opposition to each other," but recoils at the idea that current generations should be required to live in misery for the benefit of a future society: "We should have been the bondslaves of humanity, we should have drudged for it for centuries on end, and branded upon our mutilated nature the shameful traces of this servitude—in order that a later generation might devote itself in blissful indolence to the care of its moral health, and develop the free growth of its humanity!"[38] Schiller demands satisfaction in the here and now; his program of aesthetic education is the means to that end: "We must indeed, if we are to solve that political problem in practice, follow the path of aesthetics, since it is through Beauty that we arrive at Freedom."[39] Forster shares Schiller's sense of urgency, and he would indeed risk his life for the revolutionary cause, but he harbors nagging doubts about the human ability to effect permanent change. In this regard, his work anticipates that of Alexander von Humboldt, who shared Forster's liberal convictions but also voiced occasional uncertainties about human progress. "Thus do the races of men die away," writes Humboldt in conclusion to his essay on the waterfalls of the Orinoco in *Views of Nature*. "The admirable lore of the different peoples fades away," but nature as a whole lives on: "So forever will new life sprout forth from the womb of the Earth. Restlessly, procreative Nature opens her buds: unconcerned whether outrageous humanity (a forever discordant race) should trample the ripening fruit."[40]

Goethe grapples with similar questions about the ethics and efficacy of human progress in *Faust*. From a limited perspective, Faust's striving causes human suffering. In the first part of the drama, he seduces and abandons Gretchen and their child; in part two, he kills an innocent old couple to extend his commercial empire. This human tragedy unfolds within the embrace of a divine comedy, however. As Mephistopheles explains, "everything that arises / is worthy of decay" (alles, was entsteht, / Ist wert, daß es zugrunde geht), but in his role as a destructive devil, Mephistopheles inadvertently keeps creation alive, as all destruction leads to a new cycle of growth. Thus he defines himself paradoxically as "a part of that force / which, always willing evil, always produces good" (Ein Teil von jener Kraft, / Der stets das Böse will und stets das Gute schafft).[41] The same Lucretian idea informs Forster's "Look into Nature as a Whole": the individual elements of nature are in a state of constant flux, but nature itself remains unchanged. Faust's task or calling is to press nature forward, to accelerate change, not because it leads to a particular goal but because in doing so he participates most fully in the energy of creation; the ultimate crime would be to detach oneself from desire and stop striving. To win his bet with the devil, he must remain unsatisfied, driven by an insatiable lust that leaves human carnage in its wake, but in his incessant striving, Faust partakes of the larger unity of creation in its incessant mutability. In a calculated affront to Christian doctrine, Goethe makes Faust's sin the source of his salvation: "for him whose striving never ceases / we can provide redemption" (wer immer strebend sich bemüht, / Den können wir erlösen).⁴² Forster, in contrast, goes out of his way to emphasize Cook's virtues: his discoveries advance the reach of European civilization; he treats his own men with kindness and the savages with compassion. From this limited perspective, Cook does more good than evil. From the broader framework of the preface to "Cook, the Discoverer," however, we know that apparent progress is only provisional; that it will probably cause pain for some in the short run; and that ultimately, inevitably, the civilization that Cook advances will wither and die, or more to the point, it will self-destruct, as all enlightenment contains its own dialectic.

Forster follows a similar logic in "Nature as a Whole." There he turns passive admiration of nature into an ethical imperative to make it better. He ends that essay on a pessimistic note, however. Humans can drain swamps and channel rivers, but nature has a way of reasserting itself, and if humans do not continually renew their efforts, nature will reclaim control: "Everything returns to the realm of nature: nature resumes her rights, extinguishes the work of man, covers his proudest monuments with dust and moss, and, over time, destroys them completely, leaving him nothing but the agonizing realization that he has lost the property that his ancestors acquired with such difficulty due to his own fault" (8:96). Human beings have themselves to blame for their loss. "Tempted by insatiable desire and blinded by even more insatiable ambition, he renounces the feelings of humanity, uses all his powers against himself, tries to destroy himself, and succeeds in the end" (8:97). If Forster's larger thesis about nature's cycles of creation and destruction is correct, however, the human sins that cause their self-destruction are as inevitable as the virtues that drive the human desire to appreciate and improve nature. As he states in the opening pages of his essay on the colonization of Australia, there is nothing more natural than the human desire to create culture, but like all products of nature, specific human cultures are ephemeral, while nature as a whole is eternal. If Goethe sees Faust's vicious behavior as a necessary component of nature, Forster measures Cook's virtues against the same standard, admiring his accomplishments but acknowledging their ultimate ephemerality. His enlightened optimism is *aufgehoben*, both canceled and preserved, in a system that celebrates the discoverer's achievements, dismisses the negative consequences of his endeavors, and yet suggests that belief in human progress is itself an illusion within the eternal cycles of an indifferent nature.

THE CIVILIZING MISSION I: DOMESTICATING NATURE

Captain Cook's three voyages were conceived primarily as scientific expeditions, albeit ones that were undertaken in the interest of the British monarchy. Cook was appointed as the leader because of his skills as a navigator and cartographer, and the primary objective of the first mission, to observe the transit of Venus in Tahiti, was chosen because it would enable more precise navigation and produce better maps of potential colonies. The great Southern Continent that Cook sought to discover on his second voyage might have been the source of untold riches, while his final effort aimed to find the Northwest Passage that could have spurred international commerce by dramatically reducing the time it took to travel between England and China. In a narrow sense, Cook failed in each of his missions: hazy conditions rendered precise measurements of Venus's transit across the Sun impossible; he discovered no Southern Continent and no Northwest Passage.[43] And yet Cook opened vast regions of the planet to the nascent British Empire, and he did not hesitate, like conquistadors of prior centuries, to claim distant lands for the British crown. While never losing sight of potential political and economic gain for the government that sponsored the voyage, Cook and his cadre of scientists also sought knowledge for its own sake, drafting more accurate charts, cataloguing new species of plants and animals, and recording their encounters with indigenous peoples.

The spirit of Enlightenment that informed the voyage carried over into Forster's "philosophical history" of the same. Past explorers were sent out by "an interested, avaricious court" to "find great riches of silver and pearls," he contends, but such "incitements are not necessary now-a-days, when several monarchs in Europe have convinced the world that they can institute voyages of discovery, with no other view than the increase of human knowledge, and the improvement of mankind" (561). "I have adopted no particular system" (592), Forster explains, as he is motivated to learn as much as possible about all realms of knowledge. He concludes his monumental travelogue on a modest note: "the additions to the stock of human knowledge which have been made during this voyage, however considerable they may be when put in competition with what was known before, are of small moment when compared with the immense variety of unknown objects which, even in our present confined situation, are still within our reach" (685).

Cook sailed thousands of miles, often at the pace of a slow jog or leisurely stroll, meaning that he and his crew spent months sailing through mostly monotonous and occasionally terrifying oceans between remote islands in the South Pacific and around the perimeter of Antarctica. For the scientists on board, including Forster and his father, this meant almost unlimited time to observe natural phenomena and alien cultures, and to collect and catalogue specimens and artifacts. Georg Forster spent much of his time producing meticulous watercolors of the flora and fauna that his father collected, a process that engages the scientist-artist in protracted observation in a way that snapping a photograph does not.[44] The knowledge acquired might in some cases enable future colonists to exploit natural resources for imperial gain, but most of the time Forster seems motivated by curiosity and a sense of wonder at the world's infinite riches and staggering beauty.[45]

Time and again Forster interrupts his narrative to appreciate what he sees: the phosphorescence in the water as they approach South Africa, the first view of Tahiti on "one of those beautiful mornings which the poets of all nations have attempted to describe" (143), an island landscape with a waterfall that affords "a view of great beauty and grandeur" (90), a "wild and romantic spot" so charming "that the powers of description fall short of the force and beauty of nature" (91). Even life-threatening storms and violent weather are a source of sublime fascination. "Our situation during all this time was very dangerous and alarming," recalls Forster, as the ship was surrounded by giant water spouts illuminated by flashes of lightning, "a phænomenon which carried so much terrific majesty in it, and connected as it were the sea with the clouds, made our oldest mariners uneasy and at a loss how to behave" (111). "The aspect of the ocean was at once magnificent and terrific," writes Forster of a gale in the South Pacific; "now on the summit of a broad and heavy billow, we overlooked an unmeasurable expanse of sea, furrowed into numberless deep channels; now on a sudden the wave broke under us, and we plunged into a deep and dreary valley" (266–67). As they sail southward toward Antarctica, the wind dies and they find themselves surrounded by giant icebergs. "The whole scene looked like the wrecks of a shattered world, or as the poets describe some regions of hell" (291).

Such passages about nature's enchanting beauty or sublime power anticipate the affective representations of nature in Goethe's poetry, Caspar David Friedrich's paintings, and Alexander von Humboldt's travelogues. "Nature has to be felt," explains Chenxi Tang; objective depictions must be combined with subjective impressions to produce the romantic *Stimmungslandschaft* or landscape of mood. "The starting point and guiding principle of Humboldt's thinking about nature was the concept of the 'total impression' (*Totaleindruck*)," continues Tang,[46] but in espousing these views, Humboldt was following in Forster's footsteps. Writing in an era before science and the arts had diverged into the "two cultures" described in C. P. Snow's much-cited lecture, Forster, Humboldt, and Goethe could still combine scientific curiosity with aesthetic appreciation, although as we have seen, Forster already cautions against the dangers of scientific specialization in the opening pages of "A Look into Nature as a Whole."[47] In that essay, as we recall, Forster argues that passive appreciation of nature is not enough; it also has to be actively cultivated by human labor.

As both Cook and Forster describe it, the voyage is an exercise in the human effort to appreciate, understand, and improve God's creation. When setting out on the journey, Cook stocked the ships with European plants and animals designed to benefit all concerned, and he refers repeatedly in his diaries to his hopes for the success of his endeavor.[48] Before departing from New Zealand, Cook urges one of the Maoris to look after the presents he has left for them: "He made me a promise not to kill any, if he keeps his word and proper care is taken of them there were enough to stock the whole Island in due time, there being two Boars, two Sows, two Cocks and four Hens; the seeds and roots were such as are most usefull (viz) Wheat, French and Kidney Beans, Pease, Cabages, Turnips, Onions, Carrots, Parsnips, Yams &c &c."[49] When embarking on his third voyage, Cook again loaded cattle onto the ship "at His Majestys Command and expence with a view of stocking Otahiete and the Neighbouring Islands with these usefull animals." Before leaving from the island of Tonga, Cook allows himself a moment to reflect on his accomplishments: "I could not help flatering my self with the idea that some future Navigator may from the very same station behould these Medows stocked with

Cattle, the English have planted at these islands."[50] On still another Pacific island, Cook left behind a male and female dog in the hope "that they may prove an Adam and Eve of their species in this Country."[51]

Forster wholeheartedly endorses this aspect of Cook's mission. Upon their arrival in New Zealand, the men release geese that they picked up in South Africa and plant seeds brought from England, confident that they will leave the wilderness a better place. "The superiority of a state of civilization over that of barbarism could not be more clearly stated, than by the alterations and improvements we had made in this place" (105). The crew clears land for planting, scientists set up their instruments, artists sketch the landscape, and all is well: "In a word, all around us we perceived the rise of arts, and the dawn of science, in a country which had hitherto lain plunged in one long night of ignorance and barbarism!" (106). The pattern repeats itself throughout the voyage, as Cook is eager to introduce new species of plants and animals to the native cultures he encounters, while Forster provides approving commentary: "The introduction of black cattle and sheep on that fertile island [Tahiti] will doubtless increase the happiness of its inhabitants" (12). At the same time, his scientists were on the lookout for new species that might be of use to them in a process that has been variously described as "ecological imperialism," "bioprospecting," or "biopiracy."[52]

Chief among these new discoveries was the breadfruit tree, to which Forster dedicated an enthusiastic essay several years later. For centuries, he writes, Europeans have been appropriating "the Asiatic gifts of nature and those of the fourth and fifth parts of the world in general," while ignoring the benefits of the humble breadfruit.[53] Forster defines the species, speculates on its origins (Is the breadfruit native to Tahiti or was it imported by the Polynesians when they populated the Pacific islands?), describes how it is prepared (never raw, always roasted), extols its salubrious qualities, and wonders whether it might be a contributing factor in the production of an exceptionally handsome, peaceful people: "We are only certain that gentleness, love, and a tender heart are the noteworthy characteristics of people nourished by breadfruit" (6:79–80). Ironically, Forster also notes that although the breadfruit cannot be cultivated in Europe, it does thrive in the West Indies, where it could be used to feed slaves, and it was for this purpose that Bligh returned to Tahiti on his ill-fated mission of 1789.[54] Some say "that the Negroes are only bastards of apes and humans," writes Forster, but "however uncertain their origin may be, they are still undeniably human by virtue of consciousness and reason, and thus have a better right to our sympathy" than many are willing to grant them (6:64). While Forster will soon attack the institution of slavery and the racist presuppositions that support it, here he merely states that whatever their origins, enslaved Africans are humans, and as humans they deserve to be fed well. He praises breadfruit's ability to alleviate their hunger but ignores the systemic evil that has created the problem. Forster's larger point in his study of the breadfruit tree is that domesticated plants cannot be considered in isolation from the cultures that cultivate them. "The history of the products of the earth is deeply and intimately connected to human fate and the entire range of human feelings, thoughts, and actions." The scientific investigation of the external world exists in a reciprocal relation to those who study it: "Only the relationship of the outer world to our inner self gives science a general interest; just as from another perspective the public benefit of scientific truths and their influence on human happiness depends solely on their general and universal dissemination" (6:80).

Today's reader might sigh or wince at the naive confidence behind Cook's efforts to export European plants and animals to the Pacific, as we now know that the introduction of nonnative species often wreaked havoc on local ecosystems, just as European diseases decimated indigenous populations. In Alfred Crosby's words, it "did not occur to any pakeha [white man] for decades and decades that spilling and strewing alien organisms into an ecosystem can be like lighting a candle in order to lessen the gloom in a powder magazine."[55] Of more immediate concern for the sailors was the inconvenience caused by the presence of livestock on the crowded ship and the struggle to keep the cattle alive. Forster's father complained bitterly about his cramped quarters. "I was now beset with cattle & stench on both sides, having no other but a thin deal partition full of chinks between me & them. The room offered me by Capt. Cook, & which the masters obstinacy deprived me of, was now given to very peaceably bleating creatures, who on a stage raised up as high as my bed, shit & pissed on one side, whilst five Goats did the same afore on the other side."[56] The animals suffered along with the men. Scurvy-ridden sheep staggered ashore in the last stages of exhaustion after their long voyage to the Pacific islands,[57] and many died long before they reached their final destination, including those who perished in the desolate seas off Antarctica to "the Melancholy Croaking of Innumerable Penguins."[58] Their trials and tribulations were all in the name of what seemed to Cook and Forster a laudable goal, however: to transform the globe into an English garden.[59]

The negative counterpart to these efforts to introduce new species to alien environments is a casual willingness on the part of the men to exterminate the local fauna. On a regular basis throughout the voyage, Cook and his crew engage in the wholesale slaughter of birds and sea creatures. In fairness to them, the men are often on the brink of starvation as they hunt for food, but there are frequent instances in which the killing seems more for sport than survival. While sailing from New Zealand to Tahiti, for instance, they pass by a pod of whales. "They were fired at from our vessel, and one of them being shot through the head, could no longer plunge under water, but began to beat about furiously on the surface, and tinged the sea with its blood" (133). They consider bringing the cetacean aboard to examine it, but the wind is good and the ship sails on. Later in the voyage land creatures meet a similar fate. The men come ashore on a rocky island "covered with a multitude of seals" and begin shooting. Most escape into the water, but some "kept their ground, and were killed by our bullets. Several showers interrupted our sport for some time, but the weather clearing up afterwards, we killed with clubs a great number of the fattest sea-lions" (636). They are hungry, but the meat proves unpalatable and, in any case, the extent of the carnage far exceeds their need. It also proceeds with a cold-blooded matter-of-factness. While exploring an island, they come upon a sea lion so huge that they mistake it for a boulder. Instead of leaving the massive creature undisturbed, the "midshipman shot it through the head whilst it lay fast asleep." The men then turn their attention to a flock of birds, who "were so dull, as hardly to waddle from us; we easily overtook them by running, and knocked them down with sticks" (645). Even the albatrosses that encircle the ship are fair game. As the men gather fresh water from the icebergs off Antarctica, Cook notes in his diary that "Mr Forster shott an Albatross whose plumage was of a Dark grey Colour."[60] Unlike Coleridge's ancient mariner, however, the elder Forster does not suffer terrible consequences for the casual killing, nor does he come to the sentimental conclusion that God loves "all things both great and small."[61] The earth is vast, with its resources seemingly limitless and certainly capable of sustaining the occasional hunting party of a few isolated sailors; if the purposeful hunt turns into a killing frenzy, no one seems particularly disturbed.

Although Forster approves of Cook's efforts to civilize nature and seems indifferent to the crew's occasional butchery of wildlife, there are moments when he exhibits a sentimental attachment to animals of the sort that was becoming more common in the late eighteenth century.[62] When the sailors buy fifteen or twenty monkeys for their amusement on the Cape Verde Islands, only to neglect, abuse, or starve them once the novelty wears off, Forster is outraged: "A harmless race of animals, dragged from the happy recess of native shades, to wear out the rest of their lives in continual anguish and torment, deserve a pitying rememberance, though humanity would fain have drawn the veil over all acts of iron-hearted insensibility, and wanton barbarism" (37). On the same voyage south, Forster finds a little swallow in the rigging, soaked by the morning rains. He dries the bird and is delighted over the course of the next several days to watch it catch flies as it flutters about the ship. Then it disappears, probably the victim "of some unfeeling person, who caught it in order to provide a meal for a favourite cat." Clearly upset by the loss of the bird, and yet aware that most readers will find his emotions exaggerated, Forster explains that seemingly trivial incidents can take on disproportionate significance during a long sea voyage, and "it is therefore not to be wondered at, if a subject so trifling in itself as putting to death a harmless bird, should affect a heart not yet buffeted into insensibility" (39). Even the sailors are occasionally capable of showing concern for animal suffering, if in a rather roughshod fashion. When one of the shipboard dogs makes the mistake of eating some of the same fish that had just poisoned the men, it "lay several days in such exquisite torments, that it was at last thrown overboard, to put an end to its pain and misery" (597).[63]

These oscillations between random killing, occasional kindness, and the effort to export European plants and animals around the globe point to ongoing changes in the relationship between human beings and the natural environment in the late eighteenth century. In her study of Alexander von Humboldt, for instance, Andrea Wulf describes the movement "from the human-centred perspective . . . that God had given humans command over nature" to a view that placed humans in a reciprocal relation to nature in a way that denied them supreme authority. The former understanding had dominated Western thought for millennia, she observes, "from Aristotle, who had written that 'nature has made all things specifically for the sake of man,' to the botanist Carl Linnaeus, who had still echoed the same sentiment more than 2,000 years later." Even the Bible enjoined man to "be fruitful and 'replenish the earth, and subdue it: and have dominion over fish of the sea, and over fowl of the air, and over every living thing that moveth upon the earth.'"[64] In René Descartes's view, only humans "were equipped with a rational soul, from the entire spectrum of creatures, and the rest were then compressed within the mechanistic limits of purely instinctual behavior (in what has since been termed the *bête-machine* doctrine for its denial of a difference between animals and clocks or other automatons)."[65]

These rigid distinctions between humans and animals, the mind and the body, sentient beings and the physical environment, began to erode toward the end of the eighteenth century. As Chenxi Tang describes it, a static opposition between the human and natural world yielded to a new "geographic reality" conceived in terms of "the dynamic oneness of man and the earth, or the essential rootedness of the human in terrestrial nature."[66] At the same time, the old geographic reality hardly disappeared. While Alexander von Humboldt was pioneering ecological awareness and Friedrich Schelling articulated his transcendental philosophy of nature, Prussian engineers were busy taming rivers, draining swamps, and building dams. In this view, according to David Blackbourn, "nature was an adversary to be manacled, tamed, subjugated, conquered, and so on through a dozen variations."[67] The modern scientists undertook their projects in good conscience: "In the golden age of natural science, mastery over nature was supposed to mark the moral advance of humankind; it was the antithesis of war."[68] Former marshes no longer served as breeding grounds for the mosquitos that carried malaria; reclaimed lands could be settled and farmed, increasing crop yields; navigable rivers aided the distribution of natural resources and spurred commercial exchange; dams prevented catastrophic floods and provided a reliable source of hydroelectric power. Progress came at a cost, however. Fishermen and their families who had lived in the marshlands for generations lost their way of life; entire villages were inundated by the construction of new dams. The conquest of nature resulted in a "serious loss of biodiversity,"[69] while smoke from steam engines befouled the air and factory discharges polluted the waters. More ominous still were the associative links between the threat posed by invasive species, such as the insects imported from North America that caused vine disease and potato blight, and biological racism, "as Jews began to be referred to as a 'bacillus' or as 'vermin' by followers of the new, pseudoscientific anti-Semitism that arose in Germany at the end of the 1870s."[70] The Prussian penchant for draining swamps joined with the racist belief that only Germans could contain the Slavic flood and exterminate the parasitic Jews from territory destined to provide more Lebensraum for the master race.

We cannot, therefore, describe the history of human interaction with the natural world in terms of a single, clear-cut paradigm shift from anthropocentric arrogance to nascent ecological awareness or, to shift the perspective, from an Enlightenment faith in technological progress to an increasing fear of human catastrophe and ecological disaster. Instead, we witness an ongoing opposition that continues to this day, between those who exploit limited natural resources in the name of progress and profits, and those who warn of the consequences of unchecked human rapacity and seek a sustainable relationship with the earth. Forster plays an early but important role in this conflicted history. He participates in hunting expeditions, responds emotionally to natural beauty, and approves of the effort to improve God's creation, but from time to time, he also questions the efficacy of Cook's endeavors and considers the environmental impact of his explorations. Their effect on human cultures would be even more devastating.

THE CIVILIZING MISSION II: TAMING SAVAGES

The crew's violent assaults on the local fauna tend to take place when the ship is far removed from human contact; they contrast with the effort to introduce beneficial plants and animals to native communities. From early in the voyage, however, Forster is worried that their efforts may be in vain, largely because the indigenous peoples refuse to cooperate with Cook's plan for environmental improvement. When Cook brings a pair of goats to one of the islands, for instance, Forster foresees a potentially bright future: "If the natives continue to take the same care of them [as we have], they will shortly be able to turn them wild on the mountains, where they would propagate prodigiously, and afford them a new and most valuable article of food" (352). Such optimism turns out to be unwarranted: "It is hardly to be expected that these wretched savages will attend to the domestication of animals" (268). Cook also introduces cattle to Tahiti, but before they have a chance to breed, the Tahitians send them to different parts of the island. "Thus by separating the animals, and dividing them as a spoil, these barbarians effectually destroy the possibility of propagating the species. Too much occupied with the wants of the present moment, they overlook the only means of securing a certain livelihood to themselves, and reject every attempt to civilize them" (271).

Forster's exasperation with the natives who fail to appreciate the gifts of a superior culture is of a piece with John Locke's comments on the Americas in his *Second Treatise of Government*. "God gave the World to Men in Common," writes Locke, "but . . . it cannot be supposed he meant it should always remain common and uncultivated."[71] He links this general principle to the history of human cultures. "Thus in the beginning all the world was *America*," but the Europeans have progressed by dint of hard labor, while the Native Americans have failed to take advantage of the potential wealth that lies at their fingertips.[72] Thus, "for want of improving it by labour, [they] have not one hundreth part of the Conveniences we enjoy."[73] In Lisa Lowe's words, "settler powers were further justified by Locke's definition of the right to property, in which labor entitles one to possession of land, and which represents the lands in the Americas as if they were insufficiently cultivated, or devoid of inhabitants."[74] The Polynesians suffer from the same fatal character flaw, as Forster describes them, and so if they refuse to do the work, the Europeans will do it for them.

At times Forster turns the Polynesian resistance to the benefits of European civilization into a virtue. We civilized people repress our feelings, he contends, but "the simple child of nature, who inhabits these islands, gives free course to all his feelings, and glories in his affection towards the fellow-creature" (226). "They are free from cares, and happy in their ignorance" (381), "innocent and pure of heart" (402), and possessed of "an open, generous disposition, free from any mean distrust" (231–32). An old man's face is largely without wrinkles, "for cares, trouble, and disappointment, which untimely furrow our brows, cannot be supposed to exist in this happy nation" (161). The island of Tahiti "is indeed one of the happiest spots on the globe" (172), Forster concludes. "The calm contented state of the natives; their simple way of life; the beauty of the landscape; the excellence of the climate; the abundance, salubrity, and delicious taste of its fruits, were altogether enchanting, and filled the heart with rapture" (359).

Not all natives are equally blissful. The stunted inhabitants of Tierra del Fuego are particularly pitiful, in Forster's eyes.[75] They eat nothing but rancid seal meat and as a result exude "an insupportable rank stench.... This odour was so completely nauseous, that we could not continue long in their company, and with our eyes shut, could smell them at a considerable distance" (631). Dulled by their dreary diet, the pathetic creatures have "that vacant stare which is the characteristic of the most consummate stupidity" (633). At other times, Forster encounters individuals or customs that he finds revolting. On one occasion the sailors are given shore leave in New Zealand, where they "traded for curiosities, and purchased the embraces of the ladies, notwithstanding the disgust which their uncleanliness inspired." Forster finds it bad enough that the women paint their faces with ochre and oil, but "if we add to this a certain stench which announced them even at a distance, and the abundance of vermin which not only infested their hair, but also crawled on their clothes, and which they occasionally cracked between their teeth, it is astonishing that persons should be found, who could gratify an animal appetite with such loathsome objects, whom a civilized education and national customs should have taught them to hold in abhorrence" (123). On the island of Tanna, Captain Cook invites one of the natives to eat with the officers and scientists. Forster comments that the man's "manners at table were extremely becoming and decent," except that from time to time he would make "use of a stick, which he wore in his hair, instead of a fork, with which he occasionally scratched his head." The fact that his hair was heavily coated with oil and paint added to the revulsion Forster and his friends experienced, "though Fannòkko had not the least notion that such an action was reprehensible" (520). A greasy chopstick made Forster queasy, but the sight of a leprous woman selling food was worse. The individual in question was "unfortunate enough to have all her face destroyed by it [leprosy] in the most shocking manner; there was only a hole left in the place of her nose; her cheeks were swelled up and continually oozing out a purulent matter; and her eyes seemed ready to fall out of her head, being bloody and sore. These were some of the most miserable objects I recollect ever to have seen; and yet they seemed to be quite unconcerned about their misfortunes, traded as briskly as any of the rest, and what was most nauseous, had provisions to sell" (240).

Against these images of cultural decadence and personal corruption, the Polynesians stand out as an admirably clean and healthy people. Upon closer inspection, however, Forster soon realizes that even their society exhibits disturbing flaws. That the Maoris should wage war on one another is not in itself astonishing. "The state of barbarism, in which the New Zeelanders may justly be said to live, and which generally hearkens to no other voice than that of the *strongest*, might make them more liable than any other nation to resolve upon the destruction of their fellow-citizens, as soon as an opportunity offered" (103). That the inhabitants of the seemingly peaceful Society Islands should practice violent conquest and oppression of their neighbors was more of a surprise. "If we believed the accounts of the Borabora men, their native island was as fertile and desireable as these of which they had taken possession; therefore nothing but a spirit of ambition could have stimulated them to contentions." Such violent impulses seem out of keeping "with the simplicity and generous character of the people," but Forster concludes philosophically "that great imperfections cannot be excluded from the best of human societies" (213).

Evidence of inequality is one such imperfection in Polynesian society. During their first days in Tahiti, Forster and his companions imagine that they have "found at least one little spot of the world, where a whole nation, without being lawless barbarians, aimed at a certain frugal equality in their way of living." They soon discover that they were mistaken: "Our disappointment was therefore very great, when we saw a luxurious individual spending his life in the most sluggish inactivity, and without one benefit to society, like the privileged parasites of more civilized climates" (165). On an island where everyone seems to act openly and spontaneously, without artifice or guile, they are disappointed to observe the young king affecting an air of "grave or rather stiff deportment." Some may find such behavior impressive, Forster comments, "but it is unhappily a mask of hypocrisy, which we should hardly have expected at Taheitee" (169). On several occasions, Cook and his men are invited to feast on roast pork, which they soon realize is a rare treat. "They kill their hogs very seldom, perhaps only on certain solemn occasions; but at those times the chiefs eat pork with the unbounded greediness, with which certain sets of men are reproached at the turtle-feasts in England; while the common sort rarely, if ever taste a little bit" (174). The island, he concludes, "though perhaps not perfectly despotic, is yet far from being democratical" (256). On Easter Island as well, on the eastern corner of the Polynesian triangle, Forster finds evidence of social inequality in the mysterious stone sculptures that were clearly not erected by the current inhabitants. "It is therefore probable," Forster concludes, "that these people were formerly more numerous, more opulent and happy, when they could spare sufficient time to flatter the vanity of their princes by perpetuating their name by lasting monuments" (320). Forster correctly suspects that the decline in their population was due to the ecological damage their culture had inflicted on the island, thus indicating that the Europeans were not alone in their destructive impact on nature.[76]

Human sacrifice, cannibalism, and infanticide are not unknown in these seemingly paradisiacal islands. Forster is particularly disturbed by the customs of the Arioi, a privileged caste on the Society Islands who devote their lives to luxury and sensual pleasure. Servants provide them with delicacies, intoxicating beverages, and riotous entertainment. "They are amused with music and dances, which are said to be particularly lascivious at night, when no other spectators besides themselves are admitted" (390). Despite their unbridled indulgence in sexual pleasure, however, these men have no children. Forster surmises that the caste was originally supposed to be celibate, but since such a law would be "too repugnant to the impulses of nature, which must be uncommonly strong in their climate," they soon found a way to circumvent the letter of the law, and yet preserve its spirit, "by suffocating their unfortunate offspring immediately after birth" (389). In most cases, Forster is content to observe and record foreign customs, but in this instance, he and his companions feel compelled to intervene: "We endeavoured to point out the immorality and cruelty of this practice, and made use of every argument which our reflections could furnish, or our words express" (391). They attain at least a partial victory, as one individual promises not to kill his own children in the future, while assuring them that cases of infanticide are rare and limited to a very small social circle. Thus "we may comfort ourselves with the reflection, that criminal individuals are not more numerous in the Society Islands, than among other people," and we should therefore not jump to the conclusion that "a whole nation [was] accustomed to commit unnatural murders, without a sense of wrong" (392).

If read selectively, as I have done thus far, Forster's *Voyage Round the World* radiates a sense of Eurocentric complacency. Cook and his scientists strive not just to discover the world, but also to improve it, and in conclusion to his work, Forster insists that they have done just that: "From the contemplation of these different characters, the advantages, the blessings which civilization and revealed religion have diffused over our part of the globe, will become more and more obvious to the impartial enquirer." Forster proclaims that the enlightened European "will acknowledge, with a thankful heart, that incomprehensible goodness which has given him a distinguished superiority over so many of his fellow-creatures, who follow the impulse of their senses, without knowing the nature or name of virtue" (684). Thus it is not surprising that when Forster lands on a particularly attractive island, his first thought is that it "seemed to be well situated for the purpose of an European settlement." Everyone would benefit from the endeavor: "This circumstance would facilitate the establishment of a colony; and if the spirit of philanthropy could ever animate the planters, they would here have an opportunity to become the benefactors of the natives. From what we observed at Mallicollo, this race of men is very intelligent, and would readily receive the improvements of civilization" (498). During their last stay in New Zealand, Cook and his officers befriend a Maori named Peeterré and dress him up in an English outfit, which he seems to enjoy. "It is scarce to be doubted," Forster concludes, "that he felt the superiority of our knowledge, of our arts, manufactures, and mode of living." Forster is therefore perplexed when Peeterré refuses to return with them to England, "preferring the wretched precarious life of his countrymen, to all the advantages of which he saw us possessed." He concludes that Peeterré has fallen victim to a "way of thinking [that] is common to all savages; and I might have added, that it is not entirely obliterated among polished nations. The force of habit no where appears more strikingly than in such instances, where it seems alone to counterbalance the comforts of a civilized life" (615).

FROM EUROCENTRISM TO EURO-CRITIQUE

Although Forster seems quite content with his own society and correspondingly frustrated with the native peoples' failure to appreciate the same, there are moments in which he raises doubts about the Eurocentric effort to civilize the savages. For example, Forster's observation of sexual relations between the crew and the Polynesians gives him pause. He had translated Bougainville's travelogue shortly before embarking on his voyage with Cook and was therefore familiar with the French captain's account of nubile Tahitians shedding their simple garb like Venus among the Phrygian shepherds.[77] Bougainville's narrative inflamed male fantasies and established the myth of an island paradise among European readers,[78] and it is not surprising that Forster initially reinforces this stereotype. He records scenes in which smiling Tahitian women "perfectly captivated" the sailors' attention, who "carelessly disposed of their shirts and cloaths to gratify their mistresses." For men who had been at sea for months, the sight of the young women was irresistible: "The simplicity of a dress which exposed to view a well proportioned bosom and delicate hands, might also contribute to fan their amorous fire; and the view of several of these nymphs swimming nimbly all round the sloop, such as nature had formed them, was perhaps more than sufficient entirely to subvert the little reason which a mariner might have left to govern his passions" (149).

Cook describes similar scenes that quickly culminate in riotous debauchery, with sailors copulating in public with seemingly willing indigenous women. Cook never participates in the sexual revels, however, even when local chieftains offer him attractive young women for his pleasure. They find his behavior incomprehensible and more than a little ludicrous. When Cook turns down one of these offers on the island of Tonga, an old woman mocks him publicly, "Sneering in my face and saying, what sort of a man are you thus to refuse the embraces of so fine a young Woman, for the girl certainly did not [want] beauty which I could however withstand, but the abuse of the old Woman I could not."[79] Cook was a married man and the leader of the expedition, which may explain his reticence to indulge in what he probably perceived as immoral and undignified behavior. Whether Forster shared his disinclination to take advantage of sexual opportunities, or whether he did indulge and discretely left the description out of his narrative, is impossible to say. Klaus Harpprecht notes that Forster never gives the slightest hint of his own reaction to the Polynesian women; Frank Vorpahl observes that Forster wrote down the Polynesian words for "penis," "vagina," and "copulation" in his diary, although whether his interest went beyond the merely linguistic is unclear.[80]

What is clear is that Forster uses his vantage point as a detached observer to formulate a sharp critique of the ship's crew. More than one hundred men were packed into the cramped quarters of the *Resolution*, and although the ship was completely cut off from any contact with Europe, it retained the social hierarchies of home. In "Cook, the Discoverer," Forster paints a vivid picture of the crowded conditions onboard the *Resolution*. "Countless times I found myself on the quarterdeck, which was at the most twenty-four feet long, with twelve or fourteen people, who walked up and down in pairs and had to turn around every twelve or fifteen steps" (5:255–56). "Privacy was not a matter of walls," explains Greg Dening in his account of the *Bounty*. "It was a matter of behavior, closing the windows of one's soul. Except for this, the essence of a sailor's existence was to be utterly without space he could call his own."[81] The cramped confines of the ships recall Norbert Elias's analysis of court society, which he describes as a world characterized by "constant spatial proximity and constant social distance."[82] On the *Resolution*, social hierarchies were if anything more sharply defined than at court. At the top was Captain Cook, about whom we learn curiously little in Forster's travelogue, although Forster and his father dined with him regularly and shared the same close quarters. Cook appears mainly as a benevolent but inscrutable leader who issues commands but does not confide in his men. Forster and his father were listed as "supernumeraries" on the ship's manifold, scientists who associated with the officers but were distinct from them, as they were not involved with the sailing of the ship.[83] They were still more distant from the crew, from whom they were separated by an unbridgeable chasm of social difference, although the Forsters did benefit from the sailors' knowledge of the sea and its creatures when going about their scientific work, just as they learned from native informants.[84] Jürgen Goldstein points out that in the idealized image of Cook that Forster later developed in "Cook, the Discoverer," the captain's relationship with his crew serves as a model for the way an enlightened ruler should treat his subjects; in his view, Forster portrays the *Resolution* as an egalitarian society, a ship of state that anticipates the overthrow of feudal hierarchies in revolutionary Mainz.[85] There may well have been political motivations behind Forster's hagiographic essay of 1788, but in his travelogue of the late 1770s, Forster portrays rigid social hierarchies onboard ship and voices repeated sharp censures of the crew. In this context, it is worth recalling that the two Forsters traveled with a personal servant, Ernst Scholient, who remains invisible in their accounts of the voyage.[86]

As a result of these persistent social class distinctions, Forster's reflections on the differences between Europeans and indigenous peoples, between civilization and savagery, often turn into a critical commentary on the uncouth boors who sail his ship. He portrays the sailors as a breed apart, "brave, sincere, and true to each other," but also "rough, passionate," and "revengeful." While Forster does his best to understand the native peoples he encounters, the sailors do not, having "expressed a horrid eagerness" on multiple occasions "to fire upon the natives on the slightest pretences" (290). The men have a coarse sense of humor, get drunk whenever the opportunity arises, and remain in the thrall of prejudice: "Reasoning never has less weight than with sailors" (71). Blasphemy compounds the sailors' sins. Above the din of a howling storm, Forster and his more civilized companions hear the sailors "uttering horrible vollies of curses and oaths.... Inured to danger from their infancy, they were insensible to its threats; and not a single reflection bridled their blasphemous tongues. I know of nothing comparable to the dreadful energy of their curses" (267). They hoard their liquor for the holidays, and when Christmas comes—even when adrift in dangerous icefields far south in the Pacific—they are "sollicitous to get very drunk.... As long as they had brandy left, they would persist to keep Christmas 'like Christians,' though the elements had conspired together for their destruction" (290).

It is hardly surprising that these brutes should seize the opportunity for sexual debauchery whenever it presented itself. Tahiti seemed like paradise, where beautiful women offered themselves to the sailors for little or nothing in the way of reward. The native women of New Zealand, who did not bathe on a regular basis like the Tahitians, exerted a less obvious appeal, and yet there were those among the crew who were eager "to receive the caresses of the filthy female inhabitants. Perhaps it may be imagined that only brutish sailors could have such groveling appetites; but the imperious element, on which they are continually tossed about, seems to level all distinctions." And thus "the most loathsome objects in a New Zeelander's smoky and nasty hovel, were eagerly addressed" (612). Only the abject Patagonians, reeking of rancid seal meat, manage to repulse the sailors: "It almost surpasses belief, but is nevertheless an undeniable fact, that our boldest and roughest sailors were so totally overcome by this horrid exhalation, that they did not offer to contract any intimate acquaintance with the women" (631).

Upon closer inspection, Forster finds that the notoriously free love offered by the Tahitian women was not free at all: "Their favours did not depend upon their own inclination, but the men, as absolute masters, were always to be consulted upon the occasion." If the price was right—a nail or a shirt, for instance—"the lady was at liberty to make her lover happy." But not all of the women wanted to make their lovers happy. "Some among them, however, submitted with reluctance to this vile prostitution; and, but for the authority and menaces of the men, would not have complied with the desires of a set of people who could, with unconcern, behold their tears and hear their complaints" (121). Among the women who came aboard ship for sex with the crew were some who "seemed not to be above nine or ten years old, and had not the least marks of puberty" (148). Who is worse, Forster questions, the Tahitian pimps or the British johns? "Whether the members of a civilized society, who could act such a brutal part, or the barbarians who could force their own women to submit to such indignity, deserve the greatest abhorrence, is a question not easily to be decided" (121).

These individual observations about Polynesian women and girls forced into prostitution lead Forster to reflect more broadly on the role of women in society. Here again, Forster—like his father before him—develops ideas inspired by empirical observation that philosophers of the Scottish Enlightenment had extrapolated from ancient texts and modern travelogues.[87] He starts with the sad fact that women are mistreated almost everywhere: "In every country, mankind are fond of being tyrants, and the poorest Indian, who knows no wants but those which his existence requires, has already learnt to enslave his weaker helpmate, in order to save himself the trouble of supplying those wants, and cruelly exacts an obedience from her, which has been continued among savages as a curse upon the sex." To compensate for their suffering, "the Creator has wisely planted a motive in the female breast, which stands the test of every outrage, which makes them patient to suffer, and prevents their withdrawing from the power of their tyrants" (583). Forster's logic is at best awkward here, as he mitigates a pattern of male abuse, which could presumably be challenged by active women, by introducing a supposedly benevolent God who implicitly sanctions female suffering by granting them the patience to endure pain and the passivity that renders resistance impossible.

Perhaps the men can overcome their innate tendency to abuse women? Certainly not in primitive societies: "Among all savage nations the weaker sex is ill-treated, and the law of the strongest is put in force. Their women are mere drudges, who prepare raiment and provide dwellings, who cook and frequently collect their food, and are requited by blows and all kinds of severity. At New Zeeland it seems they carry this tyranny to excess, and the males are taught from their earliest age, to hold their mothers in contempt, contrary to all our principles of morality" (277). What is true among the Maoris is unfortunately the case elsewhere as well: "It is the practice of all uncivilized nations to deny their women the common privileges of human beings, and to treat them as creatures inferior to themselves" (537). On the island of Tanna, Forster finds reason to hope: "We found them unjust to their women, but not so cruel and unnatural as the New Zeelanders; on the contrary, it is rather to be supposed that they made gradual advances towards that kind of disposition which manifests itself in the good treatment of the sex at the Friendly and Society Islands" (556). Even on those islands where women are treated relatively well, Forster notes that the women are required to eat separately from the men, and that women and even young girls of the lower classes are forced into prostitution.

The basic rule of thumb is that the more civilized a people is, the better they treat their women, and the obverse is equally the case: "The more debased the situation of a nation is," writes Johann Reinhold Forster, "and of course the more remote from civilization, the more harshly we found the women treated."[88] His son confirms this impression. Georg Forster notes that the New Caledonians are superior to a neighboring tribe that still practices cannibalism, and yet that "higher degree of culture, where the understanding is sufficiently enlightened to remove the unjust contempt shewn to the fair sex, is however unknown to them" (592). In this regard, the Europeans set the standard for the proper respect for women, or at least they should. Forster takes it as a matter of course that European women are the most beautiful in the world. Their fair skin sets them apart from their less attractive counterparts.[89] In the *Resolution*'s first port of call on the Madeira Islands, for instance, Forster notes that the "common people of the island are of a tawny colour ... which may perhaps be owning to intermarriages with negroes." As a result, their women "want the florid complexion, which, when united to a pleasing assemblage of regular features, gives our Northern fair ones the superiority over all their sex" (25). Three years later, when Forster finally returns to an outpost of European civilization in South Africa, he is delighted at the sight of the women: "On entering the room, I was very agreeably surprised with the great beauty and elegance displayed in a numerous circle of ladies; I thought myself suddenly transported to the most brilliant capital of Europe, their features were regular, their forms graceful, and their complexion perfectly fair" (666).

The fascination with fair skin is not limited to the Europeans. "People of high rank in various parts of eastern Polynesia typically had their skin bleached; they were also secluded out of the sun during childhood and adolescence in order to lighten it."[90] By coincidence, the cultural practice of the Polynesians caters to the predilections of the Europeans. When in the course of his journey Forster encounters native men and women whom he finds particularly handsome, he often notes that they have lighter skin than their companions. "He was remarkably fairer than any of the natives we had yet seen" (146), Forster observes when they encounter a member of the Tahitian upper class, and the daughter of a New Zealand priest also catches his eye: "She was extremely well featured, and fairer than most of the women of this country, who seemed to pay her some degree of deference." In her very beauty, however, Forster finds the seeds of corruption—for her lighter skin can only be the result of religiously sanctioned class privileges that exempt her from daily labor in "the blaze of a tropical sun.... Must we not conclude therefore that the beginnings of luxury will be introduced even here under the cloak of religion, and that another nation will be added to the many dupes of voluptuous priest-craft?" (255–56). If humanity can be corrupted even in this relatively simple society, how much greater the potential for degradation among the more civilized! Thus the presence of moral turpitude and sexual debauchery among the Europeans is doubly depressing: their iniquities are not only worse on an absolute scale than the sins of the indigenous peoples, but they take place in a society that, if tales of human progress and the advances of the Enlightenment are to be believed, should be better.[91]

As Sankar Muthu argues in his study of Enlightenment thinkers' resistance to imperialism, rejecting the myth of the noble savage was a first step toward acknowledging the common humanity of colonizer and colonized alike.[92] Using simple savages to criticize decadent Europeans implicitly infantilizes indigenous peoples and renders them ripe for conquest by the admittedly flawed representatives of a civilization that nevertheless deems itself superior. To a certain extent, Forster falls into this pattern. His occasional praise of native simplicity slides toward impatience with their stubborn resistance to change. The Polynesians are too pure, too perfect for their own good.[93] His dismay at discovering the flaws of Polynesian culture, in contrast, prompts critical reflections on his own society: whenever they seem bad, we seem worse. "Vicious characters are to be met with in all society of men; but for one villain in these isles, we can shew at least fifty in England, or any civilized country" (210). We are not cannibals, Forster observes, but "we do not find it unnaturally and savagely cruel to take the field, and to cut one another's throats by thousands, without a single motive, besides the ambition of a prince, or the caprice of his mistress!" (280). As Montaigne had done before him, Forster questions who is the greater villain: "A New Zeelander, who kills and eats his enemy," or a "European, who, for his amusement, tears an infant from the mother's breast, in cool blood, and throws it on the earth to feed his hounds" (281). Forster concedes that the Tahitians tend to pilfer items of little value from the English ships, but here again, the Europeans outstrip them in viciousness: "In my opinion this vice is not of so heinous a nature among the Taheitians, as amongst ourselves" (188). The Patagonians live in a primitive state far below that of Europeans, but "our civilized communities are stained with vices and enormities, unknown to the wretch, who, compared with ourselves, is next to a brute, being destitute of that superior knowledge, of which, to our shame be it spoken, we do not always make the best uses" (631).

Forster plays the part of a detached and often disapproving observer of the licentiousness unleashed whenever the ship anchors off tropical islands, taking the opportunity to observe native customs and compare them to his own. He repeatedly marvels at the contrast between Europeans, who value virginity among unmarried women, and the Polynesians, who engage in promiscuous premarital sex before settling down in monogamous marriages. While he roundly condemns the sailors for their gross sexual appetites, he goes out of his way to absolve the Polynesians for their apparent iniquity. His argument often follows the same logic noted earlier:

their peccadilloes pale before our mortal sins. The "attitudes and gestures" of women in the Society Islands "might admit of being construed into wantonness, but they were entirely free from that positive degree of gross indecency which the chaste eyes of English ladies of fashion are *forced* to behold at the opera" (216). He admits that the seductive dances of the Tahitian women "did not exactly correspond with our ideas of decency" but insists that "we cannot impute that degree of unbounded licentiousness to them, with which the prostitutes of civilized Europe are unhappily reproached" (184–85). They may also have some prostitutes, but we have more; they practice infanticide, but "there are wretches" in England, "who publicly declare their skill, and offer their services, to procure abortion." The Polynesians "commit unnatural murders," but we grant "lenity towards the murderers of innocent babes" (392). The Australian Aborigines parade around naked, but fashions worn by our knights and ladies of yore "would at present be looked upon as the most indecent that can possibly be contrived" (568).

Forster's unflattering comparisons between indigenous cultures and his own cause him to question the morality of the entire voyage. In one key passage, Forster describes a moment of leisure on the island of Tanna, where the native peoples had welcomed the explorers into their midst as if they were "members of one great family." As Forster continues, it becomes clear that he imagines himself and his European companions as the father figures of a patriarchal clan: "I fell from hence into a reverie on the pre-eminence of our civilized society," Forster recalls, and he is pleased to think of himself and his companions as "the benefactors of a numerous race" (549). On his way back to the ship, however, Forster's idyll is rudely interrupted by the sight of natives holding the body of their tribesman who had just been shot to death by one of Cook's men. Cook does his best to smooth over the disturbance, but the damage is done. "Thus one dark and detestable action effaced all the hopes with which I had flattered myself. The natives, instead of looking upon us in a more favourable light than upon other strangers, had reason to detest us much more, as we came to destroy under the specious mask of friendship" (551).

This episode startles Forster into the realization that the voyage he frequently describes as a civilizing mission may in fact be leaving a trail of destruction in its wake.[94] The desire for previously unknown European goods causes the natives to force their women into prostitution and exacerbates intertribal warfare. Forster is fairly sure that the venereal disease contracted by Cook's men "was indigenous in New Zeeland. . . . But if, in spite of appearances, our conclusion should prove erroneous, it is another crime added to the score of civilized nations, which must make their memory execrated by the unhappy people, whom they have poisoned" (136). It is hardly surprising, therefore, that the native peoples do not always welcome Cook and his men with open arms: "surely from all appearances these people had a right to look on our men as a set of invaders, and what is more than all, to be apprehensive that even their liberty was at stake" (177). When a bloody altercation breaks out on one of the islands, Forster concedes that the sailors have to defend themselves when under attack, "but it is much to be lamented that the voyages of Europeans cannot be performed without being fatal to the nations whom they visit" (505). Forster and his fellow scientists seek to expand their understanding of the world, but he fears at times that the human cost is too high: "If the knowledge of a few individuals can only be acquired at such a price as the happiness of nations, it were better for the discoverers, and the discovered, that the South Sea had still remained unknown to Europe and its restless inhabitants" (200). It is too late now to prevent the contact that has already occurred, but Forster raises the vain hope "that the intercourse which has lately subsisted between Europeans and the natives of the South Sea islands may be broken off in time, before the corruption of manners which unhappily characterizes civilized regions, may reach that innocent race of men, who live in ignorance and simplicity" (168).

CULTURAL PESSIMISM

Forster sounds a Rousseauist note in the above passage that belies his awareness of imperfections among indigenous societies, whose members he describes elsewhere as neither innocent nor simple. The condemnation of civilized corruption also qualifies those passages in which he insists on the superiority of Western culture and claims that its export around the globe will be of benefit to all concerned. As in "Cook, the Discoverer," Forster combines enthusiasm for the civilizing process with an awareness of its negative potential and, indeed, its ultimate futility. The passages in *Voyage Round the World* in which he laments the destructive effects of Cook's mission can give the impression that Forster believes that if only he had never set sail, the pristine island world would have remained intact, but there are other moments in which Forster expresses a deeper, more encompassing cultural pessimism. The New Zealand beauty owes her fair skin to class privilege, just as the Tahitian chieftains live in luxury denied to common citizens. In time, the ruling class will live in complete idleness, leaving others to do all the work and suffer the consequences. "This addition of labour will have a bad effect on their bodies, they will grow ill-shaped, and their bones become marrowless: their greater exposure to the action of a vertical sun, will blacken their skins, and they will dwindle away to dwarfs, by the more frequent prostitution of their infant daughters, to the voluptuous pleasures of the great" (199). Sooner or later, the oppressed masses would have revolted even if Tahitian society had been left undisturbed—"This is the natural circle of human affairs"—but if the Europeans keep introducing "foreign luxuries" to these people, the revolution will come even sooner (200). Thus it would have been better if the Europeans had never come at all or if, having come, they were to return home and never come back again.

The logic in this passage is significantly different than in the one cited earlier. There Forster suggests that the South Sea Islands were a simple paradise corrupted by European civilization. Here he argues that their civilization—and, indeed, all civilizations—contain the seeds of their own demise.[95] From this perspective, the Europeans do not cause the downfall of Tahitian society, but they do hasten the process. This is unfortunate and to be condemned, but over time, the Tahitians would have destroyed themselves anyway. The same logic informs Forster's reflections on Cook's largely unsuccessful efforts to introduce European crops and domesticated animals to the Pacific islands. At times, as we have seen, Forster blames the natives for their failure to cooperate with Cook's well-meaning plans, but elsewhere he suggests that Cook has embarked on a futile task, as nature will quickly efface the marks of human cultivation. "We sowed indeed a quantity of European garden seeds of the best kinds; but it is obvious that the shoots of the surrounding weeds will shortly stifle every salutary and useful plant, and that in a few years our abode no longer discernible, must return to its original chaotic state" (106).

In his dystopian vision of the future, Forster predicts that the exploited Tahitian workers, reduced to sun-blackened dwarfs by back-breaking labor, will rise up and overthrow their indolent masters. Notably absent from this prediction, however, is the promise that the inevitable revolution will produce a utopian classless society of the sort that Marx and Engels envision. The rebellion may temporarily ease intolerable social inequities, but Forster never suggests that they will not return. Given the image of a "natural circle," in fact, it seems more likely that the process will simply repeat itself indefinitely. Instead of Enlightenment faith in ongoing progress, we find the eternal recurrence of social conflict that circles back to original chaos. In effect, Forster offers the negative counterpart in this passage to the ongoing cycles of nature that he praises in his essay on "Nature as a Whole." Much like Goethe's Werther, for whom nature is infused with divine spirit when he is happy in the spring and for whom nature seems nothing more than an eternally regurgitating monster when he is depressed in the fall, Forster fluctuates between a view of nature as a dynamic unity that can nevertheless be enhanced by human industry and the nagging suspicion that any attempts to advance knowledge or improve society are ultimately in vain. As a result, Forster oscillates in *A Voyage Round the World* between an endorsement of Cook's civilizing mission, a critique of its unintended consequences, and the occasional suggestion that all human cultures eventually consume themselves and sink back into the eternal flux of nature.

CHAPTER 3

Race, History, and German Classicism

When Georg Forster wrote about the eventual end to the idyll in the South Seas, whether due to the inevitable momentum of historical change or hastened by the incursion of European explorers, he had no idea how quickly it would come. William Bligh returned to Tahiti in 1792, just fifteen years after his initial trip to the island with Cook, to find that "the corruption of the natives had outstripped anything that even Diderot had imagined."[1] Increasing contact with whaling ships brought venereal disease and alcoholism to the island, while the import of European weapons rendered intertribal warfare deadlier. The first missionaries arrived in 1795, determined to convert the heathens and stamp out idolatry, and they continued until they achieved catastrophic success: "Resolutely and persistently they kept hammering away at the Tahitian way of life until it crumbled before them, and within two decades they had achieved precisely what they set out to do."[2] There were approximately 40,000 people living in Tahiti when Cook first visited in the early 1770s; missionaries estimated "that by the turn of the century not more than 15,000 or 16,000 were left, due to wars, infanticide and disease.... By the end of the 1830s the figure was down to 9,000 and it was eventually to drop to 6,000."[3] The European impact on the Pacific environment was equally devastating. The whale that Cook's men had shot in passing and then left to die was a harbinger of things to come. As Alan Moorehead observes, Cook "had stumbled upon what was probably the largest congregation of wildlife that existed in the world, and he was the first man to let the world know of its existence."[4] "Cook's intrusion into Tahiti and Australia had been bad enough for the native peoples," Moorehead continues; "for the Antarctic animals it was a holocaust." Sealers and whalers came to kill, and "the killing went on and on until there was virtually nothing left to kill, nothing at any rate that could be easily and profitably killed."[5]

Forster had become famous at an early age because he was one of the few Europeans who had actually traveled to the South Seas at a time when they were still relatively unscathed, and because he had written a bilingual travelogue that transmitted his experiences to curious readers. After returning to England in the summer of 1775, Forster spent the next three years writing and translating *Voyage Round the World*, while struggling in vain to recuperate financial losses incurred during the journey from the British admiralty. In October 1778, Forster left London and sailed for the continent, traveling through the Netherlands to Germany, where he took up his job as a professor in Kassel. For the rest of his life, with the exception of a brief trip back to England in the spring of 1790, Forster would remain in Europe. Although he worked as a teacher, translator, and librarian, he strove above all to establish his reputation as a writer. His voyage with Cook and his account of the same served as his entry ticket into the public sphere; now Forster sought to solidify his authority through further reflections on the significance of what he had seen.

Forster moved within two intellectual circles in Germany—one centered at the University of Göttingen, and another among the artists and intellectuals in Weimar. Christoph Martin Wieland was the first major artist recruited to Weimar, and he was the first to introduce Forster to the German reading public, as he published substantial excerpts of *Voyage Round the World* in *Der Deutsche Merkur*, one of Germany's leading journals, together with a glowing introduction to the young author. Goethe met Forster for the first time when he visited Kassel in September 1779; he would later host a dinner party for Forster in Weimar, and Forster returned the favor in Mainz. While in Weimar in September 1785, Forster spent an entire day with Herder, and the two men remained in close contact in the following years. Forster never met Schiller in person, but they corresponded and Schiller published some of Forster's work in his journals. Wilhelm von Humboldt visited Forster for extended periods in Mainz, while his younger brother, Alexander, accompanied Forster on his journey to the Netherlands, England, and France in the spring of 1790. Thus Forster was in personal contact with all of the leading figures of the movement subsequently known as Weimar Classicism, and each of the authors read each other's works.

Closer to Kassel lay Göttingen, home to one of Germany's leading universities. While the Weimar artists wrote about "das allgemein Menschliche," that which is common to all humankind, the distinguished scholars in Göttingen explored significant differences between human cultures. The University of Göttingen was new, by European standards, founded only in 1734, and it was considered the most modern institution of higher learning in Germany.[6] Göttingen initiated the seminar system, which enabled students to pursue independent research, and it boasted some of the leading intellectuals of the day. Although their academic disciplines varied widely, the scholars shared an interest in the course of human history and questions of ethnic and racial difference. They included Christian Gottlob Heyne, the founder of *Altertumswissenschaft* (scholarship of classical antiquity) and Forster's future father-in-law, and Johann David Michaelis, known for historical biblical criticism that changed how scholars viewed scripture, from the timeless truth of God into the cultural production of particular peoples. August Ludwig von Schlözer and Johann Christoph Gatterer pioneered a new kind of "universal" history that tried to account for all peoples past and present, including those not mentioned in the Bible. In the process, they transformed Christian salvation history, with its focus on the end of time and eternal judgment, into an ongoing process with no end in sight.[7] Anthropologists included Johann Friedrich Blumenbach, who coined the term *Caucasian* and speculated that the original white race had degenerated into Mongolian, Ethiopian, American, and Malay varieties,[8] and Christoph Meiners, a philosopher whose racist theories angered Forster and anticipated Nazi ideology.

Taken together, these thinkers sought answers to perplexing questions. If all human beings descended from a common ancestor, as the Bible insists, why do they look so different now? What color was the original couple? How did skin color change over time? Or perhaps humans evolved from multiple ancestors? If so, are different races members of the same species, or are some humans more human than others? The monogenists and polygenists approached the problem from different perspectives, but they tended to arrive at the same conclusion, agreeing "that the white male is primeval 'man,' who possesses the most harmonious countenance and has therefore rightfully achieved cultural superiority."[9] In Susanne

Zantop's summary, biological difference and cultural achievement go hand in hand: "The supremacy of the white European variety, evident in its advanced civilization... resides in physiology and anatomy, that is, in biology."[10] Not all German intellectuals believed that the peoples of the world could be divided into distinct races, however.[11] Blumenbach observes that *"innumerable varieties of mankind run into one another by insensible degrees,"*[12] while Herder contends that despite cultural differences, there is only one human race. In his view, humans vary so subtly from one another, and their cultures are so malleable over time that human diversity cannot be reduced to a limited number of discrete categories.[13] Nor were all Germans as complacent about the supremacy of European culture as Zantop suggests—we have seen that Forster was quick to counter his critique of certain aspects of Polynesian culture with reminders that Europeans were capable of greater sins.

In this chapter, I consider some of Forster's essays written between the time of his return from his voyage with Cook and his participation in the Mainz Republic. I focus first on his responses to Kant and Meiners on the topic of human racial distinctions. Forster cautiously floats the idea of polygenesis, vehemently rebukes the human rights abuses associated with slavery, and encourages his fellow Europeans to educate the Africans in the way that good parents care for their children. Beneath this condescending paternalism lies a deeper philosophical pessimism, in keeping with a tendency we noted in the previous chapter, as Forster sometimes sees historical change as inevitable and human reason ineffectual. Like Herder, although in different ways, Forster did not consider all cultures at the same level of development or equally capable of positive change. While Herder criticizes Africans, Jews, and the Chinese, Forster disapproves of the Polish during his difficult years in Vilnius. The two thinkers were united in their veneration of the ancient Greeks, however—a passion that they shared with all the figures associated with German neoclassicism, including Winckelmann, Lessing, Goethe, Schiller, Kleist, and Hölderlin. Forster's admiration of antiquity informed his critique of religious dogmatism, which led him to defend Schiller's poem about "The Gods of Greece" against charges of blasphemy. He also pondered the relationship between modern Germany and ancient Greece, which in turn inspired thoughts about European interactions with the non-European world. In the process, Forster conceives a paradoxical kind of cosmopolitan imperialism, which envisions Europe as the center of world culture rather than the site of competing nations bent on global conquest. Forster's fascination with India prompted him to grant Germany a special place in this world view, as its political disunity becomes the source of its receptivity to alien cultures.

The discussion of seemingly disparate essays allows us to consider together aspects of Forster's work that are generally kept apart. As a shorthand reference, we might refer to the twin poles of his thought as Göttingen and Weimar in the sense suggested herein. On the one hand, Forster engages with the ethnographic thought centered in Göttingen that reflects on human racial distinctions; on the other, he shares the Weimar artists' appreciation of humanity as a whole and veneration of classical antiquity. The one train of thought is eager to draw distinctions between peoples, while the other discovers similarities between ancient Greece and modern Germany and celebrates humanity as a single "family." In both cases, however, Forster thinks globally, intervening in theoretical debates about distant peoples and places he has seen, and speculating on the spiritual affinities between peoples separated by space and time. These reflections on Europe's relation to the rest of the world also engage questions of national difference within Europe. In his reflections on race, Forster joins with other thinkers in juxtaposing white Europeans to people of color from the non-European world, with the tacit or explicit assumption of European superiority. His comments on ancient Greece, in contrast, partake in a larger German tendency to underscore their special kinship with the past culture that distinguishes them from other European nations. In the preface to his translation of *Sakuntala* and other essays, Forster goes on to posit a different sort of German engagement with the world marked by cosmopolitan receptivity rather than imperialist gain, initiating a line of thought that will resonate among his contemporaries and beyond.

FORSTER ON RACE

Forster was an outgoing individual who maintained close friendships in person or through correspondence throughout his life, and he was also a socially networked writer. In his role as translator, book reviewer, and cultural intermediary, Forster depended on access to the latest literature. He had left Kassel in part because he felt intellectually isolated and, in the final months of his life, suffered not only from his worsening physical condition and loss of his wife and children but also because he was cut off from his books, his social circle in Mainz, and the international publishing network that was essential to his literary production. Nowhere did he feel more isolated than in Vilnius, however, where he had no close friends and little or no ability to keep up with current intellectual trends. "I am very ignorant of everything that is going on in German scholarship," complained Forster within days of his arrival, "since I haven't read a single journal or scholarly publication since April."[14] The loneliness only worsened as time passed. Living "in exile," Forster's only hope for escape was to write his way back into the public eye, but the prospect seemed impossible: "How can I have hope, when I am forced to starve here without literary sustenance?"[15] Despite his complaints, Forster was not entirely deprived of nourishment, for he reports to his friend Soemmerring in June of 1786 that he had come across Kant's "Defining the Concept of a Human Race," an essay "against which I have an infinite number of objections."[16] Forster immediately sensed that this was his opportunity to rejoin the literary dialogue, if not in person, then at least in print. For nearly a decade now, Forster had specialized in reviewing and translating the latest travel literature, so he knew the current accounts of alien cultures and the reflections on racial difference they provoked. Forster also had a trump card that the sedentary Kant could never play: he had circumnavigated the globe and had personal experience with indigenous peoples. He began to write immediately, and a few weeks later he sent his essay off to Herder. "I am sending you a literary trifle that I just dashed off, fresh from my pen," he wrote. "Kant's essay in the 'Berlin Journal' got me started, and I felt that I had to write to vent my spleen."[17]

Kant is known to posterity as the author of the three critiques, which treat "philosophy as a rigorous science," but John Zammito reminds us that he also dabbled in what was known as popular philosophy (Popularphilosophie), which tended to be more empirical and historical in its approach.[18] As an avid reader of travelogues, Kant was interested in the topics that concerned philosophers of history at the University of Göttingen, including the question of race.[19] Kant's comments on human racial distinctions are scattered across several of his works, but his most sustained reflections occur in the previously mentioned "Defining the Concept of a Human Race" and an earlier essay "On the Different Human Races"

(Von den verschiedenen Rassen der Menschen, 1775). Kant claims that all humans derive from a common ancestor, who was probably white, and that they all belong to the same species. Over time and under the influence of different climates, humans developed into four distinct and immutable races. He concedes that there are additional individual differences and regional variations but insists on the existence of the four fundamental racial distinctions. The white race not only was the original race but remains the best. The optimal conditions for human development lie between thirty-one and thirty-three degrees north of the equator, Kant contends, and we should consider the light-skinned brunette people from that region as the primal human race (*Stammgattung*).[20] "Negroes," in contrast, are "strong, beefy, and supple" (stark, fleischig, gelenk), but also "lazy, flaccid, and flirtatious" (faul, weichlich, und tändelnd).[21] He went on to claim that they have no feelings and no talent, remain insensitive to beauty, and are concerned only with their primitive fetish religion. They smell.

Kant is not at his best when bandying about racist stereotypes, but Christoph Meiners easily outdoes him when it comes to blatant prejudice. The future darling of the Nazis was not an ignorant man; the professor of "world wisdom" (*Weltweisheit*) at the University of Göttingen was the author of a dozen books on topics ranging from ancient Greece to modern science. If nothing else, his work proves that higher education does not always serve as a safeguard against bigotry. "I have Mr. Meiners's work too," wrote Forster upon receipt of Meiners's latest book at the time, *Outline of Human History* (Grundriß der Geschichte der Menschheit). "It is Göttingen erudition applied to an unsustainable hypothesis."[22] Meiners argues that all humans are members of the same species, which he divides into two main groups: "One of the two races is Mongolian, . . . the second comprises the white and beautiful people."[23] Meiners further subdivides the white race into Celts and Slavs. The Celts, which include the Germanic peoples, are superior in every way: more handsome, more intelligent, more courageous, and more virtuous than any other group. Meiners combines his belief in white supremacy with an explicit endorsement of colonial violence. "Whenever Europeans or other white peoples conquered weaker nations, they subjected them to much harsher servitude and mistreated them much more than when they subjugated nobler peoples," observes Meiners, but such strict treatment is unfortunately unavoidable. "Unlimited force is often necessary and also beneficial when better men exert it over less noble souls for their own gain."²⁴ In an article subsequently published in the *Göttingisches historisches Magazin,* Meiners acknowledges that the slave trade causes human suffering but argues that its benefits outweigh its unfortunate side effects—for without slavery, Europeans would have no coffee, sugar, or tobacco. He does suggest that slave owners should treat their human chattel better, but only because it is in their economic interest to maximize the value of their property.²⁵

Forster reacts allergically each time he encounters a new work by the Göttingen scholar: "the blustering Meiners [der Polterer Meiners] can only empty out his monstrous bag of crude excerpts [seinen ungeheuern Collekteensack von Crudidäten] onto the public."²⁶ When he reads a book review in which Meiners again defends the slave trade, Forster is incensed, not just by the nature of the argument but also by the fact that a journal would dignify such rubbish by putting it into print. "The *Göttingische Zeitung* is the vehicle that brings such repulsive ideas to the public and serves as the authority that they cite. I haven't been so indignant for a long time."²⁷ "Good old Meiners is incorrigible," wrote Forster sarcastically two years later; "it is a pity for a man with so much knowledge and talent!"²⁸ In his extensive review of Meiners's anthropological texts for the *Allgemeine Literatur-Zeitung,* Forster complains that Meiners reduces three-fourths of the global population to subhuman status, downplays the indebtedness of European culture to the achievements of previous civilizations, and bases his rigid racial distinctions on caricatures. Instead of criticizing other cultures from a European perspective, "it would have been more fitting to consider each people on their own terms, to describe them according to their own circumstances, and to examine precisely how they fit into the place they occupy on earth."²⁹ A man like Meiners is incapable of learning, Forster concludes, and he anticipates Meiners's reaction to the review with a mixture of Schadenfreude and disdain: "Poor Mr. Meiners! I do hope he will calm down. There was really nothing I could do for him."³⁰

Measured against Kant's open prejudice and Meiners's blatant racism, Forster appears slightly better.³¹ He challenges Kant on methodological grounds, claiming that he has a rigid system in place that blinds him to the variations revealed by empirical observation, in keeping with the spirit of Johann Reinhold Forster, who also complains about anthropologists who "study mankind only in their cabinets."³² Georg Forster acknowledges that excessive reliance on sensual impressions can hinder the development of more general ideas, but he cautions against rigid concepts that can trick us into "the most common of all illusions, . . . namely, that when searching for certain things they need, people think they have found them when they really have not."³³ As Dagmar Barnouw observes, Forster was aware that cultural prejudices and subjective opinion can color the insights of the most careful observer, but she notes that he nevertheless "argued directly against the foundations of Kant's position, namely the cognitive supremacy a priori of the conceptual over the empirical."³⁴ "Who would not prefer the limited observations of a mere, but sharp-sighted and reliable, empiricist to the many fancy notions of a prejudiced theoretician?" questions Forster (8:133). Kant claims that we cannot be certain about the skin color of the Polynesians, although he lived his entire life in Königsberg and was hardly in a position to judge; he also ignores the testimony of those who have seen the evidence with their own eyes. "Why don't we just ask the honest seafarer?" (8:135). He then questions Kant's rigid distinction between immutable races and variations caused by climate or individual differences. If humans had a common origin and gradually developed into different races, why should the current racial distinctions be set in stone? Is it not possible, and perhaps more logical, to entertain the idea that today's humans may not stem from a single source? Lord Kames raises the possibility of multiple human origins in the first of his *Six Sketches of the History of Man*, although, as David Livingstone points out, "he sort of halfheartedly tries to support the Bible's version after all."³⁵ Forster also pulls back from an unequivocal endorsement of the polygenetic theory—"I will by no means permit myself to provide a definitive answer to the question as to whether there were originally several different human races"—in keeping with his guiding principle that we should not take as fact that which we cannot empirically verify, and perhaps also to diffuse potential charges of blasphemy, in that polygenesis contradicts the biblical account of creation.³⁶ Forster is more openly concerned with the argument that the theory of polygenesis can be used to justify human rights abuses. "But if we separate the Negroes from the whites by saying that they originated from a different source, do we not cut the last thread that connected this mistreated people to us and gave them some protection and some mercy from European cruelty?" (8:154). Instead of answering his rhetorical question, Forster accuses those who assume that monogenists are any less likely to commit atrocities. "Let me rather ask if the idea that the Blacks are our brothers has anywhere, one single time, caused a slave-driver to lower his raised whip? Did he not torment the poor, patient creatures with the fury of an executioner and devilish joy, while completely convinced that they shared the same blood?" (8:154). The shift in register from a carefully reasoned argument about racial difference to an impassioned denunciation of human cruelty is a rhetorically effective strategy to win the readers' sympathy. Philosophers can debate irresolvable questions ad nauseum, while turning a blind eye to the inherent injustice in the institution of slavery.

Forster continues his emotional appeal in the concluding pages of his essay. "White man! Are you not ashamed to abuse your strength on the weak, to cast him down to the animals, to want to eradicate the last trace of reason in him?" So far, so good: in contrast to Kant, who deploys derogatory racial stereotypes with no hint of apology, Forster upbraids white Europeans for their failure to treat Africans as fellow human beings. He stops short of declaring them equal in terms of cultural development, however, as he turns his righteous indignation into a plea for paternalistic condescension.[37] The Europeans realize "that everywhere in vast, densely populated Africa the reason of the Blacks only reaches the first stage of childhood," but Europeans should not use their adult status as an excuse for child abuse. "You should be a father to him, and by developing the holy spark of reason in him, you should complete the task of ennoblement," Forster intones. "With your help he could, should become what you are, or can be, a being that is happy in the use of all its potential powers." Forster concludes his lecture by predicting that the Africans will eventually fulfill their human destiny and develop all their faculties, with or without help from the Europeans, for although the whites are currently more advanced than the Blacks, they are not intrinsically superior: "For you too are only a tool in the scheme of creation!" (8:155).

"Something More About Human Races" recapitulates in condensed form the ideas that inform Forster's *Voyage Round the World*. Here again he appears as an advocate of the Enlightenment who is convinced that Europeans are at an advanced stage of development and should therefore do their best to bring primitive cultures up to their level. There as here, Forster rebukes Europeans who fail to advance the civilizing mission and finds their faults all the more disappointing because they should know better. In the final analysis, however, Forster qualifies his argument in two ways: first, he minimizes the missionary zeal behind his exhortation to the white "fathers" to educate the African "children" by claiming that, in time, the Blacks will grow up without European tutelage; second, he reduces both cultures to the status of cogs in the wheels of creation. Belief in human agency, which would seem essential to Forster's injunction to his fellow Europeans to stop beating the enslaved Africans and start educating them, is reduced in the first step to a kind but ultimately superfluous gesture in the larger course of human development, and then removed entirely, as all humans and their cultures are mere pawns in the workings of a higher plan.

SLAVOPHOBIA AND GRAECOPHILIA

Forster begins his response to Kant's essays on human racial distinctions with an ironic reference to Vilnius, declaring the penetration of the scholarly journal "into the interior of these Sarmatian forests . . . one of the victories of the Enlightenment" (8:130). The ancient Sarmatians lived on the eastern perimeter of the Roman Empire in the region around the Black Sea. They lay outside the pale of Western civilization, therefore, and Forster's use of the term for modern Vilnius and its surroundings is a not particularly subtle way of calling them barbarians. When Forster had his private audience with Emperor Joseph II in Vienna on his way to his new job in Vilnius, the emperor had warned him about the people he would encounter—"the Poles are stubborn and stupid"[38]—and predicted that Forster would not last long in that hostile environment, so Forster was not favorably disposed to his new surroundings. In one of his early letters to his fiancée, Therese Heyne, he struggles to explain the *"polnische Wirtschaft"* around him, a derogatory term for their alleged mismanagement of the land.[39] As the months passed, Forster's antipathy toward "this bestial nation" only grew stronger.[40] Part of his hostility stemmed from self-pity, as he felt excluded from the European world of letters and blamed the Poles for his personal unhappiness. Political factors played a role as well, as Forster strongly disapproved of "the Polish grandees who are used to being surrounded by thousands of slaves. Oh, the accursed serfdom is an ugly thing! It kills and deadens human feelings down to the bone."[41]

In the end, however, Forster's dismissive comments often reek of pure prejudice, setting the tone for the next two centuries of German anti-Polish sentiment. In a long letter to Lichtenberg, Forster claims that if he did not have his wife for company, he would not be able to survive in this miserable land, and "that we have no greater fear than that of Polackization [Polackisieren]." To that end, they struggle to find intellectual sustenance, "so that degeneration doesn't creep up on us unawares" (damit uns keine Entartung unvermerkt beschleiche).[42] Forster's normal facility with languages abandons him in the case of Polish, in part "because I don't take the time to learn it," but also because "it is a difficult, barbaric language."[43] When Forster's first child is born in Vilnius, he declares that he will not allow his "little Polish girl" (meine kleine Polin)[44] to learn Polish or French before her seventh birthday, so that his plans for her education are not undermined.[45]

At the opposite end of the spectrum lay Forster's veneration for ancient Greece. When he stopped off in Weimar on the way to Vilnius, Goethe hosted "a Greek dinner" for Georg and Therese Forster, Herder, and Wieland.[46] Forster does not explain what was "Greek" about the event, but the term reflects the fascination with ancient Greece and its culture that played a central role in the movement known as Weimar Classicism. Inspired by Johann Joachim Winckelmann's impassioned descriptions of Greek sculpture, Wieland, Herder, Goethe, Schiller, and Hölderlin found in ancient Greece a model of human perfection that inspired emulation and prompted new reflections on the old debate about the relative worth of the ancients and moderns. In the run-up to the Second World War, Eliza Marian Butler went so far as to claim that the "tyranny of Greece over Germany" usurped the nation of its "normal" sense of identity and indirectly prepared the way for German National Socialism.[47] One need not accept such sensational claims today—which rely on an essentialist notion of Germany's "real" identity and follow an all-too-easy line of thought that leads directly from Winckelmann to Hitler—to acknowledge the allure of an idealized model of Greek humanism in eighteenth-century Germany. As T. J. Reed observes, German Graecophilia marks a late phase of the European Renaissance, in which "love and enthusiasm for the real world are rekindled after centuries of monotheistic gloom."[48] The Greeks offered the Germans a model of wholeness and health that promised to soothe the trauma of their shattered world. "Eternally chained to only one single little fragment of the whole, Man himself grew to be only a fragment," lamented Schiller in his letters *On the Aesthetic Education of Mankind*,[49] and Hölderlin echoed his words in the closing pages of *Hyperion*, in which he likens modern Germany to "the shards of a discarded pot. . . . I can think of no people more at odds with themselves than the Germans."[50]

When the Czarina of Russia sent word to Forster that she would like him to join a new expedition around the world, he eagerly accepted, delighted to escape his exile in Vilnius.[51] On his way back to Göttingen, where he planned to leave his wife and child and prepare for the journey, he asked Herder if he might stop for a second visit in Weimar. Forster mentioned in his letter that he and Therese "were reading with rapture" the third volume of Herder's *Ideas*, "which provides us with the most splendid entertainment."[52] In the thirteenth chapter of that volume, Herder writes with great enthusiasm about ancient Greece, which he likens, no doubt with a nod to Forster, to modern accounts of life in the Pacific islands.[53] A few months later Schiller wrote the first of his major philosophical poems, "The Gods of Greece" (Die Götter Griechenlands), in which he praises the colorful panoply of the ancient Greek gods and laments the impoverishment of modern times, in which science sucks the life out of nature and Christianity takes the fun out of life. Predictably enough, theologians were quick to condemn Schiller's work, charging him with blasphemy for his disparaging remarks about the deleterious effects of Christian faith on modern life. Friedrich Graf zu Stolberg, who had once, together with his brother, run riot with Goethe during his rebellious "Storm and Stress" period, had since turned into a pious conservative and rushed into print to condemn Schiller's poem.[54]

Stolberg's critique was part of a larger conservative turn in Prussian cultural politics that led to the "religion edict" of July 1788, which sought to suppress secularizing tendencies in keeping with the convictions of the new king, Frederick William II.[55] Wilhelm von Humboldt was vehemently opposed to this attempt on the part of the state to curtail intellectual freedom, and when he visited Mainz in October 1788, he found a fellow liberal in Georg Forster.[56] The publication of Stolberg's polemic against "The Gods of Greece" gave Forster the opportunity to intervene in the debate that he had discussed with Humboldt. Forster writes his response in the form of a letter to an unnamed German author (Stolberg), whom he sarcastically praises for daring to criticize a widely admired poem, "because it contradicts your convictions and your principles."[57] Forster states that he has read Schiller's poem "countless times" with nothing but delight, because it provides an image of "those times when the intellectual powers of the most noble human race developed under the most favorable conditions; those times, which will never come again, to which we owe everything that we have thus far become" (7:10). Forster goes on to chide Stolberg for his failure to distinguish between poetic fantasy and religious faith, as he hopes to convince him "that it is possible to admire Schiller's 'Gods of Greece' without wanting to pray to its fantastical ancient images" (fabelhaften Urbilder) (7:12). Forster, like Herder, Schiller, and Humboldt, is less concerned with the historical facts about ancient Greece than the ideal that enables a critique of religious dogmatism in the name of intellectual freedom and the poetic imagination.

Forster was not opposed to Christianity per se. In a letter of 1784, Forster assured his father that he would never convert to Catholicism and that he "was resolved to live and die as a Calvinist."[58] While in Kassel, however, Forster had become deeply involved with the Rosicrucians (*Rosenkreuzer*), the conservative counterpart to the Illuminati. This secret society was originally dedicated to "the promotion of religious piety and . . . the manufacture of gold through laboratory alchemy." As Klaus Epstein observes, "both objectives appealed to mental attitudes far different from those cherished by the *Aufklärung*."[59] In its eighteenth-century variant, the Rosicrucian order combined "an inexpressible sense of wonder about the world . . . with a passionate craving for personal union with God" in an organization that demanded "absolute obedience to secret superiors."[60] Mesmer, the hypnotist who gave his name to mesmerism, and Frederick William II, the king who inspired the religious edict that Humboldt and Forster found abhorrent, were both Rosicrucians.[61] In Kassel, in his role as "Brother Amadeus," Forster had taken the rituals and authority of the society very seriously until shortly before his departure, when he announced that he had experienced a "revolution" that had caused him to abjure "a large dose of religious mysticism" (eine gute Portion Schwärmerei).[62] Exactly what prompted the abrupt change in Forster's religious sentiments is unclear, but during his journey to Vilnius he writes of his recent past like someone who has just been cured of an illness or awakened from a dream.[63] In a moment of self-analysis, Forster concludes that his unhappy youth "had driven him into the religious enthusiasm"

(Schwärmerei) from which he has finally managed to extricate himself.[64] For the rest of his life, Forster was a born-again advocate of the Enlightenment who tolerated religion only if it tolerated free thought.

In this spirit, Forster wrote another short essay "On Proselytizers" (Über Proselytenmacherei), again in close collaboration with Wilhelm von Humboldt.[65] The Catholic widow of a Protestant man had been advised by a local official in Mainz, the Hofgerichtsrat Bender, to raise her children as Catholics (while her husband was alive, she was obligated as his subordinate to raise them as Protestants). Johann Erich Biester, the editor of the *Berlinische Monatsschrift* and a leading figure of the Berlin Enlightenment, accused Bender of proselytizing for Catholicism. Forster adopts a more moderate tone, writing that Catholics, like all believers, want to share their faith with others, but that they pose no particular threat to Protestants or anyone else. Tyranny is the enemy, not Catholicism. Forster sums up his argument at the end of his essay: "Even under the most adverse circumstances for the Protestant church, the Catholic eagerness to convert (Bekehrungseifer) has not yet succeeded in any disturbing way," he contends, "whereas freedom of conscience (Gewissensfreiheit) is always in danger under despotic regimes." There is only one solution to this predicament: "The only sure means to remedy this problem is *freedom*."[66]

Already in *Voyage Round the World*, Forster criticizes the Polynesian religious leaders who arrogate privileges for themselves while casting a nimbus of mystery around their weird rites, and in *Views of the Lower Rhine*, he voices similar critiques of Christian art. In contrast, the gods of Greece were not gods at all, at least not in the sense of divine beings that deny humans earthly pleasure, but rather expressions of a culture that venerated nature and humanity as one. But what was the relationship between ancient Greece and modern times? Did antiquity serve only as a static contrast to modernity, a model of plenitude against which the present shortcomings stood in sharp relief? Or could the past be set in motion? Could what had been lost be regained? Schiller suggested that it could. While he focused on the negative consequences of modernity in "The Gods of Greece," he soon provided the positive counterpart in "The Artists" (Die Künstler), a long philosophical poem published in March 1789. In the earlier poem, Schiller had emphasized the negative consequences of Christianity and modern science, but in "The Artists" he suggests that the loss of the poetic spirit of ancient Greece might be the necessary precondition for future gain. As Schiller explained in a letter to his friend, Christian Gottfried Körner, he had already advanced the thesis that ancient art led to modern science, but now he contends "that science itself is not the goal, but only a second stage on the way to it, ... for human perfection will only come when scientific and moral culture are again subsumed into beauty."[67] Schiller formulates an early version of the theory of history that will inform his essay *On Naive and Sentimental Poetry*, which in turn inspired works such as Heinrich von Kleist's essay on the marionette theater, in which he speculates that those who had been expelled from paradise might find a way to slip back into the garden through an unguarded gate.

In *Natural Supernaturalism*, M. H. Abrams describes the pervasive pattern of this three-phase theory of history in the works of German and British romantics.[68] Part of its appeal, no doubt, lay in its flexibility: the general structure of the argument remained the same, but its content could vary. Ancient Greeks, biblical patriarchs, and medieval minstrels could all occupy the category of the naive, as could modern children, simple peasants with their folk traditions, and even Goethe, in the stylized portrait Schiller drew in his first significant letter to his future collaborator.[69] Tahiti and other island paradises fit nicely into this format. Cook's voyages into unknown territory were also perceived as travels in time that led to the discovery of seemingly simple peoples living like Adam and Eve before the fall. The difference, however, between these modern "primitives" and idealized versions of ancient peoples was that they were alive now, and that the Europeans tended to destroy the indigenous cultures they admired. The naive worlds that served as the source of poetic fantasies were often byproducts of colonial conquests: no cracking the code of Egyptian hieroglyphs without Napoleon's military invasion into Egypt, no translation of the Sanskrit *Sakuntala* without the British presence in India, and no South Sea idyll without Cook's search for the Northwest Passage and the Southern Continent. As a participant in Cook's second expedition, who would gladly have embarked on another circumnavigation of the globe and who dreamed of a journey to India, Forster was acutely aware of the material reality behind the flights of fancy. He had already corrected Kant's racial categories with reference to empirical experience, exposed inequities in the supposedly idyllic Tahitian society, and criticized the destructive impact of the Europeans on that world. In his essays of the late 1780s and early 1790s, Forster not only expresses his admiration for ancient Greece and other seemingly pristine worlds but also considers relations between European civilization and non-European cultures. In the process, he formulates a model of cosmopolitan exchange that contrasts with the ideology of European imperialism and inspired a series of subsequent German thinkers.

COSMOPOLITAN IMPERIALISM

We begin with "On Delicacies" (Über Leckereyen), which Forster wrote for the *Goettinger Taschen Calender,* a popular venue for which he adopted an uncharacteristically jaunty tone. Forster begins by assuring his readers that he is not encroaching on the realm reserved for women by writing a cookbook—"We do not challenge the prerogative of the fair sex to teach the noble culinary arts according to rules and regulations or on the firm footing of tradition" (8:164)—and ends with an encyclopedic list of the sources of sugar in the world's cuisines. Forster is willing to consider the ecological cost of the quest for delicacies: "How many native plants were pushed aside by cultivated crops, and how many species of animals were eradicated in different lands so that deer and hares were left just for us" (8:174). He is even more concerned about the human suffering entailed in the acquisition of luxury foods. The ancient Roman who once dined on fish fed on the flesh of executed slaves is no more, "but we sell slaves so that we can enjoy a few delicacies like sugar and coffee" (8:174). Here as elsewhere in his works, Forster does not advocate for an end to civilization and the suffering it can cause. An unnamed philosopher (Rousseau) once said "that it was infinitely better to eat acorns naked in the forest than to hold forth behind the stove in a cap and nightgown" (8:166), but he failed to take his own advice. Civilization advances, whether we like it or not; without citing Kant's "Idea for a Universal History" directly, Forster expresses ideas about the advance of civilization through the antagonism of forces that he had voiced in "Cook, the Discoverer" two years earlier. "Only a push causes movement; light and fire only arise by rubbing things together harder; only in incessant partial disharmony could the grand accord of the universe arise!" (8:167). This cultural development has placed Europe at the vanguard of civilization, and one of the signs of that superiority is an ability to appreciate other cultures and their cuisines. All societies have their local delicacies, but only Europeans can rise above their particular tastes to savor the world as a whole, maintains Forster, because they have the capacity to reflect on their preferences and to articulate their ideas. "That is why only the European can determine what a delicacy is.... He alone decides and classifies the varieties of taste" (8:168). Even if you challenge Europeans' authority, "you at least have to admit that only they can provide a precise description of what they like to eat" (8:175). The world is comprised of local cultures, but only the Europeans are both local and universal.

Forster pursues these ideas in greater detail in an essay "On Local and Universal Development" (Über lokale und allgemeine Bildung).[70] He wrote the work in February 1791, in the wake of his translation of the Sanskrit play *Sakuntala* from English into German; it was the only part that Forster completed of a substantial work he planned to write about India.[71] Forster begins with sweeping statements that reflect Herder's influence. "What humans could become, they have become in accordance with the local conditions." Climate (*Klima*), in Herder's broad sense of the term, shapes particular cultures around the world. "Thus, there is nowhere where man has become everything, but he has become something different everywhere" (7:45). Here again, however, Forster reserves a special place for European culture. "The most beautiful human race could settle in the most beautiful climate on earth without maturing into the moral superiority [moralische Überlegenheit] that one cannot deny the Europeans" (7:46).[72] Other climates may be more conducive to human development, other peoples as handsome, but as luck would have it, "or, to be more serious, because the higher order of things wanted it that way," only Europeans have inherited the benefits of the historical development of culture that moved from Egypt and Asia to Greece, and then over to Rome and up into Europe. "The spirit of chivalry, the crusades, commercial enterprise, advances in navigation, the reawakening sense of human dignity, the first stirrings of the love of freedom against feudal hierarchies, the discovery of the Cape of Good Hope, the passage to India and the New World—this was all part of the reciprocal cause and effect of the accelerated activity of our spiritual strengths." This European spirit of discovery is not entirely benevolent, as Forster describes it. The circumstances that led to "a revolution in thought" produced a people in which the sense of "greed, ambition, and the craving for power were honed to the point of recklessness, for whom no task seemed too large, no exertion too strenuous" (7:47).

Their advanced civilization drives Europeans out into the world, but the world also reflects itself back onto them: "The empirical sciences, those genuine, indispensable sources of knowledge, once so muddied and despised, flow now in limpid beneficial streams from the farthest reaches of the earth down to us, and reason recognizes itself in their reflection" (7:47–48). In Forster's view, there is nothing unique about the European spirit, nothing innate or intrinsic to its character. Europe was the fortunate flower that blossomed on the stock of previous civilizations, and now it is the sponge that absorbs current world cultures. "It is not to our discredit that our knowledge contains almost nothing that is still original and distinctively ours, that it is the philosophical offshoot of our planetary research" (die philosophische Beute des erforschten Erdenrunds). In its receptive capacity, however, Europe has risen above its particular circumstances: "the distinct European character has been replaced by universality, and we are on the way to becoming an idealized people that is abstracted, as it were, from the human race, . . . that can be called the *representative* of the entire species" (7:48).

This passage combines arrogance and humility in a remarkable way.[73] The arrogance is obvious: the Europeans are the only human culture to have transcended their local setting to achieve universality. They have done this, however, only because they are the beneficiaries of forces beyond themselves that have molded a not entirely admirable character, as they are driven out into the world by greed and ambition. Their primary achievement, however, lies not in their ability to impress their culture on other parts of the world, but in their receptive capacity: they have little or nothing that is their own, and for that reason they can absorb the cultural achievements of others. Now it is their duty to send what they have received back out into the world: "One day they (non-European peoples) will receive their own ideas back again from Europe, freshly minted with the stamp of universality. The white light of reason will shine in Europe's many colonial cities, trading posts, and conquered provinces, which once were illuminated only by broken prismatic colors." Ideally—and Forster interrupts himself to acknowledge that his "speculation is bordering on the incoherent and one word more would push it into the nonsensical"—the transmogrified ideas will return to enrich their native soils without entirely eradicating the local character. Forster concedes, however, that the European-led civilizing process may only reshape the world in its image, rather than enhancing global diversity: "who can prove that the salt of Europe's universal knowledge (jenes Salz europäischer Universalkentniß) could spice them up with new humanity (mit neuer Menschheit würzen) without also transforming them into Europeans?" (7:49).

Forster wrestles with the tension between European universalism and global diversity in ways that are also central to Herder's thought and that continue to vex contemporary postcolonial theorists,[74] as suggested in the introduction to this study, although he also uses his essay to address seemingly unrelated topics. Toward the end of "On Local and Universal Development," Forster shifts the focus to reflect on universal history and Kantian ethics. At stake on an abstract level is the question of whether it might be possible to retain the advantages of reason while regaining the spontaneity of nature. "If the law of wisdom leads us to the same place where we once left the simplicity of nature behind, then our circle is closed, then freedom and necessity are reunited, the childhood innocence of the primal world and the intuition of the ultimate age are in effect the same, and the metamorphosis of the human race—" (7:49), and here Forster stops himself from concluding his utopian vision. He has already articulated the three-phase theory of history cited earlier in this study, which envisions an idyllic state of paradise regained. In ethical terms, Forster anticipates Schiller by imagining a world in which people do what they ought to do because they want to do it, rather than being ruled by a rigid concept of duty. "*Duty* is the word before which reason bows down as if to a self-created despot; the word that demands absolute obedience and transforms man into a machine, set into motion by laws" (7:51–52). In political terms, Forster condemns the tendency toward standardization in modern states in ways that will resurface in *Views of the Lower Rhine*: "But the inevitable tendency of an age that wants to restrict and stipulate everything is to annihilate all individuality. When the rules multiply, a slavish, petty uniformity of the mind arises, and then mediocrity and emptiness reign in works that have been measured and manufactured according to a formula" (7:51). In conclusion, Forster argues that art is the antidote to abstract reason and rigid morality. Only the arts can "develop and ennoble taste and the sense of beauty, not just according to rules, but through excellent examples of every kind." Their purpose is the *"representation of beautiful individuality,"* not the reproduction of a standardized norm (7:55).

Two points bear repeating about this brief but suggestive essay. First, the dialectical structure of Forster's argument allows him to preserve the form while filling it with different content. An essay that begins by reflecting on relations between Europe and the rest of the world shifts to intra-European concerns while retaining the same tension between the general and the particular. European universality, Kant's categorial imperative, and the absolutist state stand against global diversity, individual inclination, and regional differences. If the first side of the equation elevates the second without eliminating its unique features, then both parties benefit, but if it imposes a sterile uniformity by force, everyone loses. Exposing the structural commonalities behind seemingly disparate topics leads to my second point concerning the way Forster conceives of European hegemony in the imperial age. On one level, as I suggested, Forster's contention that the Europeans, and only the Europeans, are at the vanguard of human cultural development is simply arrogant, and the Eurocentric bias of his thought is clear. At the same time, however, Forster defines that supremacy in terms of absence rather than presence, in terms of the European ability to absorb and reflect rather than to conquer and control. Modern European culture owes everything to its ancient ancestors; it is in itself nothing, a cipher, a void to be filled with the accomplishments of past civilizations. The Europeans' aggressive tendencies are therefore not intrinsic to their nature, but only the inheritance of a historical process that was beyond their control: "The higher order of things wanted it that way" (7:47). The imperial aggression that drives Europe out into the world cannot mask its essential emptiness, and that emptiness enables it to receive alien cultures and reflect them back to them. To put it another way, Forster substitutes the logic of translation for the monolingual paradigm when thinking about Europe in the global context. Rather than conceiving of European culture as an essential quality that emerges out of the fatherland's native soil, expresses itself in the mother tongue, and goes on to export its civilization to the colonial "children," he describes it as a switchboard, a reflecting mirror, a site of translation and transformation that is nothing in itself, but everything in its capacity to serve as the nodal point of linguistic and cultural exchange.

But what of the intra-European differences I mentioned at the outset of this book? Where does Germany stand in relation to other European nations? In his reflections on German Orientalism, Forster appropriates the argument about Europe as a whole that he develops in "Local and Universal Development" and applies it to Germany in particular. In this modified version of his thoughts on universal history, Forster claims that other European nations are simply aggressive; they impose their will on the world. Germans, in contrast, are passive-aggressive; they extend their influence by osmosis, by their ability to absorb other cultures and mediate between them. The German lack of political unity that prevents their active acquisition of colonies becomes a source of strength, a cosmopolitan capacity for a different sort of world leadership that moves beyond the merely local without the violent imposition of a single standard on global cultures. Against Susanne Zantop's model, in which German colonial fantasies compensate for current political fragmentation and anticipate future unity, Forster finds in Germany's very disunity the capacity for a global cosmopolitanism, as opposed to an imperialist nationalism. Germany's special quality already exists now, not later; it lies in its current diversity, not in its future unity.

FORSTER'S INTEREST IN INDIA

Although Forster was best known for his travels to the South Pacific, his interest in India runs like a red thread through his works. Before departing on his journey to the Netherlands and England in the spring of 1790, Forster procured a letter of introduction from Sophie von La Roche to Warren Hastings, the former governor of Bengal, and his wife, because of his desire "to talk about India and its inhabitants with them and to see to what extent I can rediscover my Tahitians in the Indians, from whom they in all likelihood are descended."[75] Hastings had been charged with misconduct during his tenure as governor and was in the midst of a long trial; the prosecuting attorney was Sir Edmund Burke, whose *Reflections on the Revolution in France* would soon provoke Forster's displeasure. Humboldt and Forster spent an entire day observing the legal proceedings, from which Hastings was eventually acquitted.[76]

Forster also encountered Sir William Jones's translation of *Sakuntala* in London, and upon returning to Mainz, he immediately sent an excerpt of his own translation into German of Jones's English version to Schiller for publication in the journal *Thalia*; he also urged Spener to publish the entire work.[77] Incidentally, Forster's correspondence with Schiller reveals how tenuous the preservation and dissemination of literary texts could be before the advent of photocopies and electronic backup. Forster was collaborating on the translation with Ferdinand Huber, who knew Schiller from his days in Leipzig, and Huber had sent Schiller part of the sole handwritten copy of Forster's translation. "Now my agreement with my publisher [Spener] requires me to get this fragment—of which I have no copy—back as soon as possible." Forster implores Schiller to have a duplicate of the manuscript made immediately, if he thinks the fragment worthy of publication (Schiller did). "I only ask that you do me a favor now and send back my manuscript with the next postal delivery."[78]

While working on the translation, Forster continued to be preoccupied with India and questions of comparative religion. How is it possible that the Romans, Greeks, and Indians have such similar gods? It seems probable to Forster "that it was more likely that the name and the concept were communicated between peoples than that such similar ideas arose simultaneously in two different places. How useful and how in accordance with our needs it would be to have a book that gave authoritative answers and drew clear boundaries!"[79] In his survey of the latest literature from England in 1790, Forster underscores the importance of Sir William Jones's *Asiatick Researches*, which contain "many extremely important natural-historical and anthropological treatises that would be informative for the linguist, archaeologist, historian, philosopher, and mathematician,"[80] and he continues to comment on new books about India the following year. "To India!" exclaims Forster in a letter to Therese shortly after his arrival in Paris in the spring of 1793. "You see that I am seriously considering this idea."[81] A few weeks later he reports that he has an offer to direct a print shop in England, about which he has mixed feelings: "But if, on the other hand, I could raise five hundred pounds sterling, or even only three hundred, I would learn Persian and Arabic here and take the land route to India so that I could bring home new experiences and work part-time as a doctor and in a few years I would be set for life."[82] Although he must have known that he was in no condition to make the arduous journey, Forster clung to his fantasy until the end. "I am not giving up my East-Indian project yet."[83] A map of India was said to have been opened on the bed in the Parisian garret in which Forster died a few months later.[84]

Although Forster never traveled to India and lacked time and energy to immerse himself in the study of Oriental languages, others soon did. In a sense, Forster could be considered the father of German Orientalism: biblical scholars such as Johann David Michaelis had pioneered the philological study of ancient texts, but "it was the publication of Georg Forster's translation—of William Jones's translation—of the Sanskrit play, *Sakuntala*, in May 1791 that really ignited German Indophilia, offering romantics hope that they might find in ancient India a lyrical and lovely lost world unencumbered by bourgeois conventions, religious hatreds, and political polemics."[85] Within a decade of Forster's death, Novalis began incorporating poetic images of India into his works; Friedrich Schlegel studied Sanskrit in Paris, and Friedrich Creuzer and Joseph Görres began to write the sort of comparative mythologies that Forster would have liked to write himself.[86] However, Forster did manage to write a brief but dense preface to his translation of *Sakuntala* that is of crucial importance when considering the German scholarly and literary interest in world cultures at a time when other European nation-states were establishing global empires.

Forster addresses these questions directly on the opening page of his preface. "Indian literature was already an object of curiosity in England several years ago and nothing is more understandable than the fervent interest they feel for the knowledge and mentality of a people of whom fifteen million are subject to the British crown."[87] Given their colonial interests in India, it is not surprising that some London intellectuals would also be curious about the discovery of an ancient Indian drama. "Things are different in Germany. We have no capital city and no direct involvement that could make the intellectual achievements of the Indians of *immediate* interest to us." As a result, the German public does not have the benefit of the taste that "can only arise and become dominant in a refined capital city." There are advantages but also disadvantages to the artistic standards that can form in London but not in the smaller cities of the German lands. They can prevent "a ridiculously exaggerated valorization of the pitiful," but they can also blind the public to beautiful works of genius that break the rules of good taste. The lack of a direct material or political interest in India and other potential colonies also has its advantages, for it allows the Germans to curate world cultures for the benefit of humankind, rather than to exploit them in the name of a particular state: "To investigate, collect, and order what is scattered in fragments and adaptations around the world dispassionately for its own sake, until the edifice of human knowledge stands complete—or our role is over and future generations need the stones that we gathered for a new building." Forster turns Germany's political fragmentation and attendant lack of overseas colonies into a cosmopolitan virtue. "It is this general receptivity that enables us truly to pay homage to the products of good taste, no matter what nation they come from, as long as they are of high quality, whereas the French, English, and Italians find it so difficult, indeed, almost impossible to empathize with other ways of thinking and feeling, with customs and habits other than their own" (7:285–86).

GERMAN GREATNESS AND GLOBAL LITERATURE

The ideas that Forster put forth in a few brief paragraphs in his preface to *Sakuntala* would resonate throughout the romantic era and beyond. Friedrich von Hardenberg's "Christianity or Europe" (Die Christenheit oder Europa) invokes a nostalgic image of European unity in the middle ages as the model for a cosmopolitan future that transcends the national conflicts consuming Europe in the revolutionary years. In his poetic vision, Germany plays a paradoxical role as the nation that leads Europe to postnational harmony. "Germany is slowly but surely taking the lead over the other European nations."[88] Similar ideas resurface in the fragmentary poem by Friedrich Schiller known to posterity as "German Greatness" (Deutsche Größe).[89] Probably composed sometime in the course of 1801, the poem takes as its theme the contrast between Germany's crumbling Empire and its great cultural achievements. "Isolated from the political, the German established his own value, and even if the empire perished, German dignity would remain unchallenged."[90] The fragment offers a classic defense of the German *Kulturnation*: while other European nations, in particular Britain and France, consolidated their state administrations at home and extended their power abroad, the Germans joined together in the realm of the spirit. Central to Schiller's argument is the claim that the old Reich and the modern German nation are two different things: "Deutsches Reich und deutsche Nation sind zweierlei Dinge" (1:473). The former totters toward its grave, while the latter rises to new vitality: "This

Reich (the new realm of the cultural nation) is flourishing in Germany, it is thriving, and new life takes root in the midst of gothic ruins" (1:474). Lack of political unity is not to blame for Germany's problems. Just the opposite, in fact: particularism was a liberating factor in the development of diverse German cultures. "No capital city and no court exerted its tyranny over German taste. Paris. London. So many lands and rivers and customs, so many distinct impulses and characters" (1:475). The imminent collapse of the Reich is a fortunate fall, for German language and culture are now poised to extend their reach: "Our language will rule the world" (1:474) proclaims Schiller, for the Germans' time has come: "Every people has its day in history, but the day of the Germans is the harvest of all time" (1:477). He hastens to add that violent conquest is not what he has in mind:

> Das ist nicht des Deutschen Größe
> Obzusiegen mit dem Schwert,
> In das Geisterreich zu dringen
> Vorurteile zu besiegen, ringen
> Männlich mit dem Wahn zu kriegen
> Das ist s. Eifers wert. (1:475)

> German greatness does not lie in victory with the sword. To advance into the realm of the spirit, to overcome prejudices, to wrestle, to wage a manly war against illusions—that is worthy of his zeal.

Schiller reminds his readers that German Protestants once broke the bonds of the Vatican and declares that he who fights for truth and reason will always struggle in the name of humanity.

Schiller's spirited declaration that the German language will rule the world charmed the patriots who first edited Schiller's fragmentary verse, just as it might make us uncomfortable today, but it is important to focus on the text in its historical context and not in the light of subsequent events. Three points are worth emphasizing: First, Schiller explicitly and emphatically rejects military violence, citing that Germans swing their swords in the name of truth, freedom, and reason, not to subdue domestic enemies or acquire foreign colonies. Second, the sense of national solidarity he extols arises within the federated structure of the Holy Roman Empire, not in anticipation of a centralized nation-state. As Georg Schmidt observes, the link between the old Reich and the German nation was considered unfashionable among Prussian historians around 1900, as they preferred to cast the Reich as the outmoded precursor to the modern nation-state. For them, national consciousness emerged in opposition to the Reich and in anticipation of Prussian-led national unity. The reality was quite the opposite, contends Schmidt: "To summarize the debate, the German national character was at home in a federal organization."[91] Third, Schiller was not alone in articulating a vision of empire as an extension of enlightened ideals to all of humanity.[92] In addition to Novalis, who combines reactionary nostalgia with utopian dreams in "Christianity or Europe," we find Heinrich Heine, who prefaces his sarcastic sendup of German nationalism in *Germany: A Winter's Tale* (Deutschland. Ein Wintermärchen) with the claim that he would actually welcome global hegemony on the part of the Germans, but only if they conquered the world in the name of the life-affirming values of the Saint-Simonians and the liberal reforms of the French Revolution.[93] Thomas Mann extended this legacy into the twentieth century when he attacked the exclusionary, racist nationalism of the Nazis in the name of an expansive concept of cosmopolitan Germanness that he called *Weltdeutschtum*.[94]

This tendency in German thought has not gone unnoticed. Dieter Borchmeyer makes it a central theme in his monumental investigation of German identity, which he sees oscillating between two poles, inclusive and exclusive, cosmopolitan and nationalist.[95] Although it would seem that the tendency toward openness to the world would be preferable to narrow-minded nationalism, Borchmeyer notes that a smug sense of superiority clings to the self-declared German propensity for universalism and that this cosmopolitan (*weltbürgerlich*) impulse could easily flip into a desire to rule the world (*weltbeherrschend*).[96] Borchmeyer highlights a dialectic that Krishan Kumar has noted in revolutionary France, in which the effort to centralize and homogenize the nation-state within sharply drawn borders soon turned into a civilizing mission that sent armies from Madrid to Moscow.[97] The German case is the mirror image of the French, as the federated nature of the Holy Roman Empire largely precluded direct German participation in military aggression within Europe or the European conquest of the non-European world. The absence of empire becomes a source of cosmopolitan pride that inspires visions of world cultural hegemony. From one perspective, this exculpatory vision played into fantasies of future German conquests: we do not, cannot, have colonies now, which exonerates us from the guilt of those nations (in particular the Spanish) who currently mistreat their subjects, but in the future, we will establish a kinder, gentler empire of our own.[98] If we approach this phenomenon from the other side of Koselleck's proverbial saddle, however, the German cosmopolitanism in works by Forster, Schiller, Goethe, and Heine seems less an anticipation of the late-nineteenth-century quest for a place in the sun and more a secularized version of the Holy Roman Empire's Christian universalism.

Among the many variants of these ideas about Germany's place in world culture, none has garnered more attention in recent years than Goethe's concept of *Weltliteratur*. Here again, the German nation plays an ambivalent role: on the one hand, Goethe proclaims that national literatures are passé: "National literature is no longer of importance; it is the time for world literature, and all must aid in bringing it about." At a time when German scholars were just beginning to build their national literature, Goethe's dismissive comments about what he already characterizes as an anachronistic task might well have seemed deliberately provocative. At the same time, however, Goethe gives Germany pride of place in the world republic of letters: "I am convinced that a world literature is beginning to develop, in which an honorable role is reserved for us Germans. All nations are paying attention to us; they praise and criticize, accept and reject, imitate and distort, understand or misunderstand us and open or close their hearts to our concerns. We must accept this with equanimity because it is of great value to us."[99] While in this passage Goethe suggests that the intrinsic value of the new German literature has attracted widespread attention, he also describes the nation's role in economic terms, as the stock market for commercial exchange: "He who understands and studies the German language is at a marketplace where all nations offer their wares; he plays the translator as he enriches himself."[100]

Goethe viewed Weimar as one nexus of world literary circulation; Forster's Mainz was another. As Timothy Blanning observes in his history of the city, Mainz was not a major industrial center in the eighteenth century, but it did enjoy the "right of staple" (Stapelrecht), which "meant that all goods passing through the city had to be unloaded, offered for sale and then reloaded in Mainz ships to be transported to their final destinations."[101] Wines, lumber, grains, and many other commodities exchanged hands along the riverbanks, while in the center of the city Georg Forster practiced his own kind of literary *Stapelrecht*, translating, reviewing, and prefacing the latest travelogues. In the process, he transformed books about expeditions to distant places into commodities that went on journeys of their own, moving between languages and across borders in the European world of letters. B. Venkat Mani has coined the term *bibliomigrancy* for the literal movement of books and figurative exchange of ideas they fostered.[102] In doing so, he sheds new light on the German relationship to European imperialism that has been one of the central concerns of this chapter. In tracing the history of the German concept of world literature over the past two hundred years, Mani shows how it was sometimes vilified as a "Jewish" concept promulgated by "rootless cosmopolitans" who allegedly undermined the integrity of the national culture and sometimes embraced as a salutary antidote to nationalist poison. The latter view has prevailed in postwar Germany and been given new life in opposition to the current resurgence of nativist nationalism. As Mani reminds us, however, the ability of Goethe, Forster, and their contemporaries to read works of Persian, Indian, or Chinese literature depended on the presence of European powers in those regions. The Germans may not have played an active role as colonizers, but they benefitted indirectly from the activities of others. The very idea of world literature depends for its existence on the imperialist nationalism it would seek to refute.[103]

Forster's self-congratulatory preface to *Sakuntala* stands at the beginning of this tradition in German thought. Profiting directly from the booty the British brought back from India, Forster translates the English translation of the Sanskrit into German and in the process washes it clean of its implication in colonial violence; his work accrues value as the cultural equivalent of laundered money. The preface adds insult to injury, as Forster accuses the British and other imperial powers of self-absorbed insensitivity to alien cultures and praises the Germans for their disinterested pleasure in the world's cultural commodities. Novalis, Schiller, Goethe, Heine, and Thomas Mann continue this paradoxical tradition of cosmopolitan nationalism, which sets itself against garden variety national chauvinism and yet assumes the mantel of world leadership. As Herfried Münkler reminds us, empires always see themselves as benevolent forces that bring order to chaos and civilization to the barbarians,[104] and thus it is tempting to read the seemingly soaring ideals of these German writers as examples of the "utopian, innocent vision of European global authority" that Mary

Louise Pratt terms the *anti-conquest*, a belief in moral superiority that played a central role in German fantasies of future colonies.[105] In this case, however, the goal is not to conquer the world in the name of the nation but to pioneer a cosmopolitan spirit that unites all people as equals and renders violent takeovers a thing of the past. Forster's preface to his translation of *Sakuntala* offers an early articulation of the persistent pattern in German letters that mixes national pride and anti-imperialism into a paradoxical fusion of nationalist cosmopolitanism.

CHAPTER 4

Views of the Lower Rhine

Georg Forster begins *Views of the Lower Rhine* with a confession: "On the journey through the Rheingau—may my loyal compatriots forgive me!—I read a travelogue about Borneo, and warmed and refreshed my imagination on those glowing colors and massive plants of the tropics, which were nothing like this wintry region."[1] The contrast between the lush jungles of Southeast Asia and the drab banks of the Rhine on a cold March morning underscores the difference between Forster's new travelogue and the exotic locales he describes in *A Voyage Round the World*. On that journey, Forster and his companions had frequently been exposed to life-threatening danger in the most remote regions of the planet. This time, as he notes to his unnamed correspondent, it is hard to complain about a trip that allows the traveler to bring along "pen, paper, and ink" (9:1). Almost immediately, however, Forster forgets about Borneo and begins paying attention to what he sees as he travels down the Rhine. "Travel in any form, this grand, incomparable source of the most accurate education through one's own senses" (9:291), exerts its appeal even when it does not lead him to the ends of the earth. By the time he reaches Amsterdam, Forster finds himself marveling at the traditional costume worn by one of the local girls: "If a traveler had encountered this girl in the East or West Indies, he would have considered her barbaric headdress worth a sketch and written at length about the monstrous and outrageous taste of primitive peoples, because we never consider how similar we are to savages, and use this term very inappropriately for everyone in other parts of the world who is not dressed in Parisian fashion" (9:310).

Views of the Lower Rhine is an exercise in "anthropologizing the West," as Forster turns the gaze that once presumed to speak the truth about "savages" onto his own continent.[2] The journey took him and his companion, Alexander von Humboldt (who remains virtually invisible in Forster's travelogue), down the Rhine, across the English Channel, and back through revolutionary France on their return to Mainz, although we have only notes and rough drafts for Forster's account of his visit to England and Paris. The full title of the travelogue provides an itinerary of the journey: *Views of the Lower Rhine, from Brabant, Flanders, Holland, England and France, in April, May and June 1790*. As Jürgen Goldstein observes, such descriptive titles were typically reserved for accounts of expeditions to distant parts of the world; Forster appropriates this convention to describe more familiar destinations.[3] The deliberately ambivalent first word of the title, however, suggests that he intended to include more than just images of surprisingly strange headdresses worn by women in Amsterdam and similar domestic exotica. His work does offer views (*Ansichten*) of such local customs, but it also offers his opinions (*Ansichten*) about such places in the context of intra-European politics in their relation to the natural environment, global commerce, and world history.[4]

Like *A Voyage Round the World*, *Views of the Lower Rhine* stands under the sign of the Enlightenment. As the elder Forster explains in the advertisement for *Observations*, Cook made the unusual decision to include among his crew a scientist whose sole purpose was to make "a considerable addition ... to the stock of human knowledge" (lxxviii). Georg likewise prefaced *Voyage* with fulsome praise of the "enlightened monarch" (King George III) who commissioned an expedition dedicated to the comprehensive study of the planet and its inhabitants (5). The European explorer-scientists fluctuated between an appreciation of alien societies and the conviction of their own cultural superiority. If humanity comprised one great family, as the Forsters and others maintained, and yet different groups within that family were at different stages of development, it behooved the mature Europeans to work for the betterment of "savages" still in their infancy, so that "they may gradually emerge from the darkness of barbarism" to "behold the dawn of civilization."[5] As Georg Forster observed, however, the benevolent intent could have disastrous consequences, and he also raised doubts about the moral fitness of the Europeans to carry out this civilizing mission. At stake, as Forster explained in his essay "On

Local and Universal Development," was the effort to preserve the universal values of the Enlightenment without destroying the diversity of world cultures. In his preface to *Sakuntala*, Forster suggested that the Germans had the ability to understand alien cultures and facilitate the circulation of new ideas, as opposed to other nations' tendency to eradicate difference and exploit those in their control. The source of the Germans' alleged propensity for the appreciation of the foreign lay in the federated nature of their political organization. For all its shortcomings, the old Reich allowed for local autonomy within a universal framework in a way that contrasted with the centralized nation-states of modern imperial powers. Precisely this tension between German federalism and French universalism lies at the center of Forster's reflections on revolutionary politics in the final years of his life.

THE CONTEXT OF *VIEWS OF THE LOWER RHINE*

The timing of the journey gives a new edge to Forster's ideas. Forster and Humboldt left Mainz a little less than a year after King Louis XVI summoned the estates general of France to solve a looming fiscal crisis, inadvertently setting into motion the series of events that would lead to the abolition of the monarchy and his own execution. The same events would have a direct impact on Georg Forster's life as well, as French armies seeking to expand the reach of their revolution would soon occupy Mainz, turning the university librarian into one of the leaders of the short-lived Mainz Republic, before sending him into exile and a premature death in France. The journey to the Netherlands, England, and France marked a turning point in Forster's political development; in Gerhard Steiner's words, *Views* records his transformation from a humanistic representative of the Enlightenment into a revolutionary democrat.[6]

The transformation takes place on two timelines: the first involves that of the journey itself, in the spring and early summer of 1790; the second concerns the writing of the journey. Forster began work revising his rough notes and letters into the published travelogue immediately upon his return to Mainz in July 1790. Other demands on his time, including his work for the university and as a book reviewer and translator, coupled with marital discord and bouts of serious illness, delayed completion of *Views of the Lower Rhine*. Forster finally published the first volume of the work in February 1791, and the second in April 1792, but was never able to complete the planned third volume, which was to have depicted his journey to England and France.[7] The lag between the trip and the travelogue gave Forster time to research the history of the cities he had visited and to reflect on the significance of what he had seen in light of the swiftly evolving political events of the early 1790s. The interruption of the project by the incursion of French troops into Mainz meant that it would remain a torso that failed to deliver all that was promised in the travelogue's lengthy title.

The places described in the completed volumes of *Views* matter as much as the timing of the events. Forster focuses most closely on recent events in Aachen, Liège, Brussels, and the surrounding province of Brabant, rather than depicting events in revolutionary France and the British response to them. Microanalysis of local settings in border zones replaces macroanalysis of national conflicts in a global context. Forster's depiction of this region also continues a recent literary tradition, of which he was well aware. Just before he left Frankfurt for Weimar in the fall of 1775, Goethe wrote a rough draft of *Egmont*, a drama about a Flemish nobleman executed in 1568 by Spanish forces in Brussels. A few years later Schiller began work on *Don Carlos*, set in the same period, but with a focus on a Spanish prince encouraged by his friend to champion the oppressed peoples of the Netherlands against imperial tyranny. Schiller completed *Don Carlos* in May 1787 and then switched genres to write his *History of the Revolt of the Netherlands from the Spanish Government*, just as Goethe began final revisions on *Egmont* while living in Rome. Forster describes similar conflicts in the same region, although he updates the events from the early modern period to the present. All three writers engage issues of vital importance on the eve of the French Revolution. In the Netherlands, they could observe intra-European empires struggling against provincial patriots, weigh the benefits of enlightened absolutism against the pull of local traditions, and question when liberal ideals turn into demagogic ideology.

In the sixteenth century, the Netherlands, nominally part of the Holy Roman Empire, came under the control of the Spanish Habsburgs. At a time when Spain was expanding its holdings in the Americas, it also sought to control the commercial centers of northern Europe. The Protestant Netherlands eventually broke with Spain in 1581, but the predominantly Catholic regions of today's Belgium remained under Spanish control until

1714, when they were ceded to Austria. After Prussia captured Silesia from Austria in 1740, Joseph was determined to stem further losses by either maintaining control over the Austrian Netherlands or exchanging them for Bavaria. In his role as ruler of the Austrian Netherlands, Joseph imposed the same sorts of reforms he had introduced elsewhere in his realm, seeking to limit Church power, relax censorship, reform education, tolerate Jews, and abolish torture.[8] To his dismay, the conservative Belgians rejected the reforms and rebelled against his rule. As he lay on his deathbed, Joseph received the devastating news that the United States of Belgium had declared its independence from the Austrian monarchy.[9]

Efforts on the part of Prussia and Austria to gain control over Bavaria drew smaller German states, including Saxe-Weimar, into the conflict. The crisis began when the Bavarian Elector Maximilian III died without an obvious heir in December 1777. Empress Maria Theresa sent troops into Bavaria in support of one candidate; Frederick responded by leading his army into Bohemia in support of another. The so-called Potato War ensued, consisting mainly of a stalemate that finally ended when Austria relinquished Bavaria to Prussian control.[10] In the midst of this conflict, officially known as the War of Bavarian Succession, Prussia issued an ultimatum to some of the smaller states in the Holy Roman Empire, declaring that if they did not voluntarily provide Prussia with soldiers for help in their effort to expand their domain, Prussia would send in press gangs to take them by force. Weimar's secret council (*Geheimrat*) met on February 9, 1779, to debate its response. Duke Karl August suggested that they should resist Prussian power and take the matter to the imperial court, but others, including possibly Goethe, suggested that it would be more prudent to form an alliance with other small states within the Empire to create a buffer against the rival powers of Prussia and Austria.[11] This League of Princes (Fürstenbund) sought to secure the rights of small principalities within the old Empire threatened by the newly aggressive territorial states.[12]

International diplomacy and dynastic politics also played a role in the bewilderingly complex array of interests at stake in this conflict. King George III of England was also the Elector of Hannover, one of the German territories allied in the League of Princes. As Timothy Blanning explains, England was in dire straits after losing control of their American colonies in 1783, driving British diplomats to seek an alliance with Austria.[13] The

Electorate of Hannover, however, was an enemy of Austria, and German princes contacted George (in his capacity as a German Elector) to support Hannover against Austria. He readily agreed, thereby going against the wishes of his own diplomatic corps (in his capacity as the king of England). The king, who had previously referred to Hannover as "that horrid electorate," began to call it his "deutsches Vaterland" and to send his sons to be educated in Göttingen, which lay within his domain.[14] Convinced that the best way to preserve the Electorate of Hannover was to strengthen the Holy Roman Empire against Joseph's territorial ambitions (in his role as the Austrian monarch, that is, which undermined the integrity of the empire that he also led, if only nominally), George encouraged the League of Princes to form an alliance with the Kingdom of Prussia. Frederick II was only too happy to agree. When Joseph renewed efforts to gain control of Bavaria in 1785, Frederick enlisted the members of the Fürstenbund to oppose Austria, with the ostensible goal of preserving the order of the old Reich, but with the real purpose of strengthening Prussia. The League of Princes, which had been formed as a counterweight to the territorial states, had been repurposed as a pawn of Prussian hegemony.

Small wonder, then, that German artists and intellectuals took such an active interest in the Netherlands, for events there served as a reminder of how the complex web of dynastic and imperial politics could bring conflicts in seemingly distant lands into direct contact with local affairs. The long history of Spanish and Austrian rule in the Netherlands, moreover, shed light on contemporary efforts to control those provinces, while raising larger questions about the role of government in a revolutionary age. Was it better to cling to ancient traditions or embrace radical change, to live in an organic society or become a cog in a soulless machine? Should the imposition of progressive reforms on a retrograde society be considered a boon to long-suffering subjects or an act of tyranny that violated the sovereignty of independent states? Were Frederick and Joseph enlightened or despotic? Harbingers of the Revolution or defenders of the old Reich? Was there room in that Reich for constructive reform, and were there limits to the benefits of revolutionary upheavals? With these questions in mind, Goethe, Schiller, and Georg Forster turned their gaze on the Netherlands, both in its early modern past and the present day.

RELIGION AND THE ENLIGHTENED TRAVELER

In his sweeping study of Enlightenment thought, Ritchie Robertson devotes considerable attention to efforts on the part of eighteenth-century intellectuals to reconcile the demands of reason and religion.[15] While only a few were bold or foolhardy enough to declare themselves atheists, many more sought to increase the tolerance of religious differences and castigate human rights abuses perpetrated in the name of the Lord. Georg Forster is typical in this regard. As a young man in the South Pacific, he had little patience for religious superstition, although he never rejected religion per se. Nature's beauty often inspires him to give thanks to God, and he repeatedly attributes his escape from perilous situations to "the guiding hand of Providence."[16] When religion veers into delusions that block the path of human knowledge, however, Forster reacts angrily, particularly when religious fanaticism supports political despotism. He condemns "heathen priests with the idea of keeping the minds of the people in awe, by awakening their superstition." They "weave their prejudices so firmly into the web of human knowledge, that to this moment the greater part of mankind pay them homage, and blindly suffer themselves to be cheated in the grossest manner" (171). Understanding the religious beliefs of the peoples the explorers encounter poses a particularly difficult linguistic challenge, because "the dialect of the church frequently differs from the common dialect," but far worse is the fact that the same esoteric jargon keeps most of the natives in a similar state of ignorance: "and thus religion is veiled in mysteries, especially where there are priests to take advantage of the credulity of mankind" (249). Religious leaders often reserve sinful luxuries for themselves "under the cloak of religion," thus adding their communities to the list of "the many dupes of voluptuous priest-craft!" (256). Dispelling superstition therefore liberates the mind and is a source of great joy: "The destruction of vulgar prejudices is of so much service to science, and to mankind in general, that it cannot fail of giving pleasure, to every one sensible of its benefits" (621).

Forster's commitment to the principles of the Enlightenment are again on full display as he begins his journey down the Rhine. "Personal freedom is incontestably and irrevocably linked to the vocation of man and is therefore an *inalienable* right" (ein ... *unveräußerliches* Gut) (9:8) proclaims

Forster in language reminiscent of Locke, Thomas Paine, and the American Declaration of Independence.[17] Forster repeatedly asserts his faith in the power of reason and the possibility of human progress. "The more richly developed an age is, the greater the number of our concepts, the more refined our choices, the more comprehensive our range of thought and action, the more varied and attractive the relations between us and everything that surrounds us" (9:21–22). Some say that the time has passed when it was possible to question articles of religious faith, comments Forster, but he maintains "that those times can never completely end, as long as there is no means to turn people *against their own reason*, against the noblest quality that forms the foundation of their nature" (9:31).

Forster rejects anything or anyone who obstructs human development, limits human freedom, or impedes rational thought. Early in the journey, Forster recoils with horror at the sight of prisoners in the fortress of Ehrenbreitstein in Koblenz, reaching out through their barred windows to beg for alms. Against those who say that the abolition of the death penalty is a sign of progress, Forster claims that the indefinite loss of freedom is itself a cruel and unusual punishment. People argue that prisoners have the chance to reflect on their wrongdoing and amend their ways, but what good does that do if they are left to languish behind bars? Only the fear of death could make such protracted torment seem preferable to a quick execution. Political despotism and religious intolerance are among the worst sins in Forster's world. "What state can expect *public spirit* from its citizens if it mistreats them?" (9:33).[18] Worst of all is a form of religion that replaces reason with superstition and serves despotic regimes. "Nowhere does superstition appear more frightening than in Cologne," observes an outraged Forster. Here pious Catholics are duped into venerating a pile of human and horse bones that were probably picked off a battlefield and are willing to be killed or kill others for the sake of these dubious relics: "that attests to the impenetrable darkness that rules here in the realm of religion" (9:33–34).

Forster's neoclassical taste in art grows out of his humanist convictions. The man who admired Goethe's *Iphigenia*[19] and defended Schiller's "Gods of Greece" against religious zealots appreciates the Gothic cathedral of Cologne and laments that fact that it was left a fragment[20] but insists nevertheless that the cathedral's beauty pales in comparison with its ancient counterpart: "Greek architecture is incontestably the epitome of the perfected, harmonious, relevant, exquisite—in a word, the beautiful" (9:23–24). When one considers the achievements of modern artists, Forster remarks, it is hard not to think "how poor and helpless they would be in the face of the sublime and the ideal if they did not have the Greeks as their predecessors and models" (9:45). Echoing Winckelmann, Forster contends that Greek sculpture elevated human perfection to an inimitable ideal in a culture that enjoyed every advantage of a perfect climate and in which art and religion coexisted in harmony.

Christian art, in contrast, reflects a pathological hatred of the human body and a misguided suspicion of worldly experience. Forster often cites Rubens as the worst offender in this regard, as he abused his talent in the production of grotesque images of naked bodies and flabby flesh that Forster finds "unspeakably disgusting" (9:50). In Cologne, Forster sees his famous crucifixion of St. Peter, which he finds shocking. Rubens portrays a distorted image of the saint hanging upside down on the cross in a way that intensified his torture. What sort of perverted aesthetic sensibility would choose this topic for a work of art? "Are those objects worthy of depiction? Objects that I would not want to see in nature!" (9:34). Another Rubens painting shows human bodies "entwined like a disgusting coil of worms, a confused mass of limbs, and—I describe with a shudder what I see—a cannibalistic meat market" (9:44). Forster admires casts of Greek sculptures, only to be shocked when he learns that the originals had been "broken into bits to be used to build roads.... Now you tell me, are we not still the same old barbarians!" (9:81). The same spirit of humanist pleasure in the things of this world causes Forster to recoil from a group of monks he encounters on a tour of a monastery in Düsseldorf. Their octogenarian guide looks twenty years younger than he is, but only because his face radiates the complacent vapidity of a life without conflict. "What is better: to take a few more wrinkles and a mind enriched with experience and activity to the grave, or to brood away in quiet contemplation, without worries, without passion, without intellectual pleasure, and, in the end, to suffocate softly in your own fat?" Quoting Goethe's "Prometheus," Forster claims that this sort of vegetative existence has "no appeal for those who know the better destiny of man: 'to suffer, to cry, / to enjoy and to be happy'" (zu leiden, zu weinen, / zu genießen und zu freuen sich) (9:37).

AACHEN: GLOBAL COMMERCE AND ECOLOGICAL CATASTROPHE

In keeping with the spirit of the Enlightenment, Forster praises recent advances in international trade. In Coblenz, Forster reports that a businessman has established a new leather factory that uses hides imported "directly from Buenos Aires in South America. Thus, trade and industry connect the most distant parts of the world!" (9:9). His enthusiasm for the benefits of world trade soars to new levels when he reaches Aachen. Forster devotes two chapters of *Views* to his description of the city, which places local business in a world context. His initial impression of the city is negative. The former center of Charlemagne's vast empire is now in decline, its people listless and dull. The current Kaiser no longer lives there and is not even crowned there; superstition and intolerance govern the Catholic church, and an antiquated guild system stifles the local economy. Conditions got so bad that civic unrest erupted in the summer of 1786, and the Prussian government sent one of its ministers, Christian von Dohm, to investigate the matter and restore order in the Reich. Forster knew Dohm from his days in Kassel, where they had both taught at the local college. In fact, Forster had stayed with Dohm when he first arrived in the city, and Klaus Harpprecht relates the anecdote that Dohm was so excited by the arrival of the famous world traveler that he rushed to awaken his neighbor, even though it was late in the evening: "How can you sleep when Georg Forster is here?"[21] Forster's fame continued to open doors on his journey to the Netherlands, as Alexander von Humboldt recalled: "Forster's name, which awakened widespread interest,... gave us access everywhere to the leading figures."[22] These included Dohm in Aachen, and Forster drew on his former colleague's *Draft of an Improved Constitution for the Free Imperial City of Aachen* for this section of *Views of the Lower Rhine*.

In the introduction to this work, Dohm explains that the more he looked into the disturbances, the more he was convinced that the city's constitution needed reform. He is quick to assure his readers that he did not intend to create an entirely new civic order during his stay in Aachen; he only wanted to correct abuses that had corrupted the original form of government. His work was therefore revolutionary in the older sense of the term, marked by a desire to return to a previous state of affairs, rather than to create something entirely new. To this end, Dohm had to look into the city's history. Until 1450, he discovered, Aachen was ruled by a hereditary council (*Erbrath*),[23] consisting of members appointed for life. The city shifted to a rotating body of officials until 1477, when the old practice was restored, but then they reinstated the revised policy in 1513. In theory, the new system allowed greater control on the part of the people over their government, but in practice, one man ruled the dominant faction for up to thirty years at a time until another group came to power through an often-bloody struggle. Dohm sets out "to liberate the constitution from oligarchic despotism and guide it back to its original purity."[24] While conservative in its stated effort to restore the city government to its uncorrupted origins, Dohm's reforms also breathe the progressive spirit of a new age. The new constitution should inspire patriotism for the fatherland, he argues, because its laws are an expression of the general will (*der gemeine Wille*).[25] The implicit reference to Rousseau's *Social Contract* carries over into the principles stated in the opening paragraphs of Dohm's constitution. It begins on a conservative note: the burghers of Aachen are divided into fourteen guilds, and the imperial city (*Reichsstadt*) is subordinate only to the emperor. As he continues, however, Dohm introduces modern ideas into the medieval document. "A citizen of the imperial city of Aachen is a free man," he declares in the second section of his constitution; "all citizens are equal to one another" (Alle Bürger sind einander gleich).[26] Thus Dohm's efforts on the part of Aachen could be described as an exercise in progressive conservatism, in that he seeks to revitalize an ancient order with new ideas while stopping short of radical change.

Perhaps this is the best sort of reform one could hope for, concedes Forster in the opening pages of his description of Aachen, given the dreary state of affairs. He cites Margarete von Parma, the moderate regent of the Netherlands in Goethe's *Egmont*, who states that the good that she has done will look unspectacular from a distance, "simply because it is good."[27] Her replacement, the Duke of Alba, will introduce far more drastic measures in his draconian attempt to impose Spanish rule on the local governments, but she feels it is better to allow the provinces to govern themselves in accordance with their traditional customs and beliefs. What Goethe advocates as a wholesome alternative to imperial despotism turns into the best one can expect in a bad situation in Forster's more pessimistic assessment of the situation in Aachen. He offers somewhat grudging praise of Dohm's reform efforts: "Maybe it is more advisable in most cases to improve a flawed old constitution than to draft an entirely new one" (9:85–86). People ruled by a despot can hardly be expected to have the maturity to govern themselves wisely, so it is good to have a neutral third party resolve the differences. Ideals are the products of speculative reason, he continues, but constitutional reforms have to be measured "according to the current needs and circumstances" of the city in question (9:87). "So, the fourteen guilds of Aachen had to be maintained," he reluctantly concludes, "even though the guild system remains so ruinous to business and disadvantageous to the factories and workers" (9:88).

Forster goes on to describe the deleterious effect of the old guild system on the modern economy. Business has moved elsewhere, where restrictions do not hamper commerce, leaving Aachen impoverished and morally compromised. Beggars crowd the streets, compulsive gambling destroys families, and the resulting depression and despair have driven some to suicide. Women and children spin wool imported from Spain to supplement the income of impecunious peasants, even though this cottage industry is highly inefficient, while workers in the textile factories are debased into beasts of burden, "just like Negro slaves in the sugar islands, although they are not called slaves" (9:95). Meanwhile, in nearby Holland and other neighboring areas, business is booming. Large factories have sprung up in what were only recently tiny villages, and they are part of a thriving global network of commercial exchange. Forster takes pleasure in the knowledge "that thousands of people work here [in the Dutch factories] so that people can dress more beautifully or comfortably on the Euphrates and the Tigris, in Poland and Russia, in Spain and America; and that people in all those lands wear fabrics that supply thousands here with food and the various necessities of life" (9:97).

Two systems confront one another in close spatial proximity: Aachen languishes under outmoded guild restraints, while its neighbors embrace the advantages of unfettered capitalism. The contrast inspires Forster to sing the praises of global commerce and its role as a motor of human progress: "Without trade we would not yet have circumnavigated Africa, not yet have discovered America, nor undertaken or completed those things that elevate us above the other animals" (9:97). Not all climates are equally conducive to producing civilizations capable of progress, however. If conditions are too harsh, people expend all their energy in the effort to survive; if nature is too generous, society soon devolves into despotism, where the majority labors for the benefit of the few. Only in a handful of fortunate countries do we find a happy medium: the ancient Phoenicians and Greeks; Venice and Genoa in the Renaissance; and the modern Dutch, British, and other European nations. "This development was inseparably linked to civil liberty, however, and lasted only as long as it did." Among the Portuguese, for instance, commercial expansion could only be a "side effect of the spirit of conquest ... and had to disappear like something forced and unnatural in the darkness of intellectual despotism and political discord" (9:98). The Germans have had mixed success in modern times, according to Forster: municipalities open to international trade such as Hamburg and Frankfurt have done well, whereas older imperial cities like Cologne, Nuremberg, and Aachen are in decline. Freedom is the determining factor. "How small and contemptible every despot seems who has to fear the enlightenment of his subjects, in comparison with the private individual, the manufacturer of a free state, who bases his prosperity on the prosperity of his fellow citizens and on their improved education!" (9:99–100).

In summary, Forster's discussion of Aachen offers a striking instance of Enlightenment values linked to a Eurocentric narrative of universal history and faith in the benefits of global capitalism. He begins with a critical discussion of the city's religious and political conservatism that hinders economic growth. Dohm's constitutional reforms improve the situation as best as possible within the context of the old Reich, but without removing the fundamental obstacles to economic prosperity and political liberalism. Forster then expands his view to a sweeping and yet highly selective narrative of world history that follows the light of reason as it moves from ancient Greece to northern Europe, while leaving large swaths of the globe in darkness, either because savages struggle to survive in a hostile environment and have no energy left to improve their lot, or because denizens of more bountiful regions sink into indolence and Oriental despotism. Drawing on the *leyenda negra*,[28] Forster then distinguishes between northern European nations such as Holland and England, whose venture capitalism is a boon to the world economy and global culture; and Iberian nations like Portugal, which conquer lands only to extend the reach of their despotic realm; and Spain, whose ban on the import of foreign textiles limits its potential for economic expansion and exposes the evils of its authoritarian government. If Spain is to participate fully in the benefits of economic liberalism, it must begin by introducing political reforms: limit royal authority, abolish the Inquisition, "recognize irrevocably the freedom of conscience and the press, firmly establish the safety of private property together with the personal immunity of all citizens from arbitrary interventions into the power of the law" (9:102). Unfortunately, Forster concludes, no such reforms are likely in the foreseeable future.

Forster ends his thumbnail sketch of world historical development with dystopian reflections on the consequences of human-caused climate change. Before leaving Aachen, he visits a new factory for dying wool, which he describes as a large airy room with a wood-burning furnace in the middle. The sight inspires gloomy thoughts about the ecological price of economic expansion. The textile factories around Aachen require enormous amounts of fuel, which has led to the complete deforestation of the surrounding countryside. Fortunately, nature has provided "subterranean forests" (9:102) in the form of coal, and almost no one heats with wood anymore. But what if the coal reserves were also exhausted and no replacement could be found? Modern chemistry might find a solution, Forster speculates, but probably not. "It seems more likely to me that in the end, people would have to abandon the completely deforested, uninhabitable lands of ice and fog in the so-called temperate zone" (9:102–3). Driven by hunger and cold, the civilized peoples of Northern Europe will flee to the south. Turkey will blossom once again "in the beautiful light of moral culture" and "educated people will settle in Africa." The Eurocentric narrative of universal history shifts from an ascending line of progress from the Middle East to northern Europe, to a circular path that leads Europe back to the lands in which their culture originated. "The peoples of Europe will stream in light-colored hordes [in hellen Haufen] over those barbaric parts of the world." "We will defeat or expel the local barbarians and carry the torch of science back to the regions where they were first given to man" (9:103). Those eastern lands have slipped back into darkness or, in the case of Africa, have never seen the light, but the ecological catastrophe that renders northern Europe uninhabitable has a silver lining, in that it brings the benefits of civilization to benighted regions.

To this point, Forster's fantasy simply adds a new chapter to the old Orientalist tale of European supremacy. He goes on to suggest, however, that the book ends here, that the latest chapter is the last, that the environmental devastation that will send Europeans to the south marks the end of an era and not a new dawn. "The transitory nature of things convinces me that the older a human society becomes, the closer it gets to its end.... Can we bend the bow more without breaking it?" (9:103). We Northerners pride ourselves on our accomplishments and think that progress will continue indefinitely, Forster contends, but he cautions that we may be like those deluded old people who dream of a long life even as they move closer to death. In fact, we may have already reached the summit of our development. "When you have climbed to the top of the mountain, there is no alternative in this world of Ixion but to roll the wheel head over heels into the depths, and to drag yourself up from the bottom over a new mountain." It may seem foolish, Forster continues, to imagine that "a general revolution in Europe, accompanied by the collapse of political, moral, and, scientific order" (9:103–4) might be triggered by a shortage of fuel, and yet he insists that it could happen before reassuring his readers that the anticipated catastrophe will not take place for at least a thousand years.

Today's accelerating climate change suggests that Forster was right about the human impact on the planet but wrong about the timing. His speculations in *Views of the Lower Rhine* articulate an early understanding of what has come to be known as the Anthropocene, the period of earth's history in which humans have had a lasting and perhaps irreversible impact on the environment.[29] In *Voyage Round the World*, Forster had already commented on the ineffectuality of Cook's efforts to export European flora and fauna to the Pacific islands, while noting instances of wanton slaughter and cruelty on the part of the crew toward indigenous species. Alexander von Humboldt would soon make similar observations in South America, where he observed the consequences of deforestation, overfishing, and other forms of human settlement on the local ecosystems.[30] In *Views of the Lower Rhine*, Forster spins his otherwise sanguine view of industrial innovation into a nightmarish vision in which the course of human progress turns into an endless cycle of creation and destruction, or perhaps even complete and utter catastrophe with no sign of rebirth. Although Forster did not live long enough to read it, he might have been intrigued by Lord Byron's "Darkness" (1816), a poem about the extinction of the sun that pushes this doomsday scenario to its logical conclusion, until light and life on earth are gone.

LIÈGE: POLITICAL REVOLUTION AND CHTHONIC REASON

Forster's visit to Liège in today's Belgium again uses local politics as a springboard to larger reflections. As in Aachen, Christian von Dohm had been commissioned by the king of Prussia to resolve a local dispute that had larger ramifications for European politics. Liège, which Forster calls by its German name, Lüttich, was culturally French but part of the Holy Roman Empire. As in the case of Aachen, Dohm sought to place contemporary events in historical context, and to this end he published a monograph about *The Liège Revolution of 1789* just months before Forster and Humboldt visited the city.[31] As Dohm explains, the burghers of Liège established a constitution in 1316 designed to secure existing rights and freedoms against arbitrary change and to limit the exercise of power on the part of civic authorities to actions within the law. In 1684, however, the ruling prince-bishop (*Fürst-Bischoff*)[32] overthrew the constitution, a usurpation of power exacerbated by the fact that the church owned two-thirds of the land and yet paid no taxes. In the summer of 1789, the people demanded the revocation of the edict of 1684 and the restoration of their former rights. The prince-bishop signed the agreement in mid-August, but ten days later fled the city to an undisclosed location. The matter came to the court of the Holy Roman Empire (*Reichskammergericht*) in Wetzlar, which decided the dispute in favor of the prince-bishop, in part because they accepted the argument that he had signed the agreement under duress, but mainly because they were afraid that the revolutionary fever that had broken out just two months earlier in Paris was already infecting an outpost of the German Reich.

Dohm is at pains to explain to the Prussian authorities that this is not the case. Things look different from a distance, he contends, and in this case, authorities in Berlin are viewing events in Liège through the distorting lens of "the destructive French evil," "the nervous fear of revolutions." I do not know who first called the events in Liège a "revolution," he continues, but if they had called it what it was, an "agreement of opinion between the prince and his subjects to restore the old constitution," and if the timing were different, then the courts might have viewed the matter more objectively. As Dohm describes it, Liège, like Aachen, was undergoing a revolution in the older sense of the term, a return to a previous state of affairs, but the imperial court mistook their actions for a modern revolution, a complete overthrow of the existing order, which prompted "concern about the dangerous consequences of the French example for the entire Reich."[33] The Prussian king sent Dohm to look into the matter, and he discovered that some of the more radical rebels in Liège actually did want to ally themselves with the French revolutionaries. Dohm insists "that the people of Liège must not forget that they belong to the German Reich," and that any reforms have to respect the rights of the clergy and nobles as well as the third estate.[34] He nevertheless makes no secret of his sympathy for the people of Liège and encourages his readers to empathize with their concerns: a prince deserts his people; an imperial court brands the burghers as rebels, even though they had just signed an agreement with their leader; a foreign government sends in troops to keep the peace when they were not aware of any disturbance—even a less volatile people who did not have the example of revolutionary France at their doorstep would have been upset. Prussian troops under the command of General von Schlieffen entered Liège in an effort to keep the city in the German Reich, but they were reluctant to crack down too hard, in part because Schlieffen, like Dohm, was sympathetic to the people of Liège, but also because Liège, in its resistance to imperial authority, was a potential ally of Brussels in its struggle against the Austrian monarchy. As members of the Holy Roman Empire, both Austria and Prussia were allies, but as rival territorial states, they were enemies; thus, as representatives of the Reich, Prussian soldiers sought to repress the rebellion in Liège, but as enemies of Austria, they quietly encouraged resistance.[35]

Forster and Humboldt entered the city just as the Prussian troops were preparing to leave. They found the people eager to discuss politics as they wandered through town. "The names of the king of Prussia, Duke von Herzberg, General von Schlieffen, and Dohm were mentioned only with expressions of respect and love, with a kind of enthusiasm," even as they complained about the decision of the imperial court and "the German princes, who were supposed to protect them against tyranny, but treated them like rebels instead." Their outrage at the actions of the treacherous prince-bishop extended to "a general disapproval of the entire priesthood" and even "a rejection of religion itself among many" (9:110–11). Drawing on Dohm's account, Forster sketches the historical background of the current disturbances, which he leaves poised in a moment of great uncertainty: insurgents are gathering outside the city as the Prussians decide "to leave the enforcement of the Wetzlar decree to other princes of the Netherlands" (9:133). In town, everyone is wearing the black, green, white, and red cockade as a sign of local patriotism, and Forster fears that the unpredictable mob will use the call of freedom as an excuse to unleash chaos.

The events to which Dohm devotes a book of more than one hundred pages occupy no more than a few paragraphs in Forster's chapter on Liège. Forster could have updated this section of *Views* with news of the latest developments when he prepared his notes and letters for publication more than a year later, but he chose to leave things where they stood in the spring of 1790, in part to preserve the impression of immediacy for his travelogue, but mainly because he wanted to explore the larger implications of these local incidents. His argument is dense and leads us to unconventional conclusions, so it is important to follow it closely.

Forster begins with a reaffirmation of his faith in the Enlightenment: "Our reason constantly reminds us that our purpose is to attain the highest possible degree of moral perfection through the development of all of our innate capacities" (9:113). No state that denies this right or blocks this development is legitimate. And yet political change does not come about through rational means. "Violence, therefore, not gentle persuasive reason, but rather physical superiority, was the source of all changes in this small state [Liège], as in all others" (9:118). Why? No state is perfect, Forster contends, and as a result, states are always open to some doubt about their legitimacy; it is therefore logically impossible to distinguish between the valid enforcement of the law and arbitrary violence. If one party disagrees with a judge's decision, who can say where justice lies? In the case of Liège, for instance, does the fact that many people opposed a single prince-bishop make them right? "This is the massive difference between the unconditional principles of a theoretical science and their application in practical life; it is *so* difficult, *so impossible* to decide apodictically in specific cases about justice and injustice!" (9:120).

Forster has already led us to a surprising provisional conclusion: in practice, he sympathizes with the people of Liège against the prince-bishop, but in theory he is willing to concede that he may be wrong, as would be the case when assessing any political conflict. He continues with reflections about the nature of society. Given the absence of absolute justice, all societies are based on compromise. To keep the peace, people accept a law that holds society together despite ongoing discord. But this precarious situation cannot go on indefinitely. When *"positive* law" (das *positive* Recht) contradicts *"natural* laws" (*natürliche* Rechte), a form of violence ensues, and when this happens, "the constitution by its own nature is already null and void before the judgment seat of reason" (9:121). People will put up with a lot before they rebel against an illegitimate society, and governments depend on this inertia to maintain their grip on power. Few governments are despotic enough to rob their subjects of the last "little spark of divine reason" (das göttliche Fünkchen Vernunft). Poland, as so often for Forster, is the exception. "Among all European nations only the Poles have taken ignorance and barbarism so far that they have almost driven out the last trace of rational thought in their serfs" (9:122). The strategy backfires, however, as uneducated serfs are inefficient workers. Most rulers are clever enough to grant their subjects just enough freedom to prevent open rebellion; they keep them in check with threats and distractions. Eventually, however, something snaps, and at that point it only takes one man to tip the scale toward revolution. Forster uses Camille Desmoulins as an example of such an individual in recent history. He "climbed onto a stool in the Palais Royal in Paris and called out to the people: 'Gentlemen, I know they will hang me, but I risk my neck and say to you: grab your weapons!'" (9:123).

Here again, particularly in light of Forster's subsequent role in the Mainz Republic, we can assume that Forster sides with Desmoulins and endorses the French Revolution, just as he supports the people of Liège against the prince-bishop and the Wetzlar court. As he continues his argument, however, he assumes the guise of neutrality. "The most enraged democrat and the most arbitrary despot speak only *one* language today; *both* speak about the preservation and salvation of the state, about justice and the law; *both* invoke holy, inviolable contracts, *both* believe they have to risk everything, their lives and fortunes, rather than conceding the least diminishment to their rights" (9:124–25). There may well be an element of self-censorship at work here: Forster was employed by the Elector of Mainz, who, like the prince-bishop of Liège, combined secular and religious authority, and so it was in Forster's interest to pull back from an unconditional endorsement of rebellion. At the same time, Forster is using these examples to come to larger theoretical conclusions about the element of uncertainty surrounding any political decision. Both sides can use arguments to justify their actions, whether they seek to legitimate oppression or encourage rebellion, and both are potentially in the wrong: "To rebel against the sovereign is insurrection; to abuse sovereign powers is the blackest of all crimes.... You see, politics has its antinomies like every human science, and there is nothing in the world that is absolute, nothing positive, nothing unconditional, except that which exists in and of itself, which, however, we do not know" (9:125).

If absolute certainty in political affairs remains unknowable, on what basis should governments act? The simplest solution would be to establish a "universal monarchy with strong faith in the intellectual infallibility of the sole supreme ruler and his celestial existence, as the visible representative of the divinity.... *One* will, *one* wisdom, *one* moral authority above all" (9:126). The kings who attempted to establish such authority were mere mortals, however, and their subjects lost their faith in them. The alternative to a system that concentrates all power in a single individual would be a republican state that distributes power among equals. Would this "general fraternization of the human race into an all-embracing confederation" (allgemeine Verbrüderung des Menschengeschlechts zu einem allumfassenden Staatenbunde) actually solve the problems of an absolute monarchy, or would it introduce problems of its own? Forster suggests the latter: "It seems to me that the completely uniform application of those principles in practice would inevitably produce the same one-sidedness and narrowmindedness" that we already see among people who live according to strict rules. "A political mechanism" (9:127) that could achieve such uniformity seems contrary to human nature, Forster concludes. The productive diversity of conflicting opinions would be lost in such a uniform state, even if that uniformity stemmed from the seemingly positive "brotherhood of man" in an egalitarian society: "only in the conflict of opposing desires and ways of thinking is reason revealed in its sublime grandeur." A constitution that replaces the arbitrary authority of a despot with a single law that subjects everyone to "the same law of reason" would probably contribute just as little to the "general moral perfection" of humanity "as a universal monarchy" (9:128).

The opposition that Forster sets up is therefore not between monarchy (bad) and democracy (good), but between two forms of equally unacceptable totalitarianism, based on either the absolute rule of one leader or the uncompromising authority of a universal law. We have come a long way from the Enlightenment faith in reason that will guide us to a more just form of government, as Forster suggested earlier in the chapter, for he now contends that the triumph of a purely rational social order would rob us of our natural vitality. "What good would it do us to have the freedom to develop our intellectual abilities if we suddenly lacked the impetus for this development?" (9:128). We would be the secular equivalent of those placid monks who suffocate in the surfeit of their own contentment.

At this point, Forster's argument takes a final turn, as he introduces what might be termed *chthonic reason*. However threatening the image of a purely or, more precisely, merely rational society may be, it will never actually come to pass. Humanity renews itself every thirty years, and each generation develops "from simple vegetating seeds to animal physicality, and from this stage to the development of combined physical and moral capacities" (zu der gemischten physisch-sittlichen Bildung) (9:128). The term *sittlich* in this context implies more than the ethical sense of right or wrong in a given society; it extends to include all those intellectual and cultural capacities that distinguish humans as a species comprised of both body and mind, rational thought and physical desire. As Forster argues in this passage, the letter of existing laws will never suppress "the powerful dark drive" that fuels human development. This irrepressible "dark" force is neither the light of human reason nor the blind will of the body, but a combination of both, the rational expression of natural vitality, reason infused with the power of nature to produce "a combined physical-cultural development." It might seem that we have once again reached the final stage of the three-phase development outlined in Abrams's *Natural Supernaturalism*, which envisions the idyllic recuperation of naivete without the loss of "sentimental" reason, the productive fusion of mind and body, desire and duty, but Forster's world never stops changing. One generation's revitalizing power ossifies into abstract law until the next generation starts the cycle anew: "And thus the human race oscillates eternally between arbitrariness and rules," and nature is no different, as "these primal forces of the universe also struggle eternally" (9:128–29).

While the political activist seeks to effect change, the political theorist sits back to watch: "This spectacle of struggling forces is beautiful; beautiful and sublime even in its most destructive effect." At this point, Forster introduces the meteorological and geological metaphors that Jürgen Goldstein correctly identifies as an important aspect of his political thought. Against those who seek to trace "the cultural origins of the French Revolution,"[36] Forster describes revolutions as thunderstorms or volcanoes that build up force until a flash of lightning or an eruption releases the tension. "The passionate outbreaks of war have their use like physical thunderstorms; they clear and cool the political air and refresh the soil" (9:129). As Goldstein observes, such ideas about revolutions as explosive, natural calamities fly in the face of Enlightenment thought. "Revolutions are events of nature, in which reason may play a part, but nothing more."[37] Revolutions just happen from time to time, according to this view. They are not caused or guided by human reason, but rather cataclysmic natural events, and although they wreak havoc in the short run, they also revitalize decadent societies. Thus, Goldstein explains, both opponents and proponents of the Revolution seek to claim that nature is on their side: Burke condemns it as an unnatural act, while the revolutionaries plant liberty trees as living symbols of social rejuvenation.[38]

The relationship between reason and the revolution in Forster's thought is somewhat different than this paraphrase suggests, however. He oscillates between two concepts of reason in *Views of the Lower Rhine*: the one familiar and enlightened, the other that I have described as "chthonic," a primitive, amoral upwelling of natural forces. The second concept frames the first, just as Forster begins his hagiographic celebration of Cook's accomplishments with a preface suggesting that all human endeavor is part of the eternal flux of nature and thus ephemeral in the end. He concludes the reflections prompted by the situation in Liège on a similar note. "When the spontaneous combustions of reason in an entire people leave behind nothing but suffocating smoke," it would certainly be more pleasant to think that such political uprisings are only "innocent bonfires" that break out from time to time and not devasting holocausts, but Forster suggests that there may be some "good left in the residue," even in cases of catastrophic destruction. Forster voices tentative hope in the positive potential of apparent disaster, borrowing a concept from alchemy to describe the seemingly useless remainder (caput mortuum) of a chemical reaction, but he veers toward the negative as the paragraph concludes, shifting the metaphor from chemistry to the theater. We empathize with the suffering of a single tragic hero on stage, while the death of thousands in war leaves us untouched. "But if we sensitized ourselves to human misery, then we would not only cry about these events, but also find a sad side to almost everything that we see and hear, and make a sorrowful story out of the most common events in life" (9:130).

Far from celebrating the rejuvenating power of a revolutionary life force, Forster sees in major calamities only spectacular manifestations of the constant quotidian tragedies that punctuate our lives. From this perspective, revolutions accomplish nothing in the long run; they are just one more eruption of an eternally active volcano, another flash of lighting in an endless series of storms, another self-immolating outburst of human reason. "Here too, it is therefore excusable to observe events that one cannot change as spectacles" (9:130). Excusable but not inevitable: awareness of nature's endless cycles and the ultimate futility of human endeavors does not mean that we should remain in a posture of passive impartiality, nor does Forster pay mere lip service to the Enlightenment optimism that drives him to work toward positive change. Cook sails his ships and makes praiseworthy discoveries, even though Forster concedes that in advancing the human race, he causes suffering for some communities, and that his accomplishments, like all human achievements, are ultimately ephemeral. In the realm of politics as well, Forster relentlessly opposes despotism, particularly when it is abetted by religious superstition, even though when he steps back to look at the larger picture, he realizes that suffering outweighs success and that this moment will pass, like all others. But we live in the here and now, and like Faust, it is our duty to press forward and not remain in a permanent state of contemplative detachment. And thus Forster ends his philosophical excursus with a return to the present: "Now it is time to cast one more glance at Liège" (9:130).

BRUSSELS: REACTIONARY REVOLUTION

After closing out his account of the precarious situation in Liège, Forster moves on to Brussels, the center of the Catholic counterrevolution. In brief outline, the events unfolded as follows: Emperor Joseph II of Austria tried to introduce progressive reforms into the Austrian Netherlands. The people rebelled against his rule, but the rebels fell into two factions: those aligned with Heinrich van der Noot advocated for the return of the old feudal order, while followers of Jan Frans Vonck sought democratic reforms in an independent state. With the support of the church and the superstitious mob, as Forster portrays it, the conservatives won. Forster goes into considerable detail in his portrayal of the political situation in an effort to refute those "apostles of despotism" who believe "that the Enlightenment is to blame for political revolutions." In Brussels, just the opposite was true: "Yes, indeed, ignorance was never more complete, darkness never denser, the leaden yoke of faith never pressed reason more firmly into the ground. Here, fanaticism caused rebellions; superstition, stupidity, and enervated reason were its tools" (9:161). The Belgian revolution against Austrian rule succeeded, but in the process, reaction triumphed over progress and irrationality defeated the Enlightenment.

In his detailed depiction of the situation in Brussels and Brabant, Forster offers an unequivocal and relentless critique of the Catholic church. When the worst Spanish oppression of the sixteenth and seventeenth century ended, Brabant was rich and the arts flourished, "but this period passed quickly too, and everyone settled down to a long intellectual slumber under the narcotic wing of priestly education" (9:164). Soon the "Roman tyranny of the soul" (9:177) established its power, and "their clever leaders knew how to cultivate stupidity in the schools and academies in a systematic way" (9:168). While Forster marvels at the open discussion of politics among travelers he encounters on the way to the city and the vibrant exchange of ideas in public spaces, he also observes how the church manipulates opinion through the cynical use of propaganda. Clerics rouse the rabble by spreading rumors about the progressive party, and the people are only too willing to be duped. "The people? Do they not wear the chains of custom everywhere like inherited jewels that they would consider a crime to sell or exchange for a more beautiful and useful adornment?" (9:174). When offered the possibility of political reform, these "slaves of the priests" (9:194) blindly obey their leaders and reject change out of hand: "Nous ne voulons pas être libres! Even the sound of these words is so unnatural, that only the long habit of not being free explains how they could repeat what their duplicitous leaders told them to say" (9:162). Rendered docile by the religious authorities, the Belgians are incapable of change. Even the girls that Forster sees on the streets lack "the Promethean spark in their eyes; these pretty automatons can only sin and pray" (9:198).

Forster's assessment of Joseph II is considerably more nuanced. We recall that Forster had a private audience with the emperor in Vienna as he was on his way to a professorship in Vilnius, and he later requested Joseph's permission to dedicate his translation of Cook's account of his final journey, together with the introductory essay, "Cook, the Discoverer," to him. Emperor Joseph responded graciously: "Dear Professor Forster! Although I have made a general rule to forbid all book dedications, the renowned work that you are planning to transplant to German soil requires me to make an exception.... Thus I accept your dedication with pleasure and gratitude, and assure you of my complete respect and favor."[39] As a further sign of his benevolence, Emperor Joseph sent Forster a valuable diamond ring. There were certainly tactical considerations in Forster's eagerness to ingratiate himself with the emperor. It was flattering that an itinerant intellectual with no powerful connections would have been granted a personal audience with the Austrian monarch and Holy Roman emperor, and there was also the possibility that Joseph's patronage might prove useful in the future. Klaus Harpprecht suspects that Forster may have been hoping that the emperor would make him an offer to remain in Vienna in some official capacity, which would have been infinitely preferable to banishment in provincial Vilnius.[40] Even after he had accepted the appointment in Mainz, Forster had a job offer in Budapest, which he declined as diplomatically as possible, politely stating that he was reluctant to take up a new position in such a remote region (particularly since he had just escaped from what he viewed as exile in another eastern European city), but assuring the authorities "that I prefer the Kaiser's service to all others, in accordance with my personal taste and fundamental principles."[41]

Beneath the calculated flattery of the Austrian potentate lay the hope that Joseph might be a force for progressive change, and this hope—and its disappointment—informs Forster's depiction of Joseph's role in the Netherlands. On a visit to the region, according to Forster, the emperor observed that the people had great potential, even if they were currently "uneducated, sunk in superstition, lazy and indocile in the use of their intellectual powers" (9:168). With the best of intentions, Joseph began to introduce reforms. He divided the traditional lands into nine new regions, introduced a system of justice that was to extend equal protection under the law to all citizens, and abolished some of the aristocracy's old privileges. Joseph also sought to reform the University of Leuven, which he believed had been corrupted by ultramontane influence, and to improve the education of the priests. Christianity was to be returned to its simple origins, which entailed prohibiting religious processions and eliminating superfluous holy days. Joseph had fortresses razed to reduce the cost of military occupations and sought to reopen the Scheldt river to international trade.[42] "Any other people capable of recognizing its own best interest" would have appreciated the efforts of the emperor on their behalf, Forster maintains, but "the Belgian nation did not show a single spark of excitement." Joseph's frustration was understandable: "He felt a calling to encourage his subjects to make the best of themselves, as a father would teach his children," but they failed to respond to his efforts on their behalf. "Who does not pity the monarch whose people lagged so far behind him?" (9:169).

As Forster continues, however, he grows more critical in his assessment of Joseph's actions in Belgium. However good his intentions might have been, "the result of the imperial reforms was resistance, rebellion, war; the blood of thousands had to flow, the peace of millions was sacrificed—for what?—for a monarch's whim." No ruler has the right to impose even beneficial changes "through violent means" (9:170–71). Then again, Forster continues, democrats would argue that the aristocratic protest against the reforms did not necessarily represent the will of the people; indeed, he cites their claim that there is no legitimate government "'in a state in which the people are not really represented'" (9:173). Seen from this perspective—which Forster is careful to distance from his own—Joseph's actions must be measured in terms of their expediency, not justice. Was he right to do what he did? That depends on the perspective of the observer: yes, if one shares his enlightened views; no, if one does not. Was he smart to do what he did? Probably not. Above all, Forster objects to the enlightened despot's decision to ignore regional differences in the name of a single standard. "It does seem more natural to adapt the forms to the distinct character of the peoples than to force them all into *one* form" (9:174–75). Like Herder, who voices similar objections to Joseph's reforms in his *Letters Concerning the Furtherance of Humanity*, Forster notes that people develop differently in different geographical regions and that, "as in the entire organic creation," they thus have distinct cultures. "To constrain them by any sort of mechanism almost seems a sin against nature" (9:175). Herein lies Joseph's fatal flaw: he does not seem to have realized "that all good things develop slowly and gradually, that it is not a consuming fire, but a mild warming sun . . . that promotes the beautiful growth of organic nature" (9:145).

In Joseph, Forster encounters a practical example of the theoretical "antimonies" he had sketched out in his discussion of Liège: between a single absolute ruler who tolerates no dissent, and the equally unacceptable alternative of a totalitarian orthodoxy, however enlightened in its intent. The specter of uniformity (*Gleichförmigkeit*) or one-sidedness (*Einseitigkeit*) haunts German political thought around 1800. While no one was eager to advocate for the authoritarian rule of a single tyrant, there was widespread concern that enlightened reform would transform an organic society into a machine-like state. This concern informs Egmont's protest against Spanish imperialism in Goethe's drama,[43] while Schiller's *Don Carlos* not only attacks the absolute authority of the Spanish monarch and his despotic henchmen but also exposes the dangers of Posa's uncompromising idealism. The Netherlands, past and present, served as a kind of laboratory for German writers to test out the advantages and disadvantages of imperial power (either enlightened or despotic) against regional traditions. In his *History of the Revolt of the Netherlands from the Spanish Government*, for instance, Schiller describes the Netherlands as a weak alliance of autonomous principalities populated by "peaceful fishermen and shepherds in a forgotten corner of Europe."[44] "The peculiar thing about the Netherlands," writes Schiller in his review of Goethe's *Egmont*, is that they are "not *one* nation, but rather an aggregate of several smaller ones."[45] As Simon Schama explains, the Dutch "Republic was comprised not as a state but rather an alliance of seven sovereign provinces," a "loose federation" quite different from a centralized nation-state.[46] When the Spanish assumed control, however, the Dutch lost their freedom. "The Netherlands soon sensed," writes Schiller, "that they had become the province of a monarchy" (4:63). Formerly independent jurisdictions were reduced to Spanish colonies. "Now they comprised one limb of a giant body, to be used as a tool by one ambitious individual. They stopped being self-sufficient; the center of their existence was relocated in the soul of their ruler" (4:64). Having lost their sovereignty, the colonized provinces unite in opposition to Spain: "A solemn vow of the nation deposes the tyrant from his throne; the Spanish name disappears from all laws" (4:36).

A single nation emerges out of the many. And yet they join in a common cause against Spain in an effort to regain their traditional rights, not in the name of universal principles. When Philip first assumes power over the Netherlands, he vows to be "a good and just lord" who will allow his subjects to retain the "privileges and freedoms granted to them by their ancestors, and, furthermore, their habits, traditions, customs, and rights" (4:73). When he breaks that vow, he reduces human diversity to faceless uniformity, which is just how the Grand Inquisitor describes King Philip's approach to governance in *Don Carlos*. "What use are humans? For you, they are just numbers, nothing more" (Wozu Menschen? Menschen sind / Für Sie nur Zahlen, weiter nichts).[47] Schiller's indictment of the early modern Spanish Empire in the name of liberal ideals, which would entail the complete self-realization of all subjects, dovetails with his conservative resistance to the centralizing tendencies of eighteenth-century absolutism. As David Pugh suggests, "in the somewhat inchoate political climate of Germany in the later Enlightenment, it was possible for Schiller to integrate both conservative and liberal elements into his poetic presentation of the political world, in particular his denunciation of despotism."[48] In other words, for Schiller, the unity of the nation need not coincide with the unity of the state. Like Herder, who sees the strength of the ancient Greek and Hebrew nations in their decentralized alliances, or Goethe, who acknowledges the difficulties posed by the absence of a national capital for the advancement of German literature but rejects the sort of revolutionary upheavals that would lead to the formation of a unified state, Schiller also highlights the advantages of Dutch particularism over enforced standardization. He deploys the rhetoric of universal humanism in defending their right to local autonomy, however, in a way that moves him away from Goethe's conservatism and toward Georg Forster's emphatic liberalism. Looking ahead, appeals to the healthy *Gemeinschaft* of organic communities against the mechanistic leveling of the modern *Gesellschaft* will be a staple of German conservative thought for decades to come. Thomas Mann's fervent defense of a specifically German *Kultur* against the universal principles of French *Zivilisation* is only one of many examples.[49]

Forster gently chides Emperor Joseph II for imposing well-meaning reforms with a heavy hand onto a diverse realm, but he uses the same charge of enforced leveling to condemn the Catholic church in no uncertain terms. Standardization in the political realm is questionable enough, but the Catholic religion represents "a far more incomprehensible uniformity ... a uniformity of faith in invisible things that far surpass reason and its forms; a general, unconditional uniformity, that extends into the most intimate realm and arrogates to itself the right to unlimited, unquestioning authority over all the minds in the world" (9:175). To resist the reforms of an enlightened monarch in the name of an insidious religion that deceives the faithful into support of reactionary politics, even as it asserts its intrusive and uncompromising power, is to succumb to a far worse form of standardization than that of the secular state.

Given this logic, Forster can hardly support the Belgian resistance to Austrian authority in the way that Goethe's Egmont defends his people's ancient traditions. The reactionary rebels led by van der Noot seek the restoration of the feudal order that returns privileges to the aristocrats and unlimited power to the church; it tramples reason underfoot and sways the superstitious mob to do its bidding. Forster's sympathies lie more closely with the progressive faction of the Belgian resistance. He notes that Vonck, a liberal lawyer, started an underground democratic movement that quickly gained support across the region. These patriots were real progressives, not reactionaries in revolutionary garb. "It was not enough for the patriots to have driven out the Kaiser; they wanted freedom in the Netherlands, not the old tyranny under a new name" (9:204). The aristocrats were right to see Vonck and his allies as a threat, and Forster details the sequence of events that led to the defeat of the democratic party. In his view, the conservatives failed to realize "that beyond the alternative of oligarchic tyranny and French democracy there lay a third possibility; that an improved representation of the people was possible" (9:199). When on the brink of defeat, Vonck and his allies signed a petition claiming that they represented just such a moderate position. By no means were they advocating for "the frightening image of a national assembly." They insisted instead that "they intended to retain the three estates and wanted only improved representation along the lines of Flanders" (9:213). In the end, the democratic movement failed, not just because reactionary forces mobilized successfully against it but because its leaders lacked the necessary conviction to make the final sacrifice for their ideals. "It is better not to take up arms for a good cause if, having entered the fray, you are not willing either to win or die trying, with your weapon in your hand" (9:216).

Forster finally leaves Brussels and Brabant behind, shaking his head at the intransigence of a people who act against their own best interests. The second volume of *Views* concludes with a positive assessment of Dutch cities, in particular Amsterdam, whose political liberalism has enabled commercial prosperity. Had Forster been able to complete his work, he would have been able to report on his impressions of British parliamentary democracy and his visits to the English countryside, before concluding with his description of Paris, as its citizens prepared to celebrate the first anniversary of their Revolution. By the summer of 1792, however, Forster had lost the energy necessary to complete his fragmentary travelogue, and by October of that year, French troops occupied the city of Mainz and he had more pressing concerns.

The existing torso of *Views*, with its detailed reflections on Aachen, Liège, and Brussels, reveals the complexities of a political and cultural landscape in the transitional *Sattelzeit*. Looking to the future, *Views of the Lower Rhine* serves as a stepping stone on Forster's path toward political activism and advocacy of the French Revolution; looking to the past, it offers an analysis of tensions emerging out of the Holy Roman Empire in the context of European conflicts and global politics. Forster's focus remains resolutely local in his descriptions of the individual cities; his studies reveal the ambiguities of revolutionary reforms that oscillate between a desire to return to the old and embrace the new. He shows how local manufacturing is tied to a global network of raw materials and consumers, and how industry can impact the environment and potentially reverse the course of world history. *Views of the Lower Rhine* does refer to international conflicts between sovereign states, as we would understand them today, but it also reveals struggles between kingdoms and smaller principalities in the old Reich, and—as the case of King George III of England reveals—that feudal obligations did not always coincide with the interests of the nation-state. In this web of overlapping loyalties and conflicting interests, reason plays an equally ambivalent role: it serves as the driving force behind social reform and personal self-realization, the antidote to religious dogmatism and political tyranny, but also as an upwelling of tellurian forces not entirely in human control, part of a storm surge that can sweep away old injustices, but whose achievements can and probably will be washed away by future tides. Finally, even efforts to improve the world can provoke a violent backlash. Unlike Goethe's Mephistopheles, who wants to do evil and ends up doing good, Joseph II starts off with the best intentions for the Netherlands and ends up with the worst result.

CHAPTER 5

Revolution in Mainz
Liberation or Conquest?

One of the more memorable dinner parties in the history of German letters took place when Goethe visited Georg Forster on August 20, 1792, in Mainz. Actually, there were two dinner parties: Goethe returned on the following evening, although this time the guests drank beer instead of wine. They met in the home of Forster's close friend, Samuel Thomas Soemmerring, a physician, anatomist, and author of a book on human racial distinctions. Guests included Forster's wife, Therese, author of *The Seldorf Family* and many other novels; her future husband and Schiller's former friend, Ludwig Huber; Caroline Böhmer, née Michaelis, who became a central figure of German Romanticism; and Meta Forkel, who collaborated with Forster on multiple translations and was also linked to several of the leading artists and intellectuals of the era. Many of those present knew Goethe's mother and remarked on how closely he resembled her. Goethe entertained them with anecdotes about Italy and perhaps tried their patience with his anti-Newtonian theory of colors, but, as he later recalled, he studiously avoided talk of politics, "for we felt a mutual need to spare each other's feelings: while they did not altogether deny their republican sentiments, I was for my part clearly making haste to join an army which was intended to put a definite end to such sentiments and their consequences."[1]

As we recall, Forster was teaching at the University of Vilnius in 1787 when he received an invitation to join a Russian expedition to the Pacific.

Russia's war with the Ottoman Empire made the voyage impossible, but the offer gave Forster an excuse to quit his job in Vilnius and money to pay his debts. He returned to Göttingen, the home of his wife and father-in-law, to prepare for the voyage. After months of waiting, Forster finally got the bad news from Russia, but soon took advantage of a new opportunity and began work as the head librarian at the University of Mainz. Forster served at the pleasure of the Freiherr von Erthal, a Catholic bishop and one of the seven Electors in the Holy Roman Empire. Erthal was a relatively enlightened aristocrat who hired Forster to modernize the library, although in the end he did not commit the resources that would have been necessary to complete the job. As a high-ranking official in the Holy Roman Empire, the Elector was hardly an advocate of the French Revolution. He welcomed swarms of French emigres to Mainz, which strained the local economy by boosting inflation, and hosted an elaborate party in honor of the newly crowned emperor in July of 1792, just one month before Goethe arrived in Mainz.

Forster made no secret of his sympathy for the Revolution, just as Goethe was openly hostile to the turmoil, but there was enough mutual respect between the two men that they were willing to set aside their political differences for two convivial evenings. When Goethe reentered Mainz one year later, after the city had been besieged and recaptured from French occupation by Prussian forces, he "found a most lamentable situation. Things that had been built over the course of centuries were now in ruins."[2] Soemmerring's home had been particularly hard hit. A cannonball had smashed through the windows, and vandals had shredded the wallpaper and smeared some sort of grease on the walls and ceilings. "These were the same rooms where we had sat together in such friendly company the year before, jesting and conversing so cheerfully and intimately."[3] Much had happened since those evenings of the previous year. Goethe had joined the coalition of Prussian and Austrian forces intent on putting an end to the French Revolution, but their military campaign did not work out as planned. They thought they would brush aside weak French resistance on a quick march to Paris, but they bogged down instead on the rainswept plains of the Champagne and endured an ignominious retreat. At about the same time, French revolutionary armies advanced on multiple fronts, capturing Mainz and Frankfurt in the fall of 1792. Forster assumed a leading role in the revolutionary Mainz Republic, but by the time Goethe returned to the city in the summer of 1793, he was no longer there. Forster had been sent to Paris in March as a delegate of the new republic tasked with winning official recognition for France's new ally before the National Assembly. He achieved his goal, but it was an empty victory, as the Mainz Republic was already doomed.[4]

Goethe and Forster were fully aware that they were living in a time of unprecedented change. When the coalition forces found themselves stymied outside the village of Valmy, Goethe proclaimed that they had just witnessed the end of an era: "From this time and place a new epoch is beginning, and you will be able to say that you were there."[5] Whether he actually said those words at the time, or embellished the story when he prepared his memoirs for publication nearly thirty years later, is less important than the fact that Goethe was right about the significance of what took place that day in France. An allied army of Prussians, Austrians, and French emigres had tried and failed to restore the feudal order that had existed in France and elsewhere in Europe for more than a millennium. Forster was equally convinced that he was witnessing a pivotal moment in world history. "The time that we are now experiencing is extremely important and interesting," he wrote to Heyne. "All the cogs of the old machine have come to a stop."[6] The following year, he was even more emphatic: "It is one of the decisive epochs of the world that we are experiencing. History has not seen the like since the appearance of Christianity."[7]

When Forster started to write the history of the Mainz Revolution in the summer of 1793, he began with a detailed description of the festivities surrounding the coronation of the new—and what turned out to be the last—Holy Roman Emperor, Francis II. The timing of the ceremony was itself ironic, as it took place in Frankfurt on July 14, 1792, the third anniversary of the storming of the Bastille that marked the beginning of the end for European royalty. Forster was in Frankfurt on the day of the event and found himself surprisingly moved. "The Kaiser looked so young, harmless, and innocent, that the sight of him on horseback on the way to the church, with the ancestral crown on his head, brought involuntary tears to my eyes and those of others."[8] The Elector of Mainz, who in accordance with ancient tradition had summoned the electors to Frankfurt and consecrated and anointed the new emperor,[9] took the opportunity to stage an elaborate after-party in the new emperor's honor in nearby Mainz. As Forster recalled, everyone who anyone in the old German Reich was there:

"We were flattered to see the Kaiser and his wife, the king of Prussia and his princes, the Duke of Hessen, the Duke of Brunswick, a son of George III of England, and an entire pantheon of lesser earthly gods gathered all together in our Mainz."[10] All of the hotels were booked, and "from early morning on the streets were swarming with well-dressed people; toward noon the crush of coaches was loud enough to rival a capital city" (10.1:511). Concerts, balls, and firework displays entertained the well-heeled dignitaries and drained money from the city's coffers. In retrospect, Forster conceded that the general mood at the time was festive but questioned the wisdom of the rulers who had exploited the labor of "the subjugated people" for the intoxicating pleasure of a single night (10.1:512).

The event bears an eerie resemblance to the funeral of King Edward VII of England in 1910, which Barbara Tuchman used to introduce *The Guns of August*, her classic history of the First World War. The occasion this time was unhappy, but it resembled the celebration in Mainz in that it marked the end of an era: "The sun of the old world was setting in a dying blaze of splendor never to be seen again."[11] Once more, a who's who of Europe's interrelated dynastic families gathered on the eve of a conflagration that would soon render such pomp and circumstance obsolete. As Christopher Clark reminds us, however, the image "of Europe's 'last summer' as an Edwardian costume drama" is misleading in that it "suggests an array of nation-states, conceived as compact, autonomous, discrete entities, like billiard balls on a table," about to collide in mortal combat, when in fact "the sovereign structures that generated policy during the crisis were profoundly disunified." Far from viewing the early twentieth-century conflict as a quaint clash of sovereign states, Clark underscores the "raw modernity" of a struggle that resonates with today's world in the wake of the Cold War, in which "a system of global bipolar stability has made way for a more complex and unpredictable array of forces, including declining empires and rising powers—a state of affairs that invites comparison with the Europe of 1914."[12]

Clark is writing in the early twenty-first century, when international alliances, mass migration, religious fundamentalism, global finance, climate change, and contagions cut across national boundaries and challenge the notion of a world neatly divided into nation-states "like billiard balls on a table." These developments also remind us that the modern nation-state is a relatively recent invention, whose origins can be traced to precisely the period in which Goethe and Forster spent those two evenings together in August 1792. The crowning ceremony in Frankfurt and subsequent celebrations in Mainz were vivid reminders that "Germany" did not exist as a single, sovereign state but rather as what one historian has described as a "centripetal agglutination of bewilderingly heterogeneous elements."[13] The old Reich was in a state of flux: the presence of the Prussian king in Mainz was a reminder of the precarious balance of power between the Prussian and Austrian monarchies amid the diffuse hierarchies of the Holy Roman Empire. Joseph II, who had died a little more than two years earlier, was both the king of Austria and Holy Roman emperor; he focused all his energies on reforming the Austrian state and reserved only contempt for the empire.[14] Revolutionary France, for its part, had more internal diversity than we tend to recall. While the more radical of the revolutionaries advocated for a centralized government against federalizing tendencies associated with the old regime, pockets of regional resistance against Parisian rule continued to flare up from Toulon to the Vendée, and a significant percentage of Frenchmen did not speak French until well into the nineteenth century.[15] The idea of the sovereign state as a contiguous territory bound by clearly drawn borders, centered on a single capital, and governed by a common law was at best a work in progress, even in France, while many in Germany had no interest in even striving for that goal.

Goethe describes his stance on this political situation as being directly opposed to that of Forster, and in a sense, he was right: he was about to join a counterrevolutionary army, while Forster was soon to play a leading role in a revolutionary republic. As Jürgen Goldstein points out, however, both men shared the sense that politics were surface phenomena of deeper natural processes, even though Goethe tended to recoil from eruptions of revolutionary violence, while Forster embraced progressive reforms and sometimes surrendered to forces that were beyond human control.[16] In another sense, however, the two writers were more allies than enemies, for both remained skeptical of the tendency toward standardization in the modern state. Goethe, as we recall, allowed Egmont to defend Dutch traditions against the encroaching power of the Spanish Empire, in keeping with the spirit of Justus Möser, who preferred local rule to centralized authority and universal principles.[17] Forster, for his part, preferred Joseph II's enlightened reforms in the Netherlands to the reactionary politics of the existing church and state, but he also voiced concerns about

Joseph's reformist zeal that ran roughshod over the desires of the region's distinct communities. The advance of French troops onto German soil marked a new stage in the conflict between home rule and imperial aggression. Although Forster initially welcomed the French as liberators, he soon developed the nagging suspicion that they were in fact foreign conquerors.

LOCAL DISTURBANCES IN REVOLUTIONARY TIMES

The delicate balance between progressive reform and local traditions carried over into Forster's assessment of the French incursion into German territory. Although we tend to think in terms of "the" French Revolution, Forster's *Views of the Lower Rhine* reminds us that there were many local disturbances at the time, some directly, others tangentially, and still others not at all related to the unfolding events in Paris. As noted earlier in this study, *revolution* itself was a term in transition, pointing in different contexts either back to something old, forward to something new, or even in both directions at the same time. In Aachen, for instance, Dohm restored what he claimed was the spirit of the city's medieval government when he drew up a new constitution, but that constitution also voices egalitarian principles that reflect modern ideas. The burghers of Liège sought to undo the religious coup of 1684 by returning to their medieval constitution, but in the summer of 1789 that restoration looked dangerously revolutionary to the imperial court of Wetzlar. The citizens of Brussels and Brabant were united in their resistance to Austrian authority but divided on whether they wanted to restore feudal hierarchies or establish a modern republic.

While Forster was developing his observations, notes, and letters into the first two volumes of *Views*, other troubles were brewing closer to home. In February 1790, reports of an impending revolution in Aschaffenburg provoked the Elector of Mainz to send 225 troops to restore order, only to discover that the matter at hand was a squabble about who had the right to sell goods at the local market, which hardly required military intervention. "However unimportant in itself," Timothy Blanning concludes, "the Aschaffenburg episode warns against seeing every manifestation of discontent during this period as revolutionary and every popular demand as democratic."[18] New tensions broke out six months later in Mainz, as university students quarreled with local guildsmen in what threatened to become a bloody altercation, and once again, the Elector summoned troops to restore calm. The conflict was triggered by "a seemingly innocuous brawl" at a local dance,[19] but it dredged up deeper resentment on the part of the city's artisans against the privileged outsiders from the progressive university that threatened Catholic traditions. "In part at least," Blanning concludes, "the riots represented a conservative reaction against the Elector's enlightened policies."[20] The guildsmen used the opportunity, however, to present demands for the reform of local business practices, and some of "the apprentices and the journeymen [who] marched through the streets after the attack on the University . . . wore tricolour cockades and 'hats of freedom.'" Local "authorities suspected immediately that French agents were behind the disturbances," although this was never proven.[21] In Blanning's assessment, the artisans appropriated superficial symbols of the Revolution while pursuing their economic agenda. The authorities soon rounded up the protesters and sentenced the ringleaders on both sides to prison sentences or corporal punishment.[22]

Forster downplayed the incident as "a mere farce" in a letter to his father, deriding the university students as badly behaved schoolboys. He nevertheless goes on to explain the deeper tensions between the university and the Roman Catholic town, "in which a lot of the Jesuitical sourdough has remained." The many nobles employed at the Elector's court know nothing and fear learning, in his opinion; government employees resent the better-paid professors, and priests fan the flames of the workers' resentment. Together they seek "to discredit the university in the eyes of the Elector." The police could easily have diffused the conflict, but they allowed it to escalate until things threatened to get out of control. In the end, a few windows were broken but no one was killed. Most of the unruly guildsmen accepted their reprimands "like the tame sheep and asses that they are," while a few were singled out for stricter punishments. "It is a shame," concludes Forster ironically, "that they did not always get the ones who deserved it most. This is the true state of affairs."[23] Eleven days earlier in a letter to his father-in-law, Forster revealed what he suspected was the real reason for the harsh government crackdown on this local disturbance: "They probably want to show the Germans that they are not French." He goes on to suggest that the days of the authorities who enact such reactionary reprisals are numbered: "This sort of government will last as long as it can."[24]

A little more than two years later, on October 21, 1792, the government's time was up. While the defeated armies of the Prussian and Austrian troops were slogging through the mud back toward Germany, French armies under the command of General Custine advanced into the Rhineland. The Elector dispatched troops to make a stand in the town of Speyer to the south of the city, but Custine soon overwhelmed their weak resistance and marched on Mainz. Reading the writing on the wall, priests, aristocrats, emigres, and the Elector fled, the latter scratching his coat of arms off the side of his carriage in a feeble effort to obscure his identity. Amid the chaos, Forster continued to work, sending off the preface to his translation of Bligh's account of the *Bounty* and still hoping to complete the third volume of *Views*. Mainz settled into an uneasy calm as it awaited the inevitable. A few Hungarian troops of the Austrian army that had remained in Mainz behaved badly, but the advancing French army was under strict discipline. On the day before they entered town, in fact, they helped German women fold their laundry in the fields outside the city gates. Forster climbed the church tower to observe their approach, concluded that there was nothing to be done, and returned home. The next day it was all over: "Our dear Mainz [Unser gutes Mainz] is now really in French hands."[25]

FORSTER AND THE FRENCH REVOLUTION

"What did you think of the revolution in France?"[26] Forster posed this question to his father-in-law just two weeks after the storming of the Bastille, signaling his intense interest in the events in neighboring France and the ideological debates they provoked. Like many of his fellow Germans, Forster welcomed the Revolution in its initial phases, although he was one of the few who would become an active participant in revolutionary politics and eventually declare himself a French citizen. Wilhelm von Humboldt was in Paris in the summer of 1789, and when he returned to Germany, he stopped in Mainz to provide Forster with a firsthand account of the early phase of the French Revolution. In the following July, Forster had a chance to see for himself as he passed through Paris on his way back from England. Immediately after he returned to Mainz, Forster assured Heyne that enthusiasm for the Revolution was widespread in Paris and that no counterrevolution was likely, no doubt to quell rumors that the king would soon reassert his authority. "The sight of the enthusiasm among the people, particularly on the Champ de Mars, where they were preparing for the large national festival, was uplifting, because it was shared so widely among all social classes and worked so purely and simply for the common good with no concern for personal advantage."[27] Forster devoted an entire chapter of his "Memories of the Year 1790" (Erinnerungen aus dem Jahr 1790) to a description of the first annual Bastille Day celebrations. On the field where the French traditionally gathered to pay homage to their kings, they now celebrated "the first festival of regained freedom. Complete equality had just been restored among the citizens by tearing down all hereditary differences." After centuries of repression and being treated like children, the French finally had the opportunity to develop their full potential. "To be a human being was the proud accomplishment of twenty-five million people, the first and last goal of their liberation."[28]

Forster continued to follow events in France during the rapidly shifting political climate of the early 1790s, and he reports in detail about the Revolution's initial impact abroad in his annual reports about English literature. He reacted angrily when he first read Edmund Burke's *Reflections on the Revolution in France,* dismissing his antirevolutionary stance as "miserable twaddle" (elendes Gewäsch) that he refused to translate.[29] A few weeks later, Forster revised his opinion: "Burke is not so bad after all; it was just annoying at first glance to be so disappointed. In theory I'd like to agree with him, just not in the way he makes his argument."[30] In his "History of English Literature of 1790," Forster registers his surprise that Burke, who had defended the American Revolution, was so staunchly opposed to the French version of the same, while offering unqualified and, to Forster's mind, unwarranted praise of England's constitutional monarchy. "Pick whatever image you want for the French Revolution," he wrote in response to Burke, "except for one that interprets it as *violent* destruction." French revolutionaries sought to build up a new society, not just to tear down the old. Regrettable excesses were inevitable in the process, but one could hardly expect those who had languished for so long under the "festering cancer of self-indulgent despotism" not to have been infected by the "general corruption."[31] Thus Forster is willing to concede "all the bad things that Burke preaches about the new form of government in France and proclaims like a prophet of doom about what is to come; one could grant him *all* that, and still it would be no less clear that the Revolution could not be avoided, that it happened as if of its own accord, by means of the hideous collapse of the previous government, which was hopelessly rotten to the core" (7:191).

Forster often celebrates the Revolution as the triumph of human reason over political despotism and religious superstition, but in this case, Forster describes a process of natural dissolution and renewal in which humans are not driving the change but simply along for the ride: "We should really view the Revolution as a work of nature's justice" (7:191). The birth of the new requires the destruction of the old, and the very events that emancipate humans from their self-incurred immaturity, to paraphrase Kant, can also reduce them to trembling spectators. "Like the devastation of Calabria by the earthquake, the current explosion in France nothing but a noteworthy phenomenon [ein merkwürdiges Phänomen].... In both cases we recognize with awe the fate decreed by a higher, inscrutable law that grants us a peaceful, uneventful life in complete security, while outside our borders the elements and human dispositions are causing such terrible damage."[32] Jürgen Goldstein correctly emphasizes the irrationality of the Revolution as Forster describes it in such passages, but there is also an element of sarcastic critique in his contrast between Germany and France. Not every nation is fated to live in a political subduction zone, prone to earthquakes and volcanic eruptions. German soil is disturbingly stable: "No volcano will erupt under the venerable Gothic monument of our imperial constitution [Reichsverfassung] and explode its delicately embellished little towers, its slender clusters of columns and spooky pointed arches; it will not baptize us with the fire and brimstone of a political rebirth" (8:280–81). We Germans sit on our sofas or at our desks and calmly pass judgment on the world, he continues, but the French do not have that luxury: "There they are standing as if on burning ground, and they obey the omnipotence of the events that an inexorable fate prepared centuries ago" (8:285).

Two trends emerge in Forster's reflections on the Revolution in relation to German politics. On the one hand, Forster consistently criticizes the imperial court that had denied justice to the citizens of Liège and continues to do the same to other parts of the Empire: "Here it came down to protecting the German Reich, by means of a frightening example, from all foreign infection by the French malady of freedom [Ansteckung mit der französischen Freiheitseuche]."[33] The "French disease" (französische

Seuche) was a euphemism for syphilis in eighteenth-century Germany; as a result, those sympathetic with the Revolution referred to "Franken" rather than "Franzosen."[34] For representatives of the Reich, however, revolutionary France was still the source of a politically transmitted disease; if they had to "destroy the happiness of Liège's inhabitants and dole out exemplary punishments to their leaders" in order to inoculate the Holy Roman Empire from further infection, the vaccine was worth the price.[35] On the other hand, Forster insists that Germany is not yet ready for a revolution, despite the glaring flaws of its regime. "We are not at the point where a violent revolution would be the slightest help or use to us, even if it were possible, which it is not," he wrote in April 1791, although he went on to warn that if the Germans did not reform their constitution, change might come after all and catch them off guard.[36] "In no way do I belong to the *enragés* on one side or the other," he insisted the following year. "Why would it occur to me to proclaim a *revolution* that I do not want, and in fact consider such a huge disaster for Germany that I would do everything to prevent it."[37] When Custine's troops were already advancing toward Mainz, Forster continued to insist "that we in Germany should take what is happening in France as an example of what we should *not* do, because we are *not ready* for a revolution."[38] Even in December 1792, after Forster was fully committed to the revolutionary cause in Mainz, he continued to assert "that Germany is not ready for any revolution" and that reform "from the top down" would allow Germany to obtain the benefits of the French Revolution without paying the price of violent discord: "The French volcano could prevent an earthquake in Germany."[39]

The comparisons between Germany and France underscore Forster's insistence that one must take local differences into account when considering the potential for revolutionary change. In "Revolutions and Counterrevolutions in the Year 1790," which he wrote in the tumultuous days of July and August 1792, Forster mocks the notion of *a revolutionary miasma* (*Revolutions-Miasma*) "that is in the air just now and has befuddled the minds of feeble nations" (8:234). Rabies, wine, opium, and a thousand other things can cloud our judgment, Forster argues, but the idea of an infectious fog drifting from America across the Atlantic to sicken Europe with revolutionary fever makes no sense. People do not fall ill unless they are already susceptible to the disease, "and thus it obviously follows that the reputed infection with American ideas of freedom would have to have been preceded by a weakened condition that made the infection possible in the first case." Given that revolutions have broken out or threaten to break out in the most disparate parts of Europe, Forster continues, it follows "that particular local causes" must be responsible for "each of the upheavals in Holland und Brabant, in Hungary, Poland and Sweden, in Liège und France" (8:235). Not all local disturbances are new versions of the French Revolution, as the skirmish between students and artisans in Mainz demonstrated. Not all uprisings pursue progressive goals, as the reactionary revolutionaries in Brabant revealed, and sometimes, as in Liège and Aachen, the effort to restore ancient privileges inspires the modern rhetoric of universal rights.

Forster's respect for local differences in politics informs his aversion to dogmatism of any sort. In reference to his polemic against religious proselytizing, Forster asserted that "I do not like despotism of any kind, including that of *universally valid principles*. A dogmatic philosophy [Eine allein seligmachende Philosophie] is as repulsive to me as a dogmatic faith [ein allein seligmachender Glaube]."[40] In defense of his own work, Forster insists that an author must have the freedom to write what seems to be the truth in any given moment without constraint—"even though it is only relatively true, like all truth that a person can put forward; for absolute truth is a dogma and leads to despotism in thought."[41] This general dislike of inflexible ideas leads to Forster's mixed assessment of Emperor Joseph II's liberalizing reforms, as we have seen in *Views of the Lower Rhine*. He reiterates his assessment of the Austrian monarch in "Memories of the Year 1790." Joseph's intentions were good: "He wanted to make his peoples happy and judged correctly that there can be no happiness without freedom, and no political freedom without moral freedom. . . . Joseph recognized the capacity for moral perfectibility in human beings and the incomprehensible dignity of reason" (8:302). While agreeing with Joseph in theory, Forster notes that his practical attempts to improve conditions in Hungary, Holland, and Belgium—to spread religious tolerance, abolish serfdom, encourage the Hungarians to speak German, and adopt more refined customs—failed. The case of Hungary serves as one example to prove his larger point, as he observes in "Revolutions and Counterrevolutions": "But the more zealously the great Kaiser struggled to turn his barbarians into human beings, and the more gratefully the refined and better-educated Hungarian individuals received his decrees, the stronger the national hatred grew of the foreigners whom he set up as examples" (8:237). "Violence and compulsion," Forster concludes, "no matter how grand and noble the intention may be, always result only in more of the same" (8:241). Like Goethe and Schiller before him, Forster notes that the Netherlands were comprised of individual provinces that were "of completely different characters." Some, like Brabant, were Catholic and conservative, while others, like Flanders, were more likely to strive for "a form of representative government similar to that of the new French one, ... or even seriously considered a federal alliance with France" (8:244).

THE FRENCH OCCUPATION OF MAINZ

Mainz was a semiautonomous principality within the Holy Roman Empire ruled by an Elector with religious and secular authority. The court of this *Residenzstadt* was larger and more flamboyant than that of most German states, and it played a central role in the local economy, as its members were "large employers and voracious consumers."[42] The current elector, Friedrich Karl Freiherr von Erthal, began his reign in the spirit of Joseph II's enlightened absolutism: he reformed the local university, discouraged pilgrimages and religious superstition, loosened restrictions on Jews, introduced agricultural reforms, and limited corporal and capital punishment.[43] When revolution broke out in neighboring France, however, "it became clear that for Mainz the age of Enlightenment was over."[44] Erthal welcomed aristocratic French refugees, hosted the previously mentioned festivities for the new emperor, and then left town in a hurry as French troops advanced on Mainz.

The townspeople's hostility toward the university intellectuals suggests that they were even more conservative than their prince, which is probably why Forster repeatedly insists that they are not ready for radical change, but now a French revolutionary army had entered the gates. How would Mainz respond to the influx of new ideas? In this case, the army was on a proselytizing mission, spreading the good news of democratic reform. There was no absolute monarch in the mold of Joseph II commanding the troops; in fact, King Louis XVI had been apprehended in Varennes when he tried to escape France and brought back to Paris against his will in August of the previous year. Since the storming of the Tuileries on August 10, 1792, the French monarch and his family were held as virtual prisoners in Paris; Louis XVI would be tried and executed just a few months after General Custine entered Mainz. Despite the obvious differences between Joseph's enlightened absolutism and French revolutionary democracy, the question of relations between the imperial center and the colonial periphery remained the same. To what extent would the revolutionaries respect local differences as they imposed their will on Mainz and other satellite states? Were they liberators or conquerors? On the day that French troops entered Mainz, Forster wrote a long letter to Voss in which he envisions Mainz as "an important political center" of a new French territory along the left bank of the Rhine.[45] A few days later, Forster reports that Custine had delivered a speech in which he laid out the new French relations with Mainz in magnanimous terms. The citizens of Mainz were free to choose their own destiny, he declared. "If they wanted to languish on under their old despotism, he could only be sorry for them; but if they wanted to accept the French constitution, or, what would be even better (since France was big enough and desired no new territories), to form their own republic, which would be allied with France as a brother, then he promised them the most complete protection and guarantee of the French Republic and their support against all enemies."[46] On the following day, Forster speculated that France would continue to advance beyond Mainz: "If they managed to reduce Belgium and take possession of the entire Rhine, then a federation of republics would arise from Switzerland to Holland on the left bank of the Rhine. No devil could do it any harm.... The Republicans are succeeding in everything."[47]

In that same letter, Forster notes in passing that "a kind of club" has formed in support of the Revolution. "I am not afraid of the club," he added in a postscript the following day. "All they ask is that we should make an appearance, including me too. But this won't happen until I have resolved certain issues."[48] Exactly what matters Forster needed to resolve is not clear; Klaus Harpprecht speculates that Forster may have been hoping for a job offer from Berlin and wanted to wait to see what might materialize before joining the German Jacobin Club.[49] Forster also had a family to support, however troubled the state of his marriage, and he had debts. He requested a loan from his publisher, Voss, which was eventually granted on the condition that he remain a "good Prussian," prompting the indignant response cited earlier in this study, in which Forster refused to deny his democratic principles for the sake of money (although he did eventually accept the cash).⁵⁰ Aside from particular concerns, Forster must have known that if he committed himself to the French Revolution, he would have to sever his ties to Germany, which would entail not only the loss of his job at the university and exclusion from his publication network, but also risking his life as a traitor to the fatherland. By November 10, however, his mind was made up. "As far as I am concerned, I either would have had to emigrate or have remained here and not gotten involved in anything, or else I was left only with the third option: to take part, to the extent that was desired." Forster decided "to be free in the new French way."⁵¹ He assured Voss that he would continue to write his books, but that he was resolved "*to live and die as a republican.*"⁵²

Given what was at stake in making this bold declaration, Forster's passion is understandable and also in keeping with the spirit of an age in which revolutionaries did not hesitate to make grand rhetorical gestures. The practical question of Mainz's relation to France remained, however, and Forster took up this topic in his first address to the local Jacobin club on November 15, 1792. "Concerning the Relationship of the Citizens of Mainz to the French" begins by stating that the insistence on rigid national differences between the Germans and French was part of "a clever political ploy on the part of the princes designed to carefully divide peoples from one another . . . and thus to make their own sovereignty all the more secure." Such lies and distortions obscure the fundamental truth "that all men are brothers." The aristocrats want people to believe that a few men are born to lead and "the masses are made to obey; the Negro is destined by nature to be a slave of the whites, just because he has black skin and a flat nose; and similar blasphemies against sacred, healthy reason." It is time for such nonsense to end: "*To be free and equal, the motto* of rational and moral human beings, is henceforth ours as well." In just three weeks we have emerged as free men from the tutelage of priests and aristocrats, Forster marvels, and surely further transformations are possible. "Brothers! The force that could transform *us* so thoroughly can also unite France and Mainz into a single people!"⁵³

The fact remains that the French and Germans speak different languages and have different customs; just because they share a common humanity, does that mean they can share a common government? Why not? "Since when have linguistic differences made it impossible to obey the same law? Does not Russia's despot rule over a hundred peoples with different tongues? Do not the Hungarians, Bohemians, Austrians, Dutch, and Milanese each speak their own language, and are they not all subject to a single Kaiser? And were the inhabitants of half the world not once citizens of Rome?" If tyrants can forge unity out of diversity, then certainly free peoples can unite in the name of "the eternal truths that have their basis in human nature" (10.1:14). Thus Forster urges the citizens of Mainz to cast off their chains: "Become free, fellow citizens, give yourselves a free constitution. The French promise you their protection; from this moment on they are no longer conquerors, but rather brothers." If, on the other hand, the Germans fail to take advantage of this opportunity, "if you do not want to be free, then you are only the defeated subjects of a different master; then France's right of conquest comes completely into effect; then the Republic has the right to rule you like any other people defeated in battle" (10.1:25).

French soldiers have taken charge of the German city, but it is up to the people of Mainz to decide whether they come as liberators or conquerors. By encouraging the Germans to embrace their new rulers, Forster suggests that they can become active agents in control of their fate, rather than passive victims of French aggression. He does so by envisioning a future in which the French allow the Germans to retain their distinct cultural identity and language even as they form part of a greater whole. In other words, we are back to the distinction between federations, such as the old German Reich, that can tolerate regional differences within a larger unity and enlightened despots like Joseph II, who impose uniformity on disparate peoples, although in the new setting, old structural distinctions take on new meaning. On the one hand, the opposition is clear: Forster favors France over Germany, revolutionary democracy over feudal hierarchies. On the other hand, however, he transposes the federated structure of the Holy Roman Empire onto French imperial democracy. What he imagines, in other words, is an ideal fusion of progressive ideas, initiated by enlightened rulers and carried to a radical conclusion by the French Revolutionaries, with respect for local autonomy in a way that is familiar from Germany's otherwise discredited Reich.

Things did not work out as Forster had hoped, for a number of reasons. Although the French advanced almost effortlessly into western Germany in the fall of 1792, their presence did not remain uncontested. Prussian forces recaptured Frankfurt already in early December,[54] and from that point on it was only a matter of time before nearby Mainz would fall under their sway. By April, Mainz lay under siege, and after months of steady bombardment that caused great damage and inflicted enormous suffering, the city capitulated on July 23, 1793.[55] Spontaneous support for the Revolution among the people of Mainz never materialized. Already in early December, Forster noted with exasperation that "unless the general most kindly commands it," the people of Mainz "do not want to be free at all. They can and will not take a single step in that direction,"[56] following the pattern of reactionary resistance to the revolutionary change that Forster had already observed in Brussels. Two months later, Forster came to the bitter conclusion "that the mob is not ready for freedom and the enjoyment of their privileges ... they have just switched masters."[57] The leaders of the German Jacobin club also misplayed their hand. One of them decided that it would be a good idea to put out two books for citizens to sign: "One with a red binding and tricolor trim for the names of those who wanted to signal their allegiance to freedom and equality, the other black and wrapped with chains for those who freely chose to submit to the old yoke and appear as slaves before all the world, and—as the ill-considered addendum stated—wanted to be treated accordingly."[58] The heavy-handed strategy backfired: while close to a thousand citizens signed the red book (whether by choice or under duress is difficult to say), no one was eager to go on record in support of symbolic slavery, and resentment of the demand was widespread.[59] Despite the attention lavished on club members by subsequent historians either eager to embrace them as "the vanguard of the revolutionary bourgeoise," or brand them as traitors to the German nation, they were in fact a disparate group of intellectuals, white-collar professionals, and artisans who formed a brief coalition before drifting away from the revolutionary cause.[60] By the time Prussian troops reentered the city, popular resentment against those who had collaborated with the French revolutionary government had risen to a fever pitch; Goethe recounts an incident in which he intervened to prevent an angry mob from assaulting a former German Jacobin.[61]

The French Army, which had entered Mainz on its best behavior, soon began acting like an occupying force. On May 22, 1790, the French National Assembly had declared that they would never conquer foreign territories, but that policy began to change in December 1792, and soon all pretext of missionary zeal in the name of humanity was replaced with naked aggression.⁶² As the increasingly centralized government in Paris clamped down on pockets of resistance in the Vendée and elsewhere in France, it also took a harsher stance toward its newly conquered territories. Once the armies settled in for a longer stay, it became increasingly difficult to view them as a benevolent force. There were reports of theft, rape, and looting; local economies were destroyed, books and works of art were confiscated, and hunger became widespread.⁶³ Custine's soldiers, who had seemed dirty but charming when they first entered Mainz, soon clogged the gutters with their filth and threatened the local women.⁶⁴ As Timothy Blanning summarizes, the French gift to the Rhineland was impoverishment and suffering, as corrupt French officials "looked on the *pays conquis* as the conquistadores had once looked on the New World."⁶⁵ What Forster had hoped would be a liberation had turned into an invasion.⁶⁶

As club membership dwindled in the early months of 1793, Forster remained publicly loyal to the cause, but he was increasingly disturbed by reports of abuse against local citizens by the occupying forces. When the owner of an estate plundered by French soldiers turned to Forster for help in early January, he drafted a bitter complaint. "If they had said to the French administrators from the start: 'You are not here to safeguard the interests of the people of Mainz; you are mere executors of military commands that necessity or arbitrary whims decree,' we would have at least known where we stood."⁶⁷ Ludwig Uhlig notes that this vehement protest was only found among Forster's literary remains, however, and he suspects that it may never have reached its intended audience. Meanwhile, talk of a potential French federation of semi-independent German states along the west bank of the Rhine soon fades from Forster's correspondence. In late December he reports that the recent decrees of the French National Assembly were not unexpected and that "from Speyer to Bingen, there was almost unanimous support for the acceptance of the French constitution and annexation by France."⁶⁸ By mid-March, Forster and other elected officials of the Mainz Republic declared that the city would become part of France. Forster delivered a speech full of the usual pathos about the liberation of the human race by means of the French Revolution, but devoid of the earlier call for a federal alliance of distinct peoples. That evening, Forster reported to Therese that the Mainz National Assembly had unanimously declared "its desire for union with France. To that purpose they plan to send a deputation to Paris, and I will probably be among those named."⁶⁹ Forster guessed correctly, and four days later he set off with two companions for Paris, predicting that he would return to Mainz in about three weeks. In fact, he never saw the city again; Forster died in Paris on January 10, 1794.

ANCIENT ROME AND MODERN PARIS

"I arrived in the evening the day before yesterday, dear wife," wrote Forster to Therese soon after his arrival in Paris. "Yesterday I was in the National Assembly, where I spoke. I read the speech of the Mainz convention (which I also wrote) to much applause, and the result was that the annexation of the Rhine region occupied by the French was immediately decreed by acclamation."⁷⁰ Forster's triumph in the cause of the Mainz Republic would also be his last. Even as he spoke, plans were underway to recapture the city, and Forster realized almost immediately that it would be impossible for him to return as planned. But what was he to do in Paris? Despite his loyalty to the revolutionary cause, he was unlikely to be appointed to a leading role in the French capital, "because I am a foreigner, completely alone here and without any support, with no family connections, without the backing of a political party."⁷¹ He was employed for a few weeks negotiating prisoner exchanges near the city of Arras, to the north of Paris, and he was hired to translate the new French constitution into German and English,⁷² but for the most part, he had no official duties. The man who until recently had worked night and day on behalf of the Mainz Republic now seemed superfluous. "As long as I lead my current life and continue in these circumstances, I can't shake the feeling that I am doing something pointless and expending my energies in vain."⁷³

Under the circumstances, it is not surprising that Forster fantasized about learning Persian and traveling by land to India, or settling into an idyllic home in a remote Swiss village, although he must have known that both would be impossible. He could always write, and he did, but the circumstances were exceedingly difficult. He departed from Mainz on short notice with the intention of returning quickly; as a result, he left all his books and manuscripts behind, and their potential loss was a source of constant worry. Considered a renegade by the German authorities and thus unable to return to retrieve his possessions, Forster was also cut off from the literary and social networks that were essential to his existence as a writer. "When I was walking up and down alone in the Palais Royal I had involuntary tears in my eyes," he confessed to Therese, at "the thought that I should return to my room and have no one in this infinitely large city who cares about me in the least, no one who would take an interest in me, and to whom it would not be a matter of complete indifference if I disappeared tomorrow!"[74] Compounding his professional frustrations were overwhelming personal problems. His wife was living in Switzerland with another man and soon to seek a divorce, and he was unable to see his beloved children. When he did have a chance to visit them for a few days in the border town of Pontarlier, the renewed sense of loss upon his departure left him shattered. "The memory of my lost happiness and the feeling of my current inability to help us all, the tears that you all shed, and the pain that crushed us all cast me down."[75] Soon after his return to Paris, Forster's health, which had been precarious ever since he returned from his voyage around the world, broke down completely. Isolated, emaciated, and in agony, Forster lived on for several weeks, assuring Therese and the children in his final letter that although he was seriously ill, he was in no danger of dying.

Forster continued to comment on the news almost until the end, and much of what he read and witnessed with his own eyes left him deeply depressed. "I am still satisfied with the Revolution," Forster wrote in his first letter from Paris, "*although it is something completely different than what most people think.*"[76] His comments soon took a more critical turn. "Oh, ever since I learned that there is no virtue in the Revolution, it disgusts me," he cried out to Therese. "Always to find only self-interest and passion where one expects and demands greatness, always only words for feelings, always only boasting and superficial shimmer for the real essence and effectiveness—who can stand it!"[77] "If they can't persecute, denounce, and guillotine, they are nothing," he commented with disgust several days later.[78] Forster soon severed ties with all political parties and was convinced that the "local Jacobin society has been completely corrupted by its dreadful leaders."[79] As the Terror escalated, Forster was increasingly horrified. "The way things looked in ancient Rome is the way they look here now. Never did tyranny have so much brazenness, such reckless abandon, never were all principles so trampled over, never did defamation run so rampant."[80] Having devoted himself tirelessly to the cause, Forster began to wonder if his efforts had been in vain. "The last thing I need now is to become convinced that I sacrificed my last strength for an absurdity and worked with honest zeal for something that no one else took seriously, but rather used as a mere cover for the most raging passion!"[81] Having played his part in Mainz and now occupying a front-row seat in the revolutionary theater in Paris, Forster was determined to record what he saw, but he sometimes doubted his ability to do so. "Should I write the history of this horrible time? I cannot."[82] Actually, he could and did begin to write about the recent past and current events, but without conviction. "It is a great misfortune that my enthusiasm has died a natural death [de sa belle mort], which is extremely detrimental to a work like this. I write what I no longer believe."[83]

In the light of such negative comments, it would be easy to conclude that Forster had lost faith in the Revolution entirely, but this would be an oversimplification. Although he disapproves of the current course of revolutionary events, he never wishes for a return of the old regime. The French have their flaws, "but I recognize the good qualities they have alongside their failings and mistakes, and view no single nation as an ideal."[84] "I simply believe in the *importance* of the Revolution in the larger course of human events," he continued to insist; "I believe not only that it *had to* take place, but also that it will give a new direction to the way people think, enable a different development in human abilities."[85] Forster repeatedly registers his concern at the prospect of another foreign invasion into France and takes an active interest in efforts to suppress domestic insurrections. "We have *exterminated* the Vendée, and so we will *exterminate* whatever resists us."[86] "I tell you, the rebellion in the Vendée is in its death throes," Forster assured Therese in one of his final letters,[87] and he remained convinced "that the Revolution will prevail against all possible upheavals. Thousands upon thousands of families can perish, but the great achievement is irrevocable."[88]

Forster oscillates between faith in the Revolution's inexorable path toward ultimate justice and despair at the destruction it leaves in its wake. "The Revolution is a hurricane; who can stop it?"[89] Given that the leaders of the cause seem so corrupt, Forster sometimes takes recourse to the image of the Revolution as a force of nature that achieves its goals despite rather than because of human efforts on its behalf. "You see that the volcano is not yet quiet; the earth is still shaking beneath our feet; the ground is still glowing hot. But there is no doubt that the Republic will survive."[90]

It is nevertheless difficult for such a passionate advocate of the Enlightenment as Forster to concede that the damage wrought by fires and floods "are nothing in comparison with the harm that reason will cause,"[91] and to acknowledge our insignificance in the cosmic scheme of things, "because our reason is for all intents and purposes only an infinitely tiny modification, which I imagine to be subordinate to the intelligence of the universe to the same degree that I appear in relation to the universe." He goes on in this passage, however, to insist on human dignity after all, despite everything: "Who we are, what we are, we do not know; but *this* is the way we are, and this '*this*' determines how we are to live, suffer, enjoy ourselves, use our reason, enrich our intellect, ennoble our feelings. There is no other obligation than the one we have to ourselves, *to be worthy of ourselves*; this is the only basis of all true human morality."[92]

As elsewhere in Forster's work, there are echoes of Goethe's "Prometheus" in this defiant insistence on human dignity in the face of divine omnipotence and seeming indifference to human endeavors. He pushes reason to the brink of despair, acknowledges that it often does more harm than good, and seeks comfort in the belief that beneath its destructive surface, nature moves through cataclysmic fits and starts to further human progress. "The century, like humanity itself, does not move forwards in a regular tempo, but rather in an incessant rotation. The ball is hit, thrown, deflected, and touched by innumerable hands, and all these different little and big impulses drive it on."[93] As part of nature, however insignificant, it is incumbent upon humans to insist on self-worth and to use what reason they have to enrich their minds and refine their feelings, not to abrogate their responsibilities in passive despair. In keeping with this spirit, and despite his reservations, Forster did write the history of the revolution in Mainz and record his impressions of the French Revolution, although his illness made it impossible for him to complete either work. Between the fragmentary "Depiction of the Revolution in Mainz" and "Parisian Sketches," Forster also found time to write a theoretical piece, "Concerning Statesmanship in Relation to Human Happiness." Taken together, these works explore what he terms the "antinomies of politics" in *Views of the Lower Rhine* (2:519), as the reason that frees humanity from past injustice can also create new forms of tyranny. In Mainz, on the periphery of French influence, Forster had seen how liberating armies could become an oppressive force; now, at the center of the Revolution, Forster witnesses moments when the newly democratic nation unleashes vindictive rage and mob violence. Modern Paris looks like ancient Rome, the sordid seat of an empire awash in decadence and intent to impose its will on the world.

The opening chapters of Forster's fragmentary history of the Mainz revolution dispel any notion that he might have harbored sympathies for the old Reich. He begins, as noted, with the description of the revelries the Elector staged to celebrate the emperor and the feudal hierarchies he represented. As in his analysis of Aachen, Forster notes that the city should have had a thriving economy, due to its strategic position at the confluence of the Rhine and Main Rivers, but that the self-absorbed nobles squandered the opportunity and stymied growth. Forster moves on to describe the delusional coalition forces poised for what they believe will be a cakewalk into Paris, saving particular scorn for the counterproductive manifesto written by the Duke of Brunswick, full of threats inspired by embittered emigres about their plans to raze Paris and slaughter the rebels. He castigates the Elector for exhausting his small army on failed missions to punish the subjects of Liège for their disobedience to the imperial court and to stop the advance of Custine's troops in Speyer, and he mocks the priests and aristocrats who follow the Elector on his cowardly flight from the revolutionary forces poised to enter Mainz.

Once the French take charge, however, Forster's history becomes more critical of the situation in Mainz. Almost immediately, some bad elements among the Mainz population run amok and destroy some of the local vineyards. Forster attributes their misbehavior to "the sad degeneration of the Mainz citizens under the yoke of priestly despotism,"[94] but the episode reveals a character weakness that will hinder further progress of the local revolution. Forster goes on to describe the German Jacobins led by "righteous and enlightened men" cast in the glow of the "splendidly illuminated meeting hall," but surrounded by "a disparate mass of people ... suffering from all the shortcomings that resulted from their overly-hasty assembly, which in no way satisfied the noble sentiments of educated and cultivated men." Some callow students and disreputable locals filled out the ranks of the revolutionary club but did nothing to help the cause. "The naive self-satisfaction and the presumption of some, the self-interest and ambiguous intentions of others, were more detrimental to the good cause of freedom than the advocacy of the same by respectable members with insight and feeling" (10.1:553–54). The counterproductive efforts of some revolutionary zealots (*Freiheitsapostel*) to force citizens to sign one of two publicly displayed books have already been noted.

French occupying forces share the blame for mismanaging an opportunity to "win friends and sympathizers for their constitution." The French levied taxes "that ostensibly targeted only the high and mighty, but, in places where aristocratic and feudal abuses still prevailed, they inevitably fell on the working class in the end" (10.1:557). The Frankfurters were prepared to meet the foreign invaders halfway, but Custine squandered their goodwill by extorting vast sums of money from the city. The Duke of Brunswick was a fool for issuing a punitive manifesto that only provoked the wrath of the French revolutionaries, but the French armies made the same mistake by releasing their own "absurd manifesto to the Hessians that disparaged tyranny so clumsily that it awakened feelings of pride and pity among the courageous, patient people for their princes, which was the opposite of what was intended" (10.1:558). Forster intersperses these critical accounts of the French armies in the Rhineland with glances back to developments in Paris, which included the founding of the Republic, but also the indiscriminate killing of Swiss guards during the storming of the Tuileries and the September massacres, in which the people, "spurred on and led by a new kind of fanatic," broke into the prisons and "liberated themselves with horrific deeds from the deluded concern" that the prisoners might escape and threaten the Revolution. "A state shaken by revolutions is like someone ill with fever," Forster concludes; "beneficial crises and raving paroxysms alternate constantly, until either the stronger nature wins, or the dissolved organization becomes a victim of death and decay" (10.1:531).

In retrospect, Forster can only conclude that "these rash stirrings of the spirit of freedom, and, in particular, the hope of propagating French principles of democratic government on German soil, seem in some respects not only premature, but also even detrimental to the establishment of a system that would be appropriate for the true interest of humanity" (10.1:555–56). He now suspects that the Germans might have been better served if they had benefitted from "a slow, gradual process of improvement and maturation" of their own, instead of having a foreign concept of freedom forced down their throats: "They should learn from the mistakes and sufferings of their neighbors and perhaps receive gradually from above the freedom that others have to snatch violently and suddenly from below"

(10.1:556). The French liberators, in other words, had become conquerors after all, due to a fatal combination of their own mistakes and the immaturity of the German people. In reaching this conclusion, however, Forster has worked himself into a double bind: on the one hand, the French Revolution that was to bring enlightenment to the German people has become a potentially deadly disease that flings the French from crisis to cure and back again, leaving them on the brink of death, and on the other, the Germans—who have been rendered unfit for revolutionary change by the aristocrats who curtailed their freedom and kept them in a state of immaturity (*Unmündigkeit*)—are now supposed to benefit from top-down reforms from those very nobles.

"Revolution in Mainz" breaks off with the Prussian forces poised to recapture the city and Forster's plea for understanding for the foibles of his fellow Germans. "The first steps of an individual who is just escaping the bonds of slavery and starting to make his way alone through life, no matter how clumsy and awkward they may seem, still awaken hope in the breast of the humanitarian who will not let him lose faith in the providence and moral causality that guide his fate" (10.1:560). Missteps are inevitable on the path to freedom, but the journey is worth the effort. Forster switches registers in the final pages from a sober analysis of the historical events to a reaffirmation of his belief in the ultimate triumph of democracy. "Yes, it will come, the time when human value is not measured by birth or accidental rank, not by power or riches, but only in terms of virtue and wisdom" (10.1:562). The soaring rhetoric masks the dilemmas exposed by historical analysis, however, and Forster is left clinging to faith that his experience undermines.

Forster turns to more abstract questions in his final completed work, "Concerning Statesmanship in Relation to Human Happiness," in which he restates enlightenment principles as they relate to political theory. The essay begins with a basic question: How can a state confer happiness on the greatest number of its citizens? Only by granting them the freedom to develop their innate capacity for self-improvement (*Vervollkommnungsfähigkeit*) to the fullest extent. Despotic rulers keep their subjects in a state of perpetual childhood; good governments are like good parents: they know how to guide their children at first, but they also know when to let go. While Kant blames individuals for their lack of energy or courage to think for themselves, Forster points the finger at the rulers in charge. To be sure, Kant directs "What is Enlightenment?" toward a specific situation: Frederick the Great has given his Prussian subjects the freedom to develop their intellectual faculties, but most have failed to take advantage of the opportunity. Forster is less convinced of Frederick II's greatness, however. In a footnote to "Statesmanship," he writes in implicit response to Kant that although Frederick had character traits that might lead one to suspect he would be an exceptionally enlightened ruler, he disappointed in the end: "But, as highly as he valued individuals, one sees clearly that, throughout his life, his times—and his education—compelled him to despise the masses."[95]

For the most part, Forster writes in general terms about the art of governance, without naming names or indicting particular regimes. The passing reference to Frederick II suggests that Forster has his old enemies in mind, however: the absolute rulers of Europe's prerevolutionary governments. Jürgen Goldstein suggests that there may also be an implicit critique of the increasingly radical leaders of the French Revolution, which is plausible, given Forster's many critical comments about them in his letters.[96] Although he was disillusioned about what he perceived as corrupt politicians who carried out personal vendettas under the cloak of revolutionary virtue, he kept silent about such abuses in his published works. Forster's credentials as a representative of the Mainz Republic would not have saved him from the guillotine if he offended the Committee of Public Safety, as Adam Lux's example proved, and the sacrifice of this once-fervent supporter of the cause points toward the larger tendency for successive waves of radical change to wash away those who had come before. As Georg Büchner's Danton will say, "The Revolution is like Saturn: it devours its own children."[97]

If Forster is extending his critique of despotism to include revolutionary France, albeit in ways that can slip under the censor's radar, then what exactly does he criticize? Abuse of authority that curtails the freedom of individual citizens is certainly part of his charge, but he also raises the question of territorial aggression. "The secret of all prudent state policy is *expansion*," he notes sarcastically; "the secret of all politics: *cunning* and *contempt for human kind*. But what am I saying—secret!" (10.1:584). European states today strive toward "expansion and an increase in power," Forster repeats. "Should we still be allowed to flatter ourselves that this will lead to human happiness?" Should we believe that "the peace of the conqueror's subjects and all of his neighbors weighs nothing against his fame, because *perhaps*, when it is satisfied,— *perhaps*—the period will begin when the well-being of the people can become a matter of his concern?" (10.1:586). It is not my fault if placing our hopes on "such a dubious *perhaps*" sounds like a joke, Forster concludes bitterly. "The hope of future generations must be based on the *current constitution*, not just on plans of conquest and expansion, which, even if they should succeed beyond all expectations, will only accelerate the demise of the state unless it has a rock-solid foundation" (10.1:586–87). Set your own house in order first, Forster warns, before thinking about expanding your influence elsewhere.

In the "Parisian Sketches" that engaged him in the last months and weeks of his life, Forster shifts the focus from external expansion to the internal centralization of the new French nation. He registers his dismay at the accelerating use of the guillotine but still defends the Revolution, despite its flaws. He also writes at length about the importance of public opinion (*öffentliche Meinung*), or what Jürgen Habermas would term the public sphere, for disseminating the ideas that made political change possible. This "instrument and soul of the Revolution"[98] set the stage for the overturning of social class distinctions and religious hierarchies, released people from their attachment to material things, and prepared them to make sacrifices for the nation. At the beginning and end of these sketches, however, Forster focuses his attention on Paris as the center of the new revolutionary empire: "In the new republic Paris is what Rome once was in the universal empire: the monstrous head [das ungeheure Haupt] from which all actions spread out into the provinces, and in which all reactions converge" (10.1:593). The French federal system has been "shattered by a lightning bolt from the Mountain (La Montagne)" (10.1:594). "Federalism—the idea that a country could be made up of relatively autonomous local units loosely bound together—was the political system adopted by the United States," explains Jeremy Popkin, but the Montagnards vehemently opposed this strategy in France. For them, "the idea suggested a retreat to the old regime, where the provinces had had different laws, and this, the revolutionaries believed, would undermine the common national identity they wanted to promote."[99] Paris, writes Forster in mid-December 1793, remains "the source of public opinion, the heart of the Republic and the Revolution" (10.1:631). "Here, Paris is the sole measure of perfection, the pride of the nation, the north star of the Republic. . . . everything flows together here, so that it can flow back to the provinces from here" (10.1:633). In the new United States, the federal system allowed the capital to move from one city to another, Forster observes in the final pages of his fragmentary essay, but in France, "Paris will have to remain, for the time being at least, the seat of government" (10.1:635).

On the surface, Forster praises France for being everything Germany is not: a politically and culturally unified nation with a single capital city that allows the development of the public sphere and the Revolution, which, for all its flaws, is still preferable to Germany's reactionary Reich. The comparison of modern Paris to ancient Rome adds a note of ambivalence to Forster's praise, however. In the fourteenth chapter of his *Ideas*, which Forster greatly admired, Herder criticizes Rome for its insatiable lust for conquest. When we consider the pain they inflicted on the world, he concludes, "we may have to marvel at the stone-heap of Roman splendor as perhaps the pinnacle of human violence and grandeur, but also despise it as a den of tyrants and murderers of the human race."[100] Forster offered a similarly mixed assessment of Joseph II, whom he praised for his enlightened reforms but criticized for his efforts to impose a single standard on a diverse realm; he also grew increasingly critical of the French forces that occupied Mainz. Centralization and imperial expansion went hand in hand, not only in ancient Rome but also in modern territorial states such as Prussia and Austria, and in revolutionary France as well. As a young man, Forster had witnessed the extra-European variant of the same imperialist impulse, as Cook brought British culture to the indigenous peoples of the South Seas and introduced nonnative plants and animals into the local ecosystems. He had responded with a mixture of admiration and concern then, and he viewed events in Paris and its provinces with equal ambivalence now. He by no means rejects the Revolution; "Parisian Sketches" breaks off with a defiant prediction that France's enemies will fail because they are playing with a weaker hand: "Paris is still *our* card, and you have lost" (10.1:637). In more reflective passages of his final work, however, Forster returns to the themes that run through his entire oeuvre, combining rejection of the old regime with respect for its regional diversity, and advocacy of revolutionary reform with concern about its tendency toward imperial aggression and the leveling of local differences.

Conclusion
A Different Kind of Classic

Until he was ten, Georg Forster was as limited in his movements as most of his contemporaries, growing up in a village in the Polish-controlled part of Prussia and only occasionally visiting Danzig with his father. That changed when father and son set off on a journey to the interior of Russia, moved to England, and sailed around the world. Thereafter, Forster's fame and his activity as an essayist, travel writer, and translator kept him in the public eye as he catered to popular taste and participated in intellectual debates. Looking back at his brief but eventful life, we find a complicated, if not contradictory, image. As I have stressed throughout this study, Forster was a representative of the European Enlightenment, often with its attendant Eurocentric prejudices. He was confident that Europe was the heir to ancient Greece and at the vanguard of modern civilization. It was Europe's mission to understand and cultivate the natural world and improve the lives of its human inhabitants. In keeping with this spirit, Forster was an enemy of political despotism and religious obscurantism, and an advocate of the French Revolution.

At the same time, however, Forster questioned the presuppositions of this confident worldview. He endorsed Emperor Joseph's progressive reforms but worried that his imposition of a single standard onto diverse cultures would result in a machine-like leveling of local differences. He welcomed the French revolutionary armies into Mainz as liberators from feudal oppression, but he soon chafed under their abusive occupation. He won the support of the National Assembly for the incorporation of the Mainz Republic into France, but he turned away from a cause used as a cover for personal vindictiveness and political violence. He was swept away by the beauty of the South Sea islands and the innocence of their peoples, only to realize that their society had its inequities and that his own civilization was even more flawed. He discovered that human reason could exacerbate the problems it set out to resolve, that the civilizing mission could destroy indigenous cultures and wreak havoc on the environment, and that progress might be an illusion, as human cultures were eventually subsumed back into the eternal flux of nature.

It is tempting to view Forster's thought in terms of a linear development from naive optimism to jaded pessimism, but that would not do justice to the nature of his ideas. Even on his deathbed, Forster celebrated the suppression of the Vendée rebellion and continued to affirm his belief in the principles of the Revolution, even though he was deeply disappointed by daily trends and individual decisions. His plans to learn the Persian language and travel to India may have been feverish fantasies, but they also testify to his unquenchable curiosity. He acknowledged the damage caused by European explorations even as he celebrated Captain Cook's achievements in a hagiographic essay. The deeper consistency of Forster's thought lies in its antidogmatic and dialectical tendencies. Forster was deeply suspicious of anyone who claimed to possess the whole truth, whether in terms of art, religion, or politics, and he was always willing to consider the flip side of a coin, thinking things through to sometimes uncomfortable conclusions: discoveries that expand European opportunities can also destroy indigenous cultures; revolutions that remove despots can install new tyrants; industrial advances can trigger ecological catastrophe.

Forster's work suggests a different way of looking at German literature around 1800. The Age of Goethe has traditionally between described in terms of wholeness, unity, and centering; its revival of classical humanism sought to suture the wounds of modernity, as creative artists channeled the spirit of the nation in preparation for political unity. Forster's thought, in contrast, is decentered in multiple ways, moving between languages and across borders. Like Herder, and in anticipation of today's postcolonial thinkers, Forster ponders the relationship between the universal and the particular, in terms of both the European Enlightenment in the global context and intra-European tensions between feudal principalities, territorial states, and modern republics. He was one of the few Germans to support the French Revolution in action as well as thought, but like most Germans, he continued to think within the parameters of the Holy Roman Empire, weighing the desires of local communities against the demands of centralizing states. His programmatic speech of November 15, 1792, envisioned the future of the Mainz Republic as committed to the goals of the French Revolution and yet free to retain its distinct cultural identity, fusing German federalism with French universalism. His vision of a multilingual, multicultural confederation of republics along France's eastern border invoked the structure of imperial diversity exemplified by ancient Rome, modern Russia, and the Holy Roman Empire but infused with the spirit of revolutionary democracy.

While Forster's *Views of the Lower Rhine* and "Depiction of the Revolution in Mainz" examine local conflicts within Europe, *A Voyage Round the World* and subsequent essays place European thought in a global context. In the process, Forster measures the universal principles of the European Enlightenment against the diverse demands of indigenous cultures. As we have seen, Forster oscillates between an unqualified endorsement of Europe's civilizing mission and a sharp critique of its unintended consequences. From time to time, however, most notably in his essay "On Nature as a Whole" and in the introduction to "Cook, the Discoverer," Forster tries to reconcile these apparently contradictory impulses. In those essays, he lays out a Lucretian image of the world as an eternal whole whose constituent parts remain in constant flux. Like Goethe, whose Prometheus and Faust embody reckless energy, Forster suggests that those who engage most actively with the world are most in keeping with its dynamic nature. Captain Cook, for instance, displays an insatiable curiosity and limitless vitality that allow him to accomplish great things, even if his exploits cause collateral damage and are ephemeral in the end, like all human endeavors. Forster admires Cook's inquisitiveness more than his accomplishments—his willingness to challenge conventional wisdom and unsettle accepted traditions. To this extent, he provides a model for Forster's engagement with the world.

Forster was a man of many talents whose work does not fit neatly into modern disciplinary divisions: he was at various times an anthropologist, historian, literary critic, philosopher, and political theorist. Although Forster was not a creative writer, he was a gifted artist who produced arresting seascapes and detailed depictions of plants and animals discovered in the course of Cook's voyage. His diversity of talent could be used to brand him as a dilettante, a dabbler in many genres but master of none, but it can also remind us of the dynamism of the literary field in the late eighteenth century, even as the aesthetics of genius began to delimit the concept of the literary work and restrict our understanding of authorship. Forster's circumnavigation of the globe demonstrated that Europe could no longer conceive of its culture in isolation from the larger world. His interest in botany, ethnography, geology, and zoology arose out of the Enlightenment's effort to understand and categorize discrete phenomena, but it also led to increasing interest in interconnected ecosystems and the impact of human civilization on the natural environment. Forster was both a political theorist and political activist; he literally risked his life for his ideals, while acknowledging the limitations of even the most progressive efforts to improve society. As a traveler, travel writer, and translator, he opened eyes to the world and accelerated the circulation of literary texts. His fragmentary oeuvre is a work in progress, essayistic, open-ended, and undogmatic. It is tempting, therefore, to think of Forster as the exception to the rule, the almost-forgotten, unread writer in an age of literary titans, a polyglot, globe-trotting revolutionary who stands for everything that the Age of Goethe does not. Or rather, perhaps, everything that a certain version of literary historiography wanted Weimar Classicism to be. In his mobility and versatility, Forster was a classic of a different kind—a genuine cosmopolitan of German origins.

NOTES

Introduction

1. Ette, "Welterleben," 367; Vorpahl, *Der Welterkunder*, 30–37; Enzensberger, *Georg Forster*, 98–106.
2. Prinz, *Lebensgeschichte*, 94.
3. To Soemmerring, August 14, 1784, in G. Forster, *Werke*, 14:166–67. With the exception of *A Voyage Round the World*, all of Forster's works are cited from this eighteen-volume edition, with volume and page number. Unless otherwise noted, all translations are my own.
4. To J. R. Forster, November 24, 1778, 13:148.
5. See, for instance, the Xenia titled "Die unglückliche Eilfertigkeit" (The unfortunate haste): "Ach wie sie Freiheit schrien und Gleichheit, ich hörs, ich will folgen, / Und weil die Trepp mir zu lang währet, so spring ich vom Dach" (Ah, how they scream about freedom and equality, I hear it and want to follow / And because the stairs take too long, I jump from the roof). Goethe, *Gedichte 1756–1799*, 551. "So, poor Forster paid with his life for his mistakes after all!" wrote Goethe to Soemmerring shortly after Forster's death. Quoted from Enzensberger, *Georg Forster*, 296. Gervinus begins his sympathetic account of Forster's life and works with disapproving comments about how his "memory was spurned and repressed" by the German public ("Johann Georg Forster," 6).
6. Peitsch, *Georg Forster*; Scheuer, "'Apostel der Völkerfreiheit'"; Uhlig, "Zwischen Politik."
7. Vorpahl, *Der Welterkunder*, 46.
8. Zhang, *Transculturality*, 21–42.
9. Mani, *Recoding*, 68. Mani's work won the GSA/DAAD 2018 Best Book Prize.
10. Cited in Harpprecht, *Georg Forster*, 339.
11. Vorpahl, *Der Welterkunder*, 78–79; see also Harpprecht, *Georg Forster*, 263–64.
12. Roach, *It*, 1.
13. Goethe, *Werther*, in *Collected Works*, 11:3.
14. Agnew, *Enlightenment Orpheus*, 25.
15. Boone and Vickers, "Introduction," 904, 906.
16. Braudy, *Frenzy of Renown*, 313–89.
17. Darnton, "Readers Respond to Rousseau."
18. Braudy, *Frenzy of Renown*, 373, 375.
19. To Jacobi, November 2, 1779, 13:252.
20. To Jacobi, April 23, 1779, 13:198–99.
21. To Spener, December 17, 1778, 13:162.
22. To Spener, July 5, 1779, 13:217.
23. Schlegel, "Georg Forster," 89.
24. Goethe, "Response," in *Collected Works*, 3:189–92.
25. Schlegel, "Georg Forster," 92–93.
26. Ibid., 79–80.
27. Ette, *TransArea*, 10.
28. Ibid., 16.
29. Young, *White Mythologies*, 32.
30. Ibid., 163.
31. Ibid., 50.
32. Braidotti, *Posthuman*, 13.
33. Ibid., 16.
34. Young, *White Mythologies*, 161.
35. Braidotti, *Posthuman*, 11.
36. Wolin, *Seduction of Unreason*.
37. Berman, *Enlightenment or Empire*, 17.
38. Marchand, *German Orientalism*, 25.
39. Berman, *Enlightenment or Empire*, 7.
40. Chakrabarty, *Provincializing Europe*, 4.
41. Muthu, *Enlightenment Against Empire*, 1.
42. Cook, *Journals*, 2:175 (June 3, 1773). Cook's orthography is notoriously bad; the spelling mistakes in this and subsequent quotations are his own.
43. Ibid., 2:493 (August 14, 1774).
44. Muthu, *Enlightenment Against Empire*, 2.
45. Lowe, *Intimacies*, 3.
46. Tang, *Geographic Imagination*, 14–15.
47. See Strasser, Biess, and Berghoff, "Introduction."

48. Whaley, *Germany and the Holy Roman Empire*, 2:8–81.
49. Buck-Morss, "Hegel and Haiti," 838; Tautz, "Revolution, Abolition," 80. See also Tautz, *Translating the World*. On what Forster may or may not have known about the early stages of this conflict, see Kappeler, "Die globale Revolution."
50. Goldstein, *Georg Forster*, 1–10.
51. Koselleck, "Einleitung," xv.
52. Koselleck, *Futures Past*, 18.
53. Sheehan, *German History*, 14. See also P. Wilson, *Heart of Europe*, 7, 251, 284.
54. Beales, *Joseph II*, 2:68–69.
55. Blanning, *Joseph II*, 68–70, 75, 81.
56. Clark, *Iron Kingdom*, 239–40.
57. Beales, *Joseph II*, 2:1.
58. Herder, *Briefe zur Beförderung der Humanität*, in *Werke*, 7:53.
59. Ibid., 7:48.
60. Ibid., 7:56.
61. Herder, *Another Philosophy*, 49.
62. Ibid., 65.
63. Barnard, *Herder's Social and Political Thought*; Barnard, *Herder on Nationality*. Spencer, *Herder's Political Thought*, 16, 21, 130–31.
64. Spencer, *Herder's Political Thought*, 132.
65. Barnard, *Herder's Social and Political Thought*, 63–66.
66. *Vom Geist der Ebräischen Poesie*, in *Werke*, 5:1085.
67. Herder, *Ideen*, in *Werke*, 6:593.
68. Ibid., 6:580.
69. Ibid., 6:609.
70. Ibid., 6:624.
71. Popkin, *New World*, 190–91.
72. Kumar, *Visions of Empire*, 389–90.
73. Blanning, *French Revolution in Germany*, 3, 318–19; he cites Carlo Zaghi.
74. Whaley, *Germany*. See also Schmidt, *Geschichte des Alten Reiches*; Sheehan, *German History*; P. Wilson, *Heart of Europe*.
75. Blanning, *French Revolution*, 20.
76. Noyes, *Herder*, 21. See also Gomsu, "Georg Forsters Wahrnehmung," 548–50.
77. Anderson, *Imagined Communities*, 7.
78. Kittler, *Discourse Networks*.
79. See Blackall on *The Emergence of German as a Literary Language* in the eighteenth century. As Gramling argues, the very concept of monolingualism depended on the notion of discrete national languages that emerged only around this time: "Monolingualism was one of the pivotal innovations of the early modern and Enlightenment period." *The Invention of Monolingualism*, 9.

Chapter 1

1. Uhlig, *Georg Forster*, 18. On the Forster family background, see Enzensberger, *Georg Forster*, 7–15.
2. Hoare, *Tactless Philosopher*, 5.
3. To Spener, December 27, 1776, 13:76.
4. To Spener, August 25, 1783, 13:470.
5. The title pages of these first editions and the memorial plaque can be viewed on Google images.
6. To Spener, April 2, 1776, 13:34.
7. To Spener, November 9, 1775, 13:22.
8. To Vollpracht, March 12, 1776, 13:29.
9. To Heyne, May 25, 1778, 13:126.
10. Forster was born in "Polish Prussia," which included Danzig and its immediate surroundings; the region remained under Polish authority until the first partition of 1772, when Prussia took over lands adjacent to Brandenburg, but the Prussian monarchy did not gain control of Danzig until 1793. Prinz, *Lebensgeschichte*, 20.
11. To Voss, November 21, 1792, 17:248–49.
12. To Voss, November 8, 1793, 17:464.
13. Uhlig, *Georg Forster*, 28.
14. Ibid., 207, 282; Harpprecht, *Georg Forster*, 354–56, 487.
15. To Therese Forster, May 19, 1793, 17:358.
16. Harpprecht, *Georg Forster*, 24.
17. To Don Fausto d'Elhuyar y de Suvisa, December 1787, 15:74. German draft of a letter in French (December 27, 1787, 15:75–8) to a Spanish gentleman whom Forster had met in Dresden. Don Fausto tempted Forster with work for a mining operation in Mexico and the prospect of an expedition to the Philippines. See Harpprecht, *Georg Forster*, 367–72. See also Uhlig, "Der polyglotte Forster."
18. Yildiz, *Beyond the Mother Tongue*, 2.
19. Seyhan, *Writing Outside the Nation*; El-Tayeb, *European Others*.
20. I borrow the distinction between "minoritizing" and "universalizing" perspectives from Sedgwick, *Epistemology of the Closet*, 85.

21. Kramsch, "Privilege of the Nonnative Speaker," 363.
22. Yildiz, *Beyond*, 4.
23. Hokenson and Munson, *Bilingual Text*, 136–46.
24. Herder, *Abhandung über den Ursprung der Sprache*, in *Werke*, 1:787. See Trabant, "Herder and Language."
25. Schleiermacher, "Über die verschiedenen Methoden des Übersetzens." For the distinction between foreignizing and domesticating approaches to translation and Schleiermacher's advocacy of the foreignizing method, see Venuti, *Translator's Invisibility*, 19–20, 99–118.
26. Bonfiglio, *Mother Tongues and Nations*, 153–56. See also Norberg, "German Literary Studies."
27. Bonfiglio, *Mother Tongues and Nations*. See also Poliakov, *Aryan Myth*.
28. Leonhardt, *Latin*, 6. See also Hokenson and Munson, *Bilingual*, 32.
29. Leonhardt, *Latin*, 15.
30. Eibl, "Kommentar," 1003.
31. Foucault, "What Is an Author?"
32. Piper, *Dreaming in Books*, 3.
33. Ibid., 20.
34. Ibid., 21–52.
35. Withey, *Voyages of Discovery*, 189.
36. Beaglehole, *Life of Captain James Cook*, 279–305.
37. Thomas and Berghof, "Introduction," xxv–xxix.
38. Beaglehole, *Life*, 289, 439.
39. Ibid., 460–71.
40. As Martin observes, the German version of *Voyage* is not identical to the original English; Forster added some passages from Cook's account, which appeared slightly after Forster's work "Rerouting the Self."
41. Walkowitz, *Born Translated*, 1–2.
42. Thomas and Berghof, "Introduction," xviii–xxix.
43. Wales, *Remarks on Mr. Forster's Account*, 699.
44. Forster, *Reply*, 758–59.
45. Thomas and Berghof highlight many such passages in their annotations to the republished travelogue.
46. Harpprecht, *Georg Forster*, 181.
47. To Spener, July 29, 1777, 13:100.

48. To Spener, mid-August 1778, 13:130 (italics in original; the letter is undated).
49. On the long history of self-translation obscured by the monolingual paradigm and the aesthetics of genius, see Hokenson and Munson, *Bilingual Text*.
50. Esleben, "Übersetzung als interkulturelle Kommunikation"; Lüsebrink, "Interkulturelle Aneignung."
51. To Reuss, October 21, 1788, 15:199. Reuss was a professor and librarian in Göttingen.
52. To Heyne, January 9, 1789, 15:240.
53. To Heyne, June 16, 1792, 17:135.
54. Prinz, *Lebensgeschichte*, 166.
55. Harpprecht, *Georg Forster*, 397.
56. Haug, "'Ich sehe mit Verlangen'"; Haug, "'Die Arbeit unterhält mich.'"
57. To Jacobi, September 18, 1790, 16:190.
58. To Jacobi, November 1, 1789, 15:364.
59. To Jacobi, November 6, 1791, 16:366.
60. To Heyne, August 30, 1790, 16:176.
61. To Heyne, May 24, 1790, 16:151.
62. To Jacobi, November 10, 1788, 15:201.
63. To Jacobi, November 1, 1789, 15:364.
64. To Boie, July 5, 1789, 15:312. Christian Boie was a writer and editor of the *Deutsches Museum* (Harpprecht, *Georg Forster*, 237).
65. To Jacobi, January 2, 1789, 15:231.
66. Bürger, *Leben Schreiben*.
67. Woodmansee, *Author, Art, and the Market*. On the distinction between "intensive" and "extensive" reading, see Engelsing, *Der Bürger als Leser*.
68. Touaillon, *Der deutsche Frauenroman*; Becker-Cantarino, *Der lange Weg*; Blackwell and Zantop, *Bitter Healing*; Bovenschen, *Die imaginierte Weiblichkeit*; Brinker-Gabler, *Deutsche Literatur von Frauen*. In addition to Google books, see the many German texts available at Zeno.org and Projekt Gutenberg-DE.
69. Moretti, *Distant Reading*.
70. Piper, *Dreaming in Books*, 168.
71. Haug, "'Ich sehe mit Verlangen,'" 38–39.
72. Haug, "'Die Arbeit unterhält mich,'" 124.
73. Kittler, *Discourse Networks*, 77–108.
74. Uhlig, *Georg Forster*, 273. See also Enzensberger, *Georg Forster*, 209–15.
75. Uhlig, *Georg Forster*, 324.
76. Harpprecht, *Georg Forster*, 480.

77. Uhlig, *Georg Forster*, 282.
78. To Spener, July 23, 1790, 16:162–64.
79. To Spener, September 4, 1790, 16:178–80.
80. To Voss, September 4, 1790, 16:180–81.
81. To Spener, November 6, 1790, 16:202–3.
82. To Spener May 5, 1791, 16:283.
83. Anderson, *Imagined Communities*, 44–45.
84. To Spener, September 4, 1790, 16:178.
85. Weisinger, *Classical Façade*, 177.
86. Piper, *Dreaming in Books*, 6.

Chapter 2

1. Forster, *Voyage Round the World*, 653. Although I cite most of Forster's works from the standard critical edition, I make an exception for this edition in the original English of Forster's *Voyage*, as it is readily available and includes critical essays and source materials not included elsewhere. Hereafter cited in the text; the pages are numbered consecutively in the two volumes.
2. The three volumes were published in French in 1814, 1819, and 1825. They contained a total of 1,997 pages. J. Wilson, "Introduction," lxiii. On the unconventional, open-ended nature of Humboldt's narrative, see Lubrich, "Alexander von Humboldt."
3. Goldstein stresses that Forster is a storyteller who seeks a broad audience. *Georg Forster*, 38–43.
4. On Forster's "philosophical travelogue" in relation to eighteenth-century travel literature, see Neumann, "Philosophische Nachrichten."
5. Uhlig, "Theoretical or Conjectural History."
6. Goldstein, *Georg Forster*, 75.
7. Berman, *Enlightenment or Empire?*, 22–64.
8. As Thomas and Berghof suggest, the "ambivalence concerning the morality of exploration and of traffic with non-European peoples . . . runs through the entire book" ("Notes," 441). See also Zhang: "Despite his sympathetic comments, Forster still considers the Europeans 'civilized' compared to the cannibalistic islanders" (*Transculturality*, 38).
9. "Ein Blick," 8:78. Hereafter cited in the text.
10. Goethe, *Faust*, part II, act I, line 6287; Goethe, *Collected Works*, 2:161.

11. Greenblatt, *Swerve*, 103.
12. Ibid., 103.
13. Ibid., 201.
14. Tang, *Geographic Imagination*, 74.
15. Ibid., 75.
16. Ibid., 112.
17. Uhlig, *Georg Forster*, 87, 90, 133, 204; Uhlig, "Georg Forsters Anthropologie"; Uhlig, "Theoretical or Conjectural History," 404; Zhang, *Transculturality*, 34; Goldstein, *Georg Forster*, 75–80, 133–34.
18. Ferguson, *Essay*, 12.
19. Ibid., 11.
20. "Neuholland und die brittische Colonie in Botany-Bay," 5:162.
21. J. Forster, *Observations*, 99–100. See also Dettelbach, "'Kind of Linnaean Being,'" lxxi–lxxii.
22. J. Forster, *Observations*, 235.
23. "Neuholland," 5:162.
24. "Cook, the Discoverer," 5:290.
25. "Neuholland," 5:176; *Besonnenheit* is a key term in Herder's work that Forster presumably appropriates for his own. Spencer, *Herder's Political Thought*, 37. Italics in the original.
26. "Neuholland," 5:178.
27. Uhlig, *Georg Forster*, 206–7. See also Heinz, "Der Weltreisende als Heros."
28. To Lichtenberg, November 5, 1786, 14:574–75.
29. To Herder, January 21, 1787, 14:622.
30. Forster to Meyer, April 2, 1787, 14:662. Friedrich Meyer was an acquaintance from Forster's Göttingen circle of friends who later had an affair with Forster's wife, Therese. Harpprecht, *Georg Forster*, 332–34, 375–80.
31. Modern science suggests that neither sauerkraut nor malt, the other supposed antiscorbutic that Cook encouraged the sailors to consume, did much if anything to prevent disease. Cleanliness on board ship and fresh fruit and vegetables when on land did more to keep the crew as healthy as possible, although Forster and other crew members, including Cook, suffered greatly during their extended stays at sea. On this "disease of discovery," see Lamb, *Scurvy*.
32. Obeyesekere, *Apotheosis*, 127.
33. Ibid., 14. Dening confirms this view, as he argues that "it was [Bligh's] language that was seen to be his most offensive trait, not

his violence." *Mr Bligh's Bad Language*, 55. He provides a statistical analysis to show that "Cook flogged 20 percent, 26 percent and 37 percent, respectively, on his three voyages ... Bligh, on the *Bounty*, flogged 19 percent" (63).

34. Ibid., 130.
35. Zantop, *Colonial Fantasies*, 9.
36. Ibid., 29.
37. Uhlig, *Georg Forster*, 208.
38. Schiller, *Aesthetic Education*, 43, 45.
39. Ibid., 27.
40. Humboldt, *Views of Nature*, 129–30.
41. Goethe, *Faust*, lines 1339–40, 1335–36; Goethe, *Collected Works*, 2:36.
42. Goethe, *Faust*, lines 11936–37; Goethe, *Collected Works*, 2:301.
43. Beaglehole, *Life of Captain James Cook*, 531.
44. Vorpahl is particularly sensitive to Forster's artistic talents. He rediscovered a trove of Forster's watercolors (*Der Welterkunder*, 429–38) and reproduces many in color in his book. See also the lavishly produced edition of Forster's *Reise um die Welt* (2007), illustrated with Forster's drawings and watercolors.
45. Zhang underscores Forster's combined intellectual and emotional response to nature during the voyage (*Transculturality*, 27). See also Goldstein, *Georg Forster*, 41. On Forster's attentiveness to the threatening spectacle of the Antarctic icefields, see Wilke, *German Culture*, 157–64.
46. Tang, *Geographic Imagination*, 83–84.
47. Snow, *Two Cultures*; Walls, *Passage to Cosmos*, 148–72.
48. Schnickmann, "Hunde, Schweine und Pferde."
49. Cook, *Journals*, 2:279 (October 22, 1773).
50. Ibid., 3.1:158 (July 13, 1777).
51. Cited in Beaglehole, *Life of Captain James Cook*, 414.
52. Mariss, "Johann Reinhold Forster," 140.
53. Forster, "Der Brodbaum," 6:63. Hereafter cited in the text.
54. Dening, *Mr Bligh's Bad Language*, 4, 11.
55. Crosby, *Ecological Imperialism*, 229. Diamond also observes that germs killed far more indigenous peoples than European guns or steel in the course of the conquest (*Guns, Germs, and Steel*), 77–81, 195–214.

56. Cited in Hoare, *Tactless Philosopher*, 90–91.
57. Beaglehole, *Life of Captain James Cook*, 335.
58. Cited in Beaglehole, *Life of Captain James Cook*, 516.
59. Crosby, *Ecological Imperialism*, 227.
60. Cook, *Journals*, 2:76 (January 12, 1773).
61. According to Thomas and Berghof, "evidence that Coleridge read and used Forster's account for key passages remains inconclusive" ("Introduction," xlii). Lamb, in contrast, claims that Coleridge relied heavily on accounts from the *Resolution* voyage when describing the scurvy-like symptoms depicted in "Rime of the Ancient Mariner" (*Scurvy*, 3).
62. Shevelow, *For the Love of Animals*; Robertson, *Enlightenment*, 347–50.
63. The elder Forster records the same incident. J. Forster, *Observations*, 142.
64. Wulf, *Invention of Nature*, 67.
65. Shannon, "Eight Animals," 475.
66. Tang, *Geographical Imagination*, 4–5.
67. Blackbourn, *Conquest of Nature*, 5.
68. Ibid., 5.
69. Ibid., 69.
70. Ibid., 182.
71. Locke, *Second Treatise*, section 34, in Locke, *Two Treatises*, 290.
72. Ibid., section 49, 301.
73. Ibid., section 41, 297.
74. Lowe, *Intimacies*, 10.
75. Thomas and Berghof observe that Forster's harshly critical depiction of the Fuegians probably influenced Darwin's equally critical comments. Thomas and Berghof, "Introduction," xxxiii; Thomas and Berghof, "Notes," 828.
76. Thomas and Berghof, "Notes," 461, 465. They also note that Tahiti showed the adverse effects of "burning and erosion" (811).
77. Bougainville, *Voyage*, 226.
78. Moorehead, *Fatal Impact*, 59–68.
79. Cook, *Journals* 2:444 (June 28, 1774).
80. Harpprecht, *Georg Forster*, 102; Vorpahl, *Der Welterkunder*, 258.
81. Dening, *Mr Bligh's Bad Language*, 81.
82. Elias, *Court Society*, 48.
83. Uhlig, *Georg Forster*, 52.
84. Mariss, "Johann Reinhold Forster," 137. Zhang is particularly attentive to indigenous

influence on European thought, including that of Forster (*Transculturality*, 28).

85. Goldstein, *Georg Forster*, 135–36.
86. Vorpahl, *Der Welterkunder*, 201.
87. Millar devotes the first chapter of *Observations* to a discussion of "the rank and condition of women in different ages" (7–36). Lord Kames also dedicates an entire chapter to "the progress of the female sex" (*Six Sketches*, 194–255), and Johann Reinhold Forster discusses the treatment of women in different societies in *Observations* (258–67). See Uhlig, "Theoretical or Conjectural History," 406; Guest, "Looking at Women."
88. J. Forster, *Observations*, 258. Lord Kames traces "the gradual progress of women, from their low state in savage tribes, to their elevated state in civilized nations" (*Six Sketches*, 194). See also Miller, *Observations*, 48; May, "Kultur im Zeichen des Geschlechts," 185–86; and Guest, "Looking at Women," xlvi.
89. Sanches, "Dunkelheit und Aufklärung," 55, 81.
90. Thomas and Berghof, "Notes," 444.
91. See Japp on Forster's double critique of inequities in both Polynesia and Europe ("Aufgeklärtes Europa").
92. Muthu, *Enlightenment Against Empire*, 23, 68, 268.
93. As West observes, Forster is both aware of the shortcomings of Tahitian society and yet reluctant to abandon the idealized image; hence he fluctuates between praise and critique ("Limits," 159). Zhang also notes Forster's oscillation between admiration and condescension in his assessment of the Tahitians (*Transculturality*, 30–36).
94. Goldstein, *Georg Forster*, 74, 93.
95. As the editors of Johann Reinhold Forster's *Observations* note, Lord Kames also "saw the history of civilization in almost cyclical and tragic terms: an improved sociality gives way inevitably to selfishness, opulence, degeneracy, and so on." Thomas, Guest, and Dettelbach, "Notes," 424.

Chapter 3

1. Moorehead, *Fatal Impact*, 94.
2. Ibid., 99.
3. Ibid., 107.
4. Ibid., 226.
5. Ibid., 230–31.

6. Bernal, *Black Athena*, 27–28, 215–23; Zammito, *Kant, Herder*, 27–28; Robertson, *Enlightenment*, 562–64.
7. Koselleck, *Futures Past*, 17; Kuzniar, *Delayed Endings*, 29–40.
8. See excerpts of his work in Eze, *Race and the Enlightenment*, 79–90.
9. Zantop, *Colonial Fantasies*, 78. In his *Adam's Ancestors*, Livingstone provides a comprehensive overview of debates surrounding human origins in relation to the Bible, modern science, and racial prejudice. See also Poliakov, *Aryan Myth*, 155–82; Young, *Colonial Desire*, 9–13, 47–50, 64–67.
10. Zantop, *Colonial Fantasies*, 79.
11. Eze stresses that there is "no monolithic or unanimous picture of the Enlightenment, or its philosophical ideas on race." "Introduction," 6. See also the essays in Eigen and Larrimore, *German Invention of Race*, and Tautz, *Reading and Seeing*.
12. Cited from Eze, *Race*, 83; italics in original.
13. Herder, *Ideen*, in *Werke*, 6:253–56.
14. To Heyne, November 20, 1784, 14:210.
15. To Spener, April 10, 1786, 14:464–65.
16. To Sömmerring, June 8, 1786, 14:486.
17. To Herder, July 21, 1786, 14:512.
18. Zammito, *Kant, Herder*, 214. See also Shell, "Kant's Conception."
19. Zammito, *Kant, Herder*, 57, 302–7. See also the cluster of essays by Zammito, Shell, Bernasconi, and Larrimore on Kant's racial philosophy in Eigen and Larrimore, *German Invention of Race*, 33–120.
20. Kant, "Von den verschiedenen Rassen," 27.
21. Ibid., 23.
22. To Herder, January 21, 1787, 14:621.
23. Meiners, *Grundriß*, 61, 74.
24. Ibid., 218–19.
25. Meiners, "Ueber die Rechtmässigkeit," 409–11.
26. To Jacobi, November 19, 1788, 15:208.
27. To Heyne, September 7, 1789, 15:335.
28. To Heyne, January 1, 1791, 16:222.
29. "Rezension zu C. Meiners anthropologischen Abhandlungen," *Sämtliche Schriften, Tagebücher, Briefe Werke*, 11:245.
30. To Heyne, January 28, 1792, 17:35.
31. In "Dunkelheit und Aufklärung," Sanches offers a useful summary of the

debate that does not shy away from highlighting the more problematic aspects of Forster's response to Kant and Meiners. In "Pluralität und Ethos," May similarly insists that there are elements of Eurocentrism and racial bias in Forster's thought.

32. J. Forster, *Observations*, 143–44. See Enzensberger on Georg Forster's disdain for "Studierzimmergelehrten" (*Georg Forster*, 157).

33. "Noch etwas über die Menschenraßen," in *Sämtliche Schriften, Tagebücher, Briefe Werke*, 8:132. Hereafter cited in the text.

34. Barnouw, "*Eräugnis*," 333.

35. Livingstone, *Adam's Ancestors*, 60.

36. As Livingstone observes, nineteenth-century thinkers nevertheless turned intellectual cartwheels to prove that polygenesis and the biblical account of creation were not incompatible. *Adam's Ancestors*, 80–108.

37. Forster's view of Black Africans as fully human despite their cultural inferiority corresponds to that of his good friend Soemmerring, who places Africans closer to the apes and yet insists that they are part of the same human species. Soemmerring, *Ueber die körperliche Verschiedenheit*, 32.

38. To Soemmerring, February 3, 1785, 14:276.

39. Fagot, "Polen," 595. See also Kopp, *Germany's Wild East*, 15.

40. To Spener, April 10, 1786, 14:465. On Forster's antipathy to Poland, see Enzensberger, *Georg Forster*, 146–47, 156–57.

41. To Therese, January 22, 1785, 14:266.

42. To Lichtenberg, April 10, 1786, 14:460–61.

43. To Therese, December 13, 1784, 14:244.

44. Forster makes this joking reference to his daughter in a letter to Herder, December 10, 1791, 16:391.

45. To Soemmerring, August 14, 1786, 14:524.

46. To Heyne, September 19, 1785, 14:363.

47. Butler, *Tyranny*.

48. Reed, "Replacing Ancient Gods," 77.

49. Schiller, *Aesthetic Education*, 40.

50. Hölderlin, *Hyperion*, 164.

51. Harpprecht, *Georg Forster*, 361–63.

52. To Herder, September 1, 1787, 15:33.

53. Herder, *Ideen*, in *Werke*, 6:517. On the importance of Herder's chapter for both Forster and Schiller, see Uhlig, *Georg Forster*, 235.

54. Uhlig, *Georg Forster*, 234.

55. Geier, *Die Brüder Humboldt*, 87.

56. Ibid., 88–91.

57. "Fragment eines Briefes an einen deutschen Schriftsteller, über Schillers Götter Griechenlands," *Sämtliche Schriften, Tagebücher, Briefe Werke*, 7:4. Hereafter cited in the text.

58. To J. R. Forster, March 22, 1784, 14:35.

59. Epstein, *Genesis*, 105.

60. Ibid., 106–7.

61. Ibid., 109, 111.

62. To Helene Jacobi, March 9, 1784, 14:32. On Forster's engagement with the Rosicrucians, see Harpprecht, *Georg Forster*, 248–64; Enzensberger, *Georg Forster*, 107–30; and Prinz, *Lebensgeschichte*, 116–32.

63. In a letter to Soemmerring, Forster's friend and fellow former Rosicrucian, Forster writes of Spener's joy at the news "that you and I have been cured of a *certain matter*" (von einer *gewissen Sache* kuriert sind) May 14, 1784, 14:56.

64. To Therese, May 22, 1784, 14:70.

65. On Humboldt's collaboration with Forster on this essay, see Geier, *Die Brüder Humboldt*, 110–12.

66. "Über Proselytenmacherei," 8:218.

67. Schiller to Körner, February 9, 1789; Berghahn, *Briefwechsel*, 100–101. Safranski offers an insightful analysis of "The Artists" (*Schiller*, 291–92).

68. Abrams, *Natural Supernaturalism*.

69. Schiller to Goethe, August 23, 1794. On this letter, see Safranski, *Goethe*, 394–97.

70. On this essay, see Robertson, *Enlightenment*, 651–52.

71. Steiner, "Anmerkungen," 3:805.

72. Forster's use of the term *moral* in this context encompasses more than ethics in the narrow sense of right or wrong. It refers rather to the entire range of intellectual development and cultural refinement peculiar to the human race.

73. Gomsu acknowledges elements of Eurocentrism in this essay but insists on Forster's general lack of racial and cultural prejudice. "'Über lokale,'" 334; Sanches, "Dunkelheit und Aufklärung"; May, "Pluralität und Ethos," take a more critical stance.

74. Noyes, *Herder*, 21. See also Gomsu, "Georg Forsters Wahrnehmung," 548–50.

75. To La Roche, March 15, 1790, 16:30.
76. Harpprecht, *Georg Forster*, 455. Agnani draws parallels between Burke's rejection of British imperialism, which motivated his denunciation of Hastings and the East India Company during the trial, and his rejection of the Jacobins as "colonial conquerors" who exerted equally despotic authority over revolutionary France. *Hating Empire*, 109–32, 131.
77. To Spener, July 23, 1790, 16:164.
78. To Schiller, August 20, 1790, 16:173.
79. To Heyne, August 30, 1790, 16:175.
80. "Geschichte der Englischen Litteratur vom Jahre 1790," 7:177.
81. To Therese, June 10, 1793, 17:366.
82. To Therese, June 4, 1793, 17:363.
83. To Therese, June 14, 1793, 17:368.
84. Harpprecht, *Georg Forster*, 24.
85. Marchand, *German Orientalism*, 22.
86. Kontje, *German Orientalisms*; Marchand, *German Orientalism*; Williamson, *Longing for Myth*.
87. "Vorrede zu *Sakontala*," 7:285. The spelling of the Sanskrit play varies between *Sakontala* and *Sakuntala*; I follow Marchand's lead and use *Sakuntala*. Hereafter cited in the text.
88. Hardenberg (Novalis), *Schriften*, 2:519; Kontje, *German Orientalisms*, 87–90.
89. The title was introduced by Bernhard Suphan in his monumental Schiller edition of 1902; it has since become standard in editions of Schiller's works (Kaufmann, *Nation und Nationalismus*, 38–41; Wittkop, "Deutsche Größe").
90. Schiller, *Sämtliche Werke*, 1:473. Hereafter cited in the text.
91. Schmidt, "Friedrich Meinecke's Kulturnation," 607.
92. Schmidt, "Staat, Nation und Universalismus."
93. Heine, *Germany: A Winter Tale*, ii.
94. Boes, "*Weltdeutschtum*."
95. Borchmeyer, *Was ist Deutsch?*, 13.
96. Ibid., 22.
97. Kumar, *Visions of Empire*, 387–464.
98. Zantop, *Colonial Fantasies*.
99. Goethe, "On World Literature," in *Collected Works*, 3:224–25.
100. Goethe, *Werke*, 12:362.
101. Blanning, *Reform and Revolution*, 73.

102. Mani, *Recoding*, 10.
103. Ibid., 65–67.
104. Münkler, *Imperien* 8. See also Kumar, *Visions of Empire*, 6.
105. Pratt, *Imperial Eyes*, 39; Zantop, *Colonial Fantasies*, 7–8.

Chapter 4

1. Forster, *Ansichten vom Niederrhein*, 9:1. Hereafter cited in the text.
2. Rabinow, "Representations," 241. See also Steiner, "Naturerkenntnis," 940; Goldstein, *Georg Forster*, 155, 163.
3. Goldstein, *Georg Forster*, 154.
4. On the deliberate ambivalence of the title, see Steiner, "Naturerkenntnis," 941; Wuthenow, "Zur Form der Reisebeschreibung"; Saine, *Georg Forster*, 96–97; Uhlig, *Georg Forster*, 262.
5. J. Forster, *Observations*, lxxviii.
6. Steiner, *Georg Forster*, 63. Harpprecht suggests a similar teleology in his chapter title on *Views*: "Unterwegs zur Revolution" (On the way to the Revolution); Harpprecht, *Georg Forster*, 431–64. Goldstein also argues that the work is designed to prepare Forster's fellow citizens for the coming Revolution. *Georg Forster*, 162.
7. Saine, *Georg Forster*, 100–101.
8. Beales, *Joseph II*, 2:503.
9. Blanning, *Joseph II*, 172.
10. Clark, *Iron Kingdom*, 216–18.
11. Umbach, *Federalism*, 165–66.
12. Umbach, *Federalism*, 37; Schmidt, *Geschichte des Alten Reiches*, 295–305; Schmidt, "Goethe: Politisches Denken," 208–11.
13. Blanning, "'That Horrid Electorate."
14. Ibid., 338.
15. Robertson, *Enlightenment*, 82–260.
16. Forster, *Voyage*, 78.
17. Saine, *Georg Forster*, 121.
18. Forster italicizes *public spirit* in English; Habermas credits him with introducing the concept to German readers in his *Parisian Sketches* of 1793, but Forster uses the term already here in *Views*. Habermas, *Structural Transformation*, 93, 101–2. Goldstein calls attention to Forster's influence on Habermas. *Georg Forster*, 142.
19. When Forster was deeply disappointed with Goethe's *Groß-Cophta*, a farce about the

French "affair of the diamond necklace," he speculated that Goethe may have been mocking the German public for its failure to appreciate "the beauties of his *Egmont, Tasso*, and *Iphigenie*." To Heyne, April 7, 1792, 17:92.

20. Forster's comment helped to inspire the patriotic effort to complete the church and was one of the reasons that *Views* was Forster's most widely read work in the nineteenth century (Steiner, "Naturerkenntnis," 946–47; Harpprecht, *Georg Forster*, 436–37; Saine, *Georg Forster*, 102).

21. Harpprecht, *Georg Forster*, 205.

22. Cited in Steiner, "Naturerkenntnis," 938.

23. Dohm, *Entwurf einer verbesserten Constitution*, xvi.

24. Ibid., xiii.

25. Ibid., xvi.

26. Ibid., 3.

27. Goethe, *Egmont*, act III, scene 1; Goethe, *Collected Works*, 7:115.

28. In Zantop's words, "the 'black legend' (*la leyenda negra*) is invoked to denounce Spanish cruelties, particularly in the seventeenth and eighteenth centuries" (*Colonial Fantasies*, 219–20).

29. Chakrabarty, "Climate of History"; Boes and Marshall, "Writing the Anthropocene."

30. Ette, *Alexander von Humboldt*; Wulf, *Invention of Nature*.

31. Dohm, *Die Lütticher Revolution im Jahr 1789* appeared in February 1790.

32. As the title indicates, the city's leader combined secular and sacred authority.

33. Dohm, *Die Lütticher Revolution*, 38–39.

34. Ibid., 50.

35. Uhlig, *Georg Forster*, 253–54.

36. Chartier, *Cultural Origins*; Darnton, *Literary Underground*.

37. Goldstein, *Georg Forster*, 164.

38. Ibid., 12–13.

39. Cited from Harpprecht, *Georg Forster*, 360.

40. Ibid., 300.

41. To Heyne, January 9, 1789, 15:240.

42. Blanning, *Joseph II*, 138.

43. Borchmeyer, *Goethe der Zeitbürger*, 95–105.

44. Schiller, *Geschichte des Abfalls der vereinigten Niederlande von der spanischen Regierung*, in *Sämtliche Werke*, 4:27–361, here 35. Hereafter cited in the text.

45. Schiller, "Über Egmont, Trauerspiel von Goethe," in *Sämtliche Werke*, 5:932–42, here 938.

46. Schama, *Patriots and Liberators*, 46.

47. Act V, scene 10; Schiller, *Werke*, 2:213.

48. Pugh, "Enlightenment and Absolutism," 102.

49. Kontje, *Imperial Fictions*, 195–201.

Chapter 5

1. Goethe, *Campaign in France*, in *Collected Works*, 5:619. According to Goldstein, Goethe's unpublished notes suggest that they may have talked about politics after all (*Georg Forster*, 199).

2. *Siege of Mainz*, in *Collected Works*, 5:770.

3. Ibid., 5:771.

4. For detailed accounts of Mainz history and the revolutionary upheavals of the early 1790s, see Blanning, *Reform and Revolution*, and Saine, *Black Bread–White Bread*.

5. *Campaign in France*, 5:652.

6. To Heyne, July 25, 1791, 16:321.

7. To Voss, November 21, 1792, 17:250.

8. To Heyne, July 17, 1792, 17:143.

9. Blanning, *Reform and Revolution*, 46.

10. Forster, "Darstellung der Revolution in Mainz," 10.1:514. Hereafter cited in the text.

11. Tuchman, *Guns*, 1.

12. Clark, *Sleepwalkers*, xxiv–xxvi.

13. R. J. W. Evans, cited in Blanning, *Joseph II*, 17.

14. Blanning, *Joseph II*, 148; Beales, *Joseph II*, 403.

15. Popkin, *New World*, 342, 363, 391. Weber's *Peasants into Frenchman* reveals that the unification of French society was still not complete one hundred years after the Revolution.

16. Goldstein, *Georg Forster*, 96, 200.

17. On Möser's life and works, see Epstein, *Genesis of German Conservatism*, 297–338. On Möser's influence on Goethe's political thought and *Egmont*, see Borchmeyer, *Goethe der Zeitbürger*, 95–105.

18. Blanning, *Reform and Revolution*, 251. Blanning provides a detailed account of the issues at stake in the local dispute and finds "not the slightest whisper of a revolutionary

mood or of opposition based on principle" (249).

19. Ibid., 253.
20. Ibid., 257.
21. Ibid., 258.
22. Ibid., 259–60.
23. To J. R. Forster, September 18, 1790, 16:189–90.
24. To Heyne, Sptember 7, 1790, 16:184.
25. To Voss, October 21, 1792, 17:208.
26. To Heyne, July 30, 1789, 15:319.
27. To Heyne, July 13, 1790, 16:157.
28. "Erinnerungen aus dem Jahr 1790," 8:285–86.
29. To Heyne, December 9, 1790, 16:213.
30. To Heyne, January 1, 1791, 16:222.
31. "Geschichte der Englischen Litteratur vom Jahre 1790," 7:190.
32. "Erinnerungen," 8:280.
33. Forster, "Revolutionen und Gegenrevolutionen aus dem Jahr 1790," 8:257.
34. Uhlig, *Georg Forster*, 288–89.
35. Forster, "Revolutionen," 8:257.
36. To Dohm, April 5, 1791, 16:265.
37. To Heyne, February 21, 1792, 17:46.
38. To Voss, October 2, 1792, 17:189.
39. To Voss, December 21, 1792, 17:279.
40. To Jacobi, November 1, 1789, 15:363.
41. To Heyne, August 30, 1790, 16:176.
42. Blanning, *Reform and Revolution*, 80–81.
43. Ibid., 163–93.
44. Ibid., 272.
45. To Voss, October 21, 1792, 17:209.
46. To Huber, October 24, 1792, 17:214.
47. To Huber, October 25, 1792, 17:218.
48. To Huber, October 26, 1792, 17:220.
49. Harpprecht, *Georg Forster*, 505–6.
50. See chapter 2. Forster outlines his objections in a long letter to Voss of November 21, 1792, 17:248–54.
51. To Voss, November 10, 1792, 17:240.
52. To Voss, November 21, 1792, 17:252.
53. "Über das Verhältniss der Mainzer gegen die Franken," 10.1:13.
54. Harpprecht, *Georg Forster*, 520.
55. Blanning, *Reform and Revolution*, 300.
56. To Huber, December 4, 1792, 17:257.
57. To Therese, January 28, 1793, 17:322.
58. "Darstellung der Revolution," 10.1:557.

59. Harpprecht, *Georg Forster*, 516–17; Uhlig, *Georg Forster*, 302–3. Goldstein notes that four brave souls actually did sign the black book (*Georg Forster*, 193).
60. Blanning, *Mainz*, 295–98.
61. Goethe, *Siege of Mainz*, in *Collected Works* 5:768.
62. Harpprecht, *Georg Forster*, 511; Uhlig, *Georg Forster*, 311; Blanning, *French Revolution*, 272.
63. Ibid., 82–134.
64. Blanning, *Reform and Revolution*, 282.
65. Blanning, *French Revolution*, 176.
66. Ibid., 319.
67. Uhlig, *Georg Forster*, 316.
68. To Huber, December 28, 1792, 17:288.
69. To Therese, March 21, 1973, 17:334.
70. To Therese, March 31, 1993, 17:336.
71. To Therese, August 21, 1793, 17:426.
72. Uhlig, *Georg Forster*, 332, 334.
73. To Therese, August 26, 1793, 17:431.
74. To Therese, May 4, 1793, 17:351.
75. To Therese, November 6, 1793, 17:463.
76. To Therese, March 31, 1793, 17:337.
77. To Therese, April 16, 1793, 17:334.
78. To Therese, April 27, 1793, 17:349.
79. To Therese, May 16, 1793, 17:354.
80. To Therese, June 26, 1793, 17:376.
81. To Therese, April 13, 1793, 17:342.
82. To Therese, April 16, 1793, 17:344.
83. To Therese, October 8, 1793, 17:459.
84. To Therese, April 5, 1793, 17:338.
85. To Therese, June 10, 1793, 17:364.
86. To Therese, October 24, 1793, 17:461.
87. To Therese, December 14, 1793, 17:488.
88. To Therese, November 27, 1793, 17:480.
89. To Therese, December 28, 1793, 17:498.
90. To Therese, December 2, 1793, 17:483.
91. To Therese, April 16, 1793, 17:345.
92. To Therese, September 25, 1793, 17:448.
93. To Jacobi, January 2, 1789, 15:231.
94. "Darstellung der Revolution," 10.1:550.
95. "Über die Beziehung der Staatskunst auf das Glück der Menschheit," 10.1:582.
96. Goldstein, *Georg Forster*, 222–23.
97. Büchner, *Danton's Death*, act I, scene 5, 19.
98. "Parisische Umrisse," 10.1:602.
99. Popkin, *New World Begins*, 342.
100. Herder, *Ideen*, in *Werke*, 6:620.

BIBLIOGRAPHY

Primary Sources

Berghahn, Klaus L., ed. *Briefwechsel zwischen Schiller und Körner*. Munich: Winkler, 1973.

Bougainville, Louis-Antoine de. *Voyage autour du monde par la frégate du Roi La Boudeuse et la flute L'Étoile*. Paris: Gallimard, 1982.

Büchner, Georg. *Danton's Death*. In *Georg Büchner, Complete Plays and Prose*, translated by Carl Richard Mueller, 1–71. New York: Hill and Wang, 1963.

Cook, James. *The Journals of Captain James Cook on His Voyages of Discovery*. Edited from the original manuscripts by J. C. Beaglehole. Vol. 2, *The Voyage of the Resolution and Adventure, 1772–1775*. Cambridge: Cambridge University Press, 1961. Vol. 3, part 1, *The Voyage of the Resolution and Discovery, 1776–1780*. Cambridge: Cambridge University Press, 1967.

Dohm, Christian Wilhelm von. *Entwurf einer verbesserten Constitution der Kaiserlichen freyen Reichsstadt Aachen*. Frankfurt: n.p., 1790.

———. *Die Lütticher Revolution im Jahr 1789 und das Benehmen seiner königlichen Majestät von Preussen bei derselben*. Berlin: Decker und Sohn, 1790.

Ferguson, Adam. *An Essay on the History of Civil Society*. Dublin: Grierson, 1767.

Forster, Georg. *Reise um die Welt: Illustriert von eigener Hand*. With a biographical essay by Klaus Harpprecht and an afterword by Frank Vorpahl. Frankfurt am Main: Eichborn, 2007.

———. *A Reply to Mr. Wales's Remarks*. In George Forster, *A Voyage Round the World*, edited by Nicholas Thomas and Oliver Berghof, 754–83. Honolulu: University of Hawai'i Press, 2000.

———. *A Voyage Round the World*. 2 vols, continuous pagination. Edited by Nicholas Thomas and Oliver Berghof. Honolulu: University of Hawai'i Press, 2000.

———. *Werke: Sämtliche Schriften, Tagebücher, Briefe*. Edited by Deutsche Akademie der Wissenschaften zu Berlin, Institut für Deutsche Sprache und Literatur. 18 volumes. Berlin: Akademie, 1958–.

Forster, Johann Reinhold. *Observations Made During a Voyage Round the World*. Edited by Nicholas Thomas, Harriet Guest, and Michael Dettelbach, with a linguistics appendix by Karl H. Rensch. Honolulu: University of Hawai'i Press, 1996.

Goethe, Johann Wolfgang von. *Campaign in France, 1792. Siege of Mainz*. Edited and translated by Thomas P. Saine. In *Goethe's Collected Works*, edited by Thomas P. Saine and Jeffrey L. Sammons, 5:607–776. New York: Suhrkamp, 1987.

———. *Egmont: A Tragedy*. Translated by Michael Hamburger. In *Goethe's Collected Works*, edited by Thomas P. Saine and Jeffrey L. Sammons, 7:83–151. New York: Suhrkamp, 1988.

———. *Essays on Art and Literature*. Translated by Ellen von Nardroff and Ernest H. von Nardroff. In *Goethe's Collected Works*, edited by John Gearey, 3. New York: Suhrkamp, 1986.

———. *Faust I & II*. Edited and translated by Stuart Atkins. In *Goethe's Collected Works*, vol. 2, edited by

Thomas P. Saine and Jeffrey L. Sammons. New York: Suhrkamp, 1984.
———. *Gedichte 1756–1799*. Edited by Karl Eibl. Berlin: Deutscher Klassiker Verlag, 2010.
———. *The Sorrows of Young Werther*. Translated by Victor Lange and Judith Ryan. In *Goethe's Collected Works*, edited by David Wellbery, 11:1–87. New York: Suhrkamp, 1988.
———. *Werke*. Edited by Herbert von Einem, Wolfgang Kayser, Dorothea Kuhn, Josef Kunz, Waltraud Loos, Hans Joachim Schrimpf, Erich Trunz, and Rike Wankmüller. 14 vols. Hamburg: Wegner, 1948–60.
Hardenberg, Friedrich von [Novalis, pseud.]. *Schriften*. Edited by Paul Kluckhohn and Richard Samuel. 2nd rev. ed., 1960. 4 vols. Reprint: Stuttgart: Kohlhammer, 1977.
Heine, Heinrich. *Germany: A Winter Tale*. Translated by Edgar Alfred Bowring. Bilingual edition. New York: Mondial, 2007.
Herder, Johann Gottfried. *Another Philosophy of History and Selected Political Writings*. Translated by Ioannis D. Evrigenis and Daniel Pellerin. Indianapolis: Hackett, 2004.
———. *Werke in zehn Bänden*. Edited by Martin Bollacher. Frankfurt am Main: Deutscher Klassiker Verlag, 1985–2000.
Hölderlin, Friedrich. *Hyperion, or the Hermit in Greece*. Translated by Willard R. Trask. New York: Ungar, 1965.
Home, Henry (Lord Kames). *Six Sketches of the History of Man* (1774). Philadelphia: Bell, 1776.
Humboldt, Alexander von. *Views of Nature*. Edited by Stephen T. Jackson and Laura Dassow Walls, translated by Mark W. Person. Chicago: University of Chicago Press, 2014.
Kant, Immanuel. "Bestimmung des Begriffs einer Menschenrasse." *Schriften zur Anthropologie, Geschichtsphilosophie, Politik und Pädagogik I*. In Kant, *Werkausgabe*, edited by Wilhelm Weischedel, 11:65–102. Frankfurt am Main: Suhrkamp, 1968.
———. "Von den verschiedenen Rassen der Menschen." *Schriften zur Anthropologie, Geschichtsphilosophie, Politik und Pädagogik I*. In Kant, *Werkausgabe*, edited by Wilhelm Weischedel, 11: 9–30. Frankfurt am Main: Suhrkamp, 1968.
Locke, John. *Two Treatises of Government*. Edited by Peter Laslett. Cambridge: Cambridge University Press, 1988.
Meiners, Christoph. *Grundriß der Geschichte der Menschheit*. 2nd ed. Lemgo: Meyer, 1793.
———. "Über die Rechtmässigkeit des Negern-Handels." *Göttingisches historisches Magazin* 2 (1788): 398–416.
Millar, John. *Observations Concerning the Distinction of Ranks in Society* (1771). 2nd ed. London: Murray, 1773.
Schiller, Friedrich. *On the Aesthetic Education of Man in a Series of Letters*. Translated by Reginald Snell. New York: Ungar, 1965.
———. *Sämtliche Werke*. 5 vols. Edited by Gerhard Fricke and Herbert G. Göpfert. Munich: Hanser, 1980.
Schlegel, Friedrich. "Georg Forster: Fragment einer Charakteristik der deutschen Klassiker." In *Kritische Friedrich-Schlegel-Ausgabe*, edited by Hans Eichner, 2: 78–99. Zurich: Thomas, 1967.
Schleiermacher, Friedrich. "Ueber die verschiedenen Methoden des Übersetzens." In *Das Problem des Übersetzens*, edited by Hans Joachim Störig, 38–69. Stuttgart: Goverts, 1963.
Soemmerring, Samuel Thomas. *Über die körperliche Verschiedenheit des Mohren vom Europäer*. Mainz: n.p., 1784.
Wales, William. *Remarks on Mr. Forster's Account of Captain Cook's Last Voyage Round the World, in the Years 1772, 1773, 1774, and 1775*. London: Nourse, 1778. In George Forster, *A Voyage Round the World*, edited by Nicholas Thomas and Oliver

Berghof, 2:698–753. Honolulu: University of Hawai'i Press, 2000.

Secondary Sources

Abrams, M. H. *Natural Supernaturalism: Tradition and Revolution in Romantic Literature*. New York: Norton, 1971.

Agnani, Sunil M. *Hating Empire Properly: The Two Indies and the Limits of Enlightenment Anticolonialism*. New York: Fordham University Press: 2013.

Agnew, Vanessa. *Enlightenment Orpheus: The Power of Music in Other Worlds*. Oxford: Oxford University Press, 2008.

Anderson, Benedict. *Imagined Communities: Reflections on the Origin and Spread of Nationalism*. Rev. ed. London: Verso, 2006.

Barnard, F. M. *Herder on Nationality, Humanity, and History*. Montreal: McGill-Queen's University Press, 2003.

———. *Herder's Social and Political Thought: From Enlightenment to Nationalism*. Oxford: Oxford University Press, 1965.

Barnouw, Dagmar. "*Eräugnis*: Georg Forster on the Difficulties of Diversity." In *Impure Reason: Dialectic of Enlightenment in Germany*, edited by W. Daniel Wilson and Robert C. Holub, 322–43. Detroit: Wayne State University Press, 1993.

Beaglehole, J. C. *The Life of Captain James Cook*. Stanford: Stanford University Press, 1974.

Beales, Derik. *Joseph II*. Vol. 2, *Against the World, 1780–1790*. Cambridge: Cambridge University Press, 2009.

Becker-Cantarino, Barbara. *Der lange Weg zur Mündigkeit: Frau und Literatur (1500–1800)*. Stuttgart: Metzler, 1987.

Berman, Russell A. *Enlightenment or Empire? Colonial Discourse in German Culture*. Lincoln: University of Nebraska Press, 1998.

Bernal, Martin. *Black Athena: The Afroasiatic Roots of Classical Civilization*. Vol. 1, *The Fabrication of Ancient Greece, 1785–1985*. Rutgers: Rutgers University Press, 1987.

Blackall, Eric A. *The Emergence of German as a Literary Language, 1700–1775*. 2nd ed. Ithaca: Cornell University Press, 1978.

Blackbourn, David. *The Conquest of Nature: Water, Landscape, and the Making of Modern Germany*. New York: Norton, 2006.

Blackbourn, David, and Geoff Eley. *The Peculiarities of German History: Bourgeois Society and Politics in Nineteenth-Century Germany*. Oxford: Oxford University Press, 1984.

Blackwell, Jeannine, and Susanne Zantop, eds. *Bitter Healing: German Women Writers, 1700–1830: An Anthology*. Lincoln: University of Nebraska Press, 1990.

Blanning, T. C. W. *The French Revolution in Germany: Occupation and Resistance in the Rhineland, 1792–1802*. New York: Oxford University Press, 1983.

———. *Joseph II*. London: Longman, 1994.

———. *Reform and Revolution in Mainz, 1743–1803*. Cambridge: Cambridge University Press, 1974.

———. "'That Horrid Electorate' or 'Ma Patrie Germanique'? George II, Hanover, and the Fürstenbund of 1785." *Historical Journal* 20, no. 2 (1977): 311–44.

Boes, Tobias. "*Weltdeutschtum*: On the Notion of a German World Community from Schiller to Thomas Mann." In *German in the World*, edited by James Hodkinson and Benedict Schofield, 58–73. Rochester: Camden House, 2020.

Boes, Tobias, and Kate Marshall. "Writing the Anthropocene: An Introduction." *Minnesota Review* 83 (2014): 60–72.

Bonfiglio, Thomas Paul. *Mother Tongues and Nations: The Invention of the Native Speaker*. New York: De Gruyter, 2010.

Boone, Joseph A., and Nancy J. Vickers. "Introduction: Celebrity Rites." *PMLA* 126, no. 4 (2011): 900–911.

Borchmeyer, Dieter. *Goethe: Der Zeitbürger*. Munich: Hanser, 1999.

———. *Was ist Deutsch? Die Suche einer Nation Nach Sich Selbst*. Berlin: Rowohlt, 2017.

Bovenschen, Silvia. *Die imaginierte Weiblichkeit: Exemplarische Untersuchungen zu kulturgeschichtlichen und literarischen Präsentationsformen des Weiblichen*. Frankfurt am Main: Suhrkamp, 1979.

Braidotti, Rosi. *The Posthuman*. Cambridge: Polity, 2013.

Braudy, Leo. *The Frenzy of Renown: Fame and Its History*. New York: Oxford University Press, 1986.

Brinker-Gabler, Gisela, ed. *Deutsche Literatur von Frauen*. 2 vols. Munich: Beck, 1988.

Buck-Morss, Susan. "Hegel and Haiti." *Critical Inquiry* 26, no. 4 (2000): 821–65.

Bürger, Christa. *Leben Schreiben: Die Klassik, die Romantik und der Ort der Frauen*. Stuttgart: Metzler, 1990.

Butler, E. M. *The Tyranny of Greece over Germany: A Study of the Influence Exercised by Greek Art and Poetry over the Great German Writers of the Eighteenth, Nineteenth, and Twentieth Centuries*. 1935. Reprint, Boston: Beacon, 1958.

Chakrabarty, Dipesh. "The Climate of History." *Critical Inquiry* 35, no. 2 (2009): 197–222.

———. *Provincializing Europe: Postcolonial Thought and Historical Difference*. Princeton: Princeton University Press, 2000.

Chartier, Roger. *The Cultural Origins of the French Revolution*. Translated by Lydia G. Cochrane. Durham: Duke University Press, 1991.

Clark, Christopher. *Iron Kingdom: The Rise and Downfall of Prussia, 1600–1947*. Cambridge, MA: Harvard University Press, 2006.

———. *The Sleepwalkers: How Europe Went to War in 1914*. New York: Harper, 2012.

Crosby, Alfred W. *Ecological Imperialism: The Biological Expansion of Europe, 900–1900*. Cambridge: Cambridge University Press, 2004.

Darnton, Robert. *The Literary Underground of the Old Regime*. Cambridge, MA: Harvard University Press, 1985.

———. "Readers Respond to Rousseau: The Fabrication of Romantic Sensitivity." In Robert Darnton, *The Great Cat Massacre and Other Episodes in French Cultural History*, 215–56. New York: Random House, 1984.

Dening, Greg. *Mr Bligh's Bad Language: Passion, Power and Theatre on the Bounty*. Cambridge: Cambridge University Press, 1992.

Dettelbach, Michael. "'A Kind of Linnaean Being': Forster and Eighteenth-Century Natural History." In Johann Reinhold Forster, *Observations Made During a Voyage Round the World* (1778), edited by Nicholas Thomas, Harriet Guest, and Michael Dettelbach, with a linguistics appendix by Karl H. Rensch, lv–lxxiv. Honolulu: University of Hawai'i Press, 1996.

Diamond, Jared. *Guns, Germs, and Steel: The Fates of Human Societies*. New York: Norton, 1999.

Eibl, Karl. "Kommentar." In Johann Wolfgang Goethe, *Gedichte 1756–1799*, 727–1266. Berlin: Deutscher Klassiker Verlag, 1987. Vol. 1 of Johann Wolfgang Goethe, *Sämtliche Werke, Briefe, Tagebücher und Gespräche*. Berlin: Deutscher Klassiker Verlag, 2010.

Eigen, Sara, and Mark Larrimore, eds. *The German Invention of Race*. Albany: SUNY Press, 2006.

Elias, Norbert. *The Court Society*. Translated by Edmund Jephcott. New York: Pantheon, 1983.

El-Tayeb, Fatima. *European Others: Queering Ethnicity in Postnational Europe*. Minneapolis: University of Minnesota Press, 2011.

Engelsing, Rolf. *Der Bürger als Leser: Lesergeschichte in Deutschland 1500–1800*. Stuttgart: Metzler, 1974.

Enzensberger, Ulrich. *Georg Forster: Ein Leben in Scherben*. Frankfurt am Main: Eichborn, 1996.

Epstein, Klaus. *The Genesis of German Conservatism*. Princeton: Princeton University Press, 1966.

Esleben, Jörg. "Übersetzung als interkulturelle Kommunikation bei Georg Forster." *Georg Forster Studien* 9 (2004): 165–79.

Ette, Ottmar. *Alexander von Humboldt und die Globalisierung*. Frankfurt am Main: Insel, 2009.

———. *TransArea: A Literary History of Globalization*. Place of publication not identified. De Gruyter Mouton, 2016.

———. "Welterleben / Weiterleben: Zur Vektopie bei Georg Forster, Alexander von Humboldt und Adelbert von Chamisso." In *Forster—Humboldt—Chamisso: Weltreisende im Spannungsfeld der Kulturen*, edited by Julian Drews, Ottmar Ette, Tobias Kraft, Barbara Schneider-Kempf, and Jutta Weber, 383–427. Göttingen: V & R unipress, 2017.

Eze, Emmanuel Chukwudi. "Introduction." In *Race and the Enlightenment: A Reader*, edited by Emmanuel Chukwudi Eze, 1–9. Cambridge, MA: Blackwell, 1997.

———, ed. *Race and the Enlightenment: A Reader*. Cambridge, MA: Blackwell, 1997.

Fagot, Pascal. "Polen als Georg Forsters Gegenstück zu Tahiti." *Georg Forster Studien* 11 (2006): 595–610.

Foucault, Michel. "What Is an Author?" In *Language, Counter-Memory, Praxis: Selected Essays and Interviews by Michel Foucault*, edited by Donald F. Bouchard, 113–38. Ithaca: Cornell University Press, 1977.

Geier, Manfred. *Die Brüder Humboldt: Eine Biographie*. Reinbek bei Hamburg: Rowohlt, 2009.

Gervinus, Georg Gottfried. "Johann Georg Forster." In *Georg Forsters Sämmtliche Schriften*, edited by G. G. Gervinus and Therese Forster, 7:1–78. Leipzig: Brockhaus, 1843.

Goldstein, Jürgen. *Georg Forster: Voyager, Naturalist, Revolutionary*. Translated by Anne Janusch. Chicago: University of Chicago Press, 2019.

Gomsu, Joseph. "Georg Forsters Wahrnehmung neuer Welten." *Zeitschrift für Germanistik* 8 (1998): 538–50.

———. "'Über lokale und allgemeine Bildung': Georg Forsters Projekt einer anderen Moderne." *Georg Forster Studien* 11 (2006): 323–34.

Gramling, David. *The Invention of Monolingualism*. New York: Bloomsbury, 2016.

Greenblatt, Stephen. *The Swerve: How the World Become Modern*. New York: Norton, 2011.

Guest, Harriet. "Looking at Women: Forster's Observations in the South Pacific." In Johann Reinhold Forster, *Observations Made During a Voyage Round the World (1778)*, edited by Nicholas Thomas, Harriet Guest, and Michael Dettelbach, with a linguistics appendix by Karl H. Rensch, xli–liv. Honolulu: University of Hawai'i Press, 1996.

Habermas, Jürgen. *The Structural Transformation of the Public Sphere: An Inquiry into a Category of Bourgeois Society*. Translated by Thomas Burger and Frederick Lawrence. Cambridge, MA: MIT Press, 1991.

Harpprecht, Klaus. *Georg Forster oder die Liebe zur Welt: Eine Biographie*. Reinbek bei Hamburg: Rowhlt, 1990.

Haug, Christine. "'Die Arbeit unterhält mich, ohne mich zu ermüden': Georg Forsters Übersetzungsmanufaktur in Mainz in den 1790er Jahren." *Georg Forster Studien* 13 (2008): 99–128.

———. "'Ich sehe mit Verlangen der Stunde entgegen, die mich von

Brod-Arbeit befreien soll': Georg Forster im Beziehungsgeflecht seiner Verleger um 1800." *Georg Forster Studien* 12 (2007): 25–55.

Heinz, Jutta. "Der Weltreisende als Heros der praktischen Urteilskraft: Georg Forsters Cook der Entdecker." *Georg Forster Studien* 20 (2015): 17–32.

Hoare, Michael E. *The Tactless Philosopher: Johann Reinhold Forster (1729–98)*. Melbourne: Hawthorn, 1976.

Hokenson, Jan Walsh, and Marcella Munson. *The Bilingual Text: History and Theory of Literary Self-Translation*. New York: Routledge, 2014.

Japp, Uwe. "Aufgeklärtes Europa und natürliche Südsee: Georg Forsters *Reise um die Welt*." In *Reise und Utopie: Zur Literatur der Spätaufklärung*, edited by Hans Joachim Piechotta, 10–56. Frankfurt am Main: Suhrkamp, 1976.

Kappeler, Floran. "Die globale Revolution: Forster und Haiti." *Georg Forster Studien* 19 (2014): 17–43.

Kaufmann, Hans A. *Nation und Nationalismus in Schillers Entwurf "Deutsche Größe" und im Schauspiel Wilhelm Tell: Zu ihrer kulturpolitischen Funktionalisierung im frühen 20. Jahrhundert*. Frankfurt am Main: Lang, 1993.

Kittler, Friedrich A. *Discourse Networks: 1800/1900*. Translated by Michael Metteer, with Chris Cullens. Stanford: Stanford University Press, 1990.

Kontje, Todd. *German Orientalisms*. Ann Arbor: University of Michigan Press, 2004.

———. *Imperial Fictions: German Literature Before and Beyond the Nation-State*. Ann Arbor: University of Michigan Press, 2018.

Kopp, Kristin. *Germany's Wild East: Constructing Poland as Colonial Space*. Ann Arbor: University of Michigan Press, 2012.

Koselleck, Reinhart. "Einleitung." In *Geschichtliche Grundbegriffe: Historisches Lexikon zur politisch-sozialen Sprache in Deutschland*, edited by Otto Brunner, Werner Conze, and Reinhart Koselleck, 1:xiii–xxvii. Stuttgart: Klett, 1972.

———. *Futures Past: On the Semantics of Historical Time*. Translated by Keith Tribe. New York: Columbia University Press, 2004.

Kramsch, Claire. "The Privilege of the Nonnative Speaker." *PMLA* 112, no. 3 (1997): 359–69.

Kumar, Krishnan. *Visions of Empire: How Five Imperial Regimes Shaped the World*. Princeton: Princeton University Press, 2017.

Kuzniar, Alice A. *Delayed Endings: Nonclosure in Novalis and Hölderlin*. Athens: University of Georgia Press, 1987.

Lamb, Jonathan. *Scurvy: The Disease of Discovery*. Princeton: Princeton University Press, 2017.

Leonhardt, Jürgen. *Latin: Story of a World Language*. Translated by Kenneth Kronenberg. Cambridge, MA: Harvard University Press, 2013.

Livingstone, David N. *Adam's Ancestors: Race, Religion, and the Politics of Human Origins*. Baltimore: Johns Hopkins University Press, 2008.

Lowe, Lisa. *The Intimacies of Four Continents*. Durham: Duke University Press, 2015.

Lubrich, Oliver. "Alexander von Humboldt: Revolutionizing Travel Literature." *Monatshefte* 96 (2004): 360–87.

Lüsebrink, Hans-Jürgen. "Interkulturelle Aneignung und wissenschaftliche Erkenntnis: Zum Zusammenhang von Übersetzung, Rezensionstätigkeit und Erforschung fremder Kulturen im Werk Georg Forsters." *Georg Forster Studien* 19 (2014): 1–13.

———. "Zivilisatorische Gewalt: Zur Wahrnehmung kolonialer Entdeckung und Akkulturation in Georg Forsters Reiseberichten und Rezensionen." *Georg Forster Studien* 8 (2003): 123–38.

Mani, B. Venkat. *Recoding World Literature: Libraries, Print Culture, and*

Germany's Pact with Books. New York: Fordham University Press, 2017.

Marchand, Suzanne L. *German Orientalism in the Age of Empire: Religion, Race, and Scholarship.* Cambridge: Cambridge University Press, 2009.

Mariss, Anne. "Johann Reinhold Forster and the Ship *Resolution* as a Space of Knowledge Production." In *Explorations and Entanglements: Germans in Pacific Worlds from the Early Modern Period to World War I*, edited by Hartmut Berghoff, Frank Biess, and Ulrike Strasser, 127–52. New York: Berghahn, 2019.

Martin, Alison E. "Rerouting the Self: Georg Forster's *Reise um die Welt.*" In *Translating Selves: Experience and Identity between Languages and Literatures*, edited by Paschalis Nikolaou and Maria-Venetia Kyritsi, 155–68. New York: Continuum, 2008.

May, Yomb. "Kultur im Zeichen des Geschlechts: Eine genderorientierte und postkoloniale Lektüre von Georg Forsters *Reise um die Welt.*" *Georg Forster Studien* 13 (2008): 5–20.

———. "Pluralität und Ethos in Georg Forsters Anthropologie." *Georg Forster Studien* 11 (2006): 335–57.

Moorehead, Alan. *The Fatal Impact: The Invasion of the South Pacific, 1767–1840.* New York: Harper & Row, 1966.

Moretti, Franco. *Distant Reading.* New York: Verso, 2013.

Münkler, Herfried. *Imperien: Die Logik der Weltherrschaft vom Alten Rom bis zu den Vereinigten Staaten.* Reinbek bei Hamburg: Rowohlt, 2007.

Muthu, Sankar. *Enlightenment Against Empire.* Princeton: Princeton University Press, 2003.

Neumann, Michael. "Philosophische Nachrichten aus der Südsee: Georg Forsters *Reise um die Welt.*" In *Der ganze Mensch: Anthropologie und Literatur im 18. Jahrhundert*, edited by Hans-Jürgen Schings, 517–44. DFG-Symposion 1992. Stuttgart: Metzler, 1992.

Norberg, Jakob. "German Literary Studies and the Nation." *German Quarterly* 91 (2018): 1–17.

Noyes, John K. *Herder: Aesthetics against Imperialism.* Toronto: University of Toronto Press, 2015.

Obeyesekere, Gananath. *The Apotheosis of Captain Cook: European Mythmaking in the Pacific.* Princeton: Princeton University Press, 1992.

Peitsch, Helmut. *Georg Forster: A Critical History of His Reception.* New York: Lang, 2001.

Piper, Andrew. *Dreaming in Books: The Making of the Bibliographic Imagination in the Romantic Age.* Chicago: University of Chicago Press, 2009.

Poliakov, Leon. *The Aryan Myth: A History of Racist and Nationalist Ideas in Europe.* Translated by E. Howard. London: Sussex University Press, 1974.

Popkin, Jeremy D. *A New World Begins: The History of the French Revolution.* New York: Basic Books, 2019.

Pratt, Mary Louise. *Imperial Eyes: Travel Writing and Transculturation.* London: Routledge, 1992.

Prinz, Alois. *Die Lebensgeschichte des Georg Forster.* Frankfurt am Main: Insel, 2008.

Pugh, David V. "Enlightenment and Absolutism in Schiller's Classical Drama." In *A Reassessment of Weimar Classicism*, edited by Gerhart Hoffmeister, 96–116. Lewiston: Mellen, 1996.

Rabinow, Paul. "Representations are Social Facts: Modernity and Post-Modernity in Anthropology." In *Writing Culture: The Poetics and Politics of Ethnography*, edited by James Clifford and George E. Marcu, 234–61. Berkeley: University of California Press, 1986.

Reed, T. J. "Replacing Ancient Gods: Weimar Classicism and After." In *The Reception of Classical Antiquity in German Literature*, edited by Anne Simon and Katie Fleming, 64–81. Munich: Iudicium, 2013.

Roach, Joseph. *It*. Ann Arbor: University of Michigan Press, 2007.

Robertson, Ritchie. *The Enlightenment: The Pursuit of Happiness, 1680–1790*. New York: HarperCollins, 2021.

Safranski, Rüdiger. *Goethe: Kunstwerk des Lebens. Biographie*. Munich: Hanser, 2013.

———. *Schiller, oder Die Erfindung des Deutschen Idealismus: Biographie*. Munich, Hanser, 2004.

Saine, Thomas P. *Black Bread–White Bread: German Intellectuals and the French Revolution*. Columbia, SC: Camden House, 1988.

———. *Georg Forster*. New York: Twayne, 1972.

Sanches, Manuela Ribeiro. "Dunkelheit und Aufklärung—Rasse und Kultur: Erfahrung und Macht in Forsters Auseinandersetzungen mit Kant und Meiners." *Georg Forster Studien* 8 (2003): 53–82.

Schama, Simon. *Patriots and Liberators: Revolution in the Netherlands, 1780–1813*. 1977. Reprint New York: Vintage, 1992.

Scheuer, Helmut. "Apostel der Völkerfreiheit oder 'Vaterlandsverräter'? Georg Forster und die Nachwelt." *Georg Forster Studien* 1 (1997): 1–18.

Schmidt, Georg. "Friedrich Meineckes Kulturnation: Zum historischen Kontext nationaler Ideen in Weimar-Jena um 1800." *Historische Zeitschrift* 284, no. 3 (2007): 597–621.

———. *Geschichte des Alten Reiches: Staat und Nation in der Frühen Neuzeit 1495–1806*. Munich: Beck, 1999.

———. "Goethe: Politisches Denken und regional orientierte Praxis im Alten Reich." *Goethe Jahrbuch* (1995): 197–212.

———. "Staat, Nation und Universalismus: Weimar-Jena als Zentrum deutscher Identitätssuche im späten Alten Reich." In *Identitäten: Erfahrungen und Fiktionen um 1800*, edited by Gonthier-Louis Fink and Andreas Klinger, 33–70. Frankfurt am Main: Lang, 2004.

Schnickmann, Heiko. "Hunde, Schweine und Pferde: Tiere als Mittel des Interkulturellen im Umfeld der Cookschen Reisen." *Georg Forster Studien* 19 (2014): 175–89.

Sedgwick, Eve Kosofsky. *Epistemology of the Closet*. Berkeley: University of California Press, 1990.

Seyhan, Azade. *Writing Outside the Nation*. Princeton: Princeton University Press, 2001.

Shannon, Laurie. "The Eight Animals in Shakespeare; or, Before the Human." *PMLA* 124, no. 2 (2009): 472–79.

Sheehan, James J. *German History, 1770–1866*. Oxford: Clarendon, 1989.

Shell, Susan M. "Kant's Conception of a Human Race." In *The German Invention of Race*, edited by Sara Eigen and Mark Larrimore, 55–72. Albany: SUNY Press, 2006.

Shevelow, Kathryn. *For the Love of Animals: The Rise of the Animal Protection Movement*. London: Holt, 2009.

Snow, C. P. *The Two Cultures*. Cambridge: Cambridge University Press, 2012.

Spencer, Vicki A. *Herder's Political Thought: A Study of Language, Culture, and Community*. Toronto: University of Toronto Press, 2012.

Steiner, Gerhard. "Anmerkungen." In Georg Forster, *Werke in vier Bänden*, edited by Gerhard Steiner, 3:777–851. Reprint Leipzig: Insel, no date listed.

———. *Georg Forster*. Stuttgart: Metzler, 1977.

———. "Naturerkenntnis und Praktische Humanität: Georg Forsters kleine Schriften zur Naturgeschichte, Länder- und Völkerkunde und die Ansichten vom Niederrhein." In Georg Forster, *Werke in Vier Bänden*, edited by Gerhard Steiner, 2:907–52. Reprint Leipzig: Insel, no date listed.

Strasser, Ulrike, Frank Biess, and Hartmut Berghoff. "Introduction: German Histories and Pacific Histories." In *Explorations and Entanglements: Germans in Pacific Worlds from the*

Early Modern Period to World War I, edited by Hartmut Berghoff, Frank Biess, and Ulrike Strasser, 1–32. New York: Berghahn, 2019.

Tang, Chenxi. *The Geographic Imagination of Modernity: Geography, Literature, and Philosophy in German Romanticism*. Stanford: Stanford University Press, 2008.

Tautz, Birgit. *Reading and Seeing Ethnic Differences in the Enlightenment: From China to Africa*. New York: Palgrave, 2007.

———. "Revolution, Abolition, Aesthetic Sublimation: German Responses to News from France in the 1790s." In *(Re-)Writing the Radical: Enlightenment, Revolution and Cultural Transfer in 1790s Germany, Britain and France*, edited by Maike Oergel, 72–87. Berlin: De Gruyter, 2012.

———. *Translating the World: Toward a New History of German Literature Around 1800*. University Park: Pennsylvania State University Press, 2018.

Thomas, Nicholas, and Oliver Berghof. "Introduction." In George Forster, *A Voyage Round the World*, edited by Nicholas Thomas and Oliver Berghof, xix–xliii. Honolulu: University of Hawai'i Press, 2000.

———. "Notes." In George Forster, *A Voyage Round the World*, edited by Nicholas Thomas and Oliver Berghof, 425–75, 811–34. Honolulu: University of Hawai'i Press, 2000.

Thomas, Nicholas, Harriet Guest, and Michael Dettelbach. "Notes." In Johann Reinhold Forster, *Observations Made During a Voyage Round the World*, edited by Nicholas Thomas, Harriet Guest, and Michael Dettelbach, 401–32. Honolulu: University of Hawai'i Press, 1996.

Touaillon, Christine. *Der deutsche Frauenroman des 18. Jahrhunderts*. Vienna: Braumüller, 1919.

Trabant, Jürgen. "Herder and Language." In *A Companion to the Works of Johann Gottfried Herder*, edited by Hans Adler and Wulf Koepke, 117–39. Rochester: Camden House, 2009.

Tuchman, Barbara W. *The Guns of August*. New York: Ballantine, 1962.

Uhlig, Ludwig. *Georg Forster: Lebensabenteuer eines gelehrten Weltbürgers: 1754–1794*. Göttingen: Vandenhoeck & Ruprecht, 2004.

———. "Georg Forsters Anthropologie in wechselnden Umfeldern." *Georg Forster Studien* 10 (2005): 283–303.

———. "Der polyglotte Forster: Fremdsprachige Bekenntnisse im Zusammenhang seines Lebens." *Georg Forster Studien* 18 (2013): 135–78.

———. "Theoretical or Conjectural History: Georg Forsters *Voyage Round the World* im zeitgenössischen Kontext." *Germanisch-Romanische Monatsschrift*, Neue Folge 53.4 (2003): 399–414.

———. "Zwischen Politik, Belletristik und Literaturwissenschaft: Georg Forsters Bild in der Kulturtradition des 19. Jahrhunderts." *Georg Forster Studien* 6 (2001): 1–24.

Umbach, Maiken. *Federalism and Enlightenment in Germany, 1740–1806*. London: Hambledon, 2000.

Venuti, Lawrence. *The Translator's Invisibility: A History of Translation*. New York: Routledge, 1995.

Vorpahl, Frank. *Der Welterkunder: Auf der Suche nach Georg Forster*. Berlin: Galiani, 2018.

Walkowitz, Rebecca L. *Born Translated: The Contemporary Novel in an Age of World Literature*. New York: Columbia University Press, 2015.

Walls, Laura Dassow. *The Passage to Cosmos: Alexander von Humboldt and the Shaping of America*. Chicago: Chicago University Press, 2009.

Weber, Eugen. *Peasants into Frenchmen: The Modernization of Rural France, 1870–1914*. Stanford: Stanford University Press, 1976.

Weisinger, Kenneth D. *The Classical Façade: A Nonclassical Reading of*

Goethe's Classicism. University Park: Pennsylvania State University Press, 1988.

West, Hugh. "The Limits of Enlightenment Anthropology: Georg Forster and the Tahitians." *History of European Ideas* 10, no. 2 (1989): 147–60.

Whaley, Joachim. *Germany and the Holy Roman Empire.* Vol. 1, *Maximilian I to the Peace of Westphalia, 1493–1648.* Oxford: Oxford University Press, 2012.

Wilke, Sabine. *German Culture and the Modern Environmental Imagination: Narrating and Depicting Nature.* Leiden, Netherlands: Brill, 2015.

Williamson, George S. *The Longing for Myth in Germany: Religion and Aesthetic Culture from Romanticism to Nietzsche.* Chicago: University of Chicago Press, 2004.

Wilson, Jason. "Introduction." In Alexander von Humboldt, *Personal Narrative of a Journey to the Equinoctial Regions of the New Continent*, abridged and translated by Jason Wilson, xxxv–lxiv. London: Penguin, 1995.

Wilson, Peter H. *Heart of Europe: A History of the Holy Roman Empire.* Cambridge, MA: Harvard University Press, 2016.

Withey, Lynne. *Voyages of Discovery: Captain Cook and the Exploration of the Pacific.* Berkeley: University of California Press, 1987.

Wittkop, Gregor. "Deutsche Größe: Misstrauische Notizen zu einem Gedichtentwurf Friedrich Schillers." In *Friedrich Schiller*, edited by Heinz Ludwig Arnold and Mirjam Springer, 32–39. Munich: text + kritik, 2005.

Wolin, Richard. *The Seduction of Unreason: The Intellectual Romance with Fascism. From Nietzsche to Postmodernism.* Princeton: Princeton University Press, 2004.

Woodmansee, Martha. *The Author, Art, and the Market: Rereading the History of Aesthetics.* New York: Columbia University Press, 1994.

Wulf, Andrea. *The Invention of Nature: Alexander von Humboldt's New World.* New York: Vintage, 2015.

Wuthenow, Rainer. "Zur Form der Reisebeschreibung: Georg Forsters Ansichten vom Niederrhein." *Lessing Yearbook* 1 (1969): 234–54.

Yildiz, Yasemin. *Beyond the Mother Tongue: The Postmonolingual Condition.* New York: Fordham University Press, 2012.

Young, Robert J. C. *Colonial Desire: Hybridity in Theory, Culture and Race.* London: Routledge, 1995.

———. *White Mythologies: Writing History and the West.* 2nd ed. London: Routledge, 2004.

Zammito, John H. *Kant, Herder, and the Birth of Anthropology.* Chicago: Chicago University Press, 2002.

Zantop, Susanne. *Colonial Fantasies: Conquest, Family, and Nation in Precolonial Germany, 1770–1870.* Durham, NC: Duke University Press, 1997.

Zhang, Chunjie. *Transculturality and German Discourse in the Age of European Colonialism.* Evanston, IL: Northwestern University Press, 2017.

INDEX

Abrams, M. H., 98, 133
Adorno, Theodor, 7, 22
Age of Goethe, 12, 23, 29, 37, 42, 172, 174
    aesthetics of genius, 18–19, 29, 36–38,
        40–42, 45, 106, 174
Agnani, Sunil M., 182n76
Agnew, Vanessa, 4
Anderson, Benedict, 18, 40
Anthropocene, 19, 127
Archenholz, Johann Wilhelm von, 11, 35

Banks, Joseph, 30
Barnouw, Dagmar, 91
Becher, Johann, 11
Berghof, Oliver, 177n45, 178n8, 179n61
Berman, Russell, 8, 46
Biester, Johann Erich, 97
Blackall, Eric A., 176n79
Blackbourn, David, 65–66
Blanning, Timothy, 17, 110, 117, 148–49, 160, 183n18
Bligh, William, 26, 52, 61, 83, 150, 178n, 179n
Blumenbach, Johann Friedrich, 85, 86
Böhmer-Schelling, Caroline, 38, 143
Boie, Christian, 177n64
Bonfiglio, Thomas, 28
Boone, Joseph A., 5
Borchmeyer, Dieter, 109
Bougainville, Louis-Antoine de, 1, 7, 72
    Voyage autour du mond, 26
Braidotti, Rosi, 8
Braudy, Leo, 5
Brunswick, Karl Wilhelm Ferdinand, Duke of, 146, 165–66
Büchner, Georg, 168
Buck-Morss, Susan, 11
Buffon, Georges-Louis Leclerc comte de, 1, 5
Bürger, Christa, 36
Burke, Edmond, 104, 182n76
    Reflections on the Revolution in France, 104, 134, 151
Butler, E. M., 94
Byron, Lord George Gordon, 127

Chakrabarty, Dipesh, 8–9
Chamisso, Adelbert von, 11

Charlemagne, 13, 122
Clark, Christopher, 14, 146
Coleridge, Samuel Taylor, 63, 179n61
Columbus, Christopher, 7, 51–52
Cook, James, 1, 3, 7, 9, 10, 17, 19, 25, 26, 30–31, 34, 36, 43–46, 51–53, 57–64, 66–69, 71–73, 76, 79–84, 86, 98, 114, 127, 134–37, 170, 172–74, 175n42, 177n40, 178n31, 179n33
    Voyage Towards the South Pole, A, 3, 31
Creuzer, Friedrich, 106
Crosby, Alfred, 62
Custine, Adam Philippe comte de, 22, 150, 153, 156, 160, 165–66

Darwin, Charles, 179n75
Declaration of Independence, 120
Dening, Greg, 73, 178n33
Descartes, René, 65
Desmoulins, Camille, 131
Diamond, Jared, 179n55
Diderot, Denis, 83
Dohm, Christian von, 122–25, 148
    Draft of an Improved Constitution (Entwurf einer verbesserten Constitution), 122–23
    Liège Revolution of 1789 (Die Lütticher Revolution), 128–30

Eigen, Sara, 180n19
Elias, Norbert, 73
Engels, Friedrich, 82
Engelsing, Rolf, 177n67
Enzensberger, Ulrich, 176n1, 181n32, 181n40, 181n62
Epstein, Klaus, 96
Erthal, Friedrich Karl Freiherr von, Archbishop and Elector of Mainz, 131, 144–45, 148–50, 155, 165
Ette, Ottmar, 7, 10
Eze, Emmanuel Chukwudi, 180n11

Fanon, Frantz, 7
Ferguson, Adam,
    Essay on the History of Civil Society, 45–46, 49

Fichte, Johann Gottlieb
  Addresses to the German Nation (*Reden an die deutsche Nation*), 28
Forkel-Liebeskind, Meta, 38–39, 143
Forster, Georg (George)
  and ancient Greece, 19–20, 86–87, 94–99, 120–21, 125, 171
  as book reviewer, 12, 20, 29, 34, 87, 88, 115
  as cosmopolitan, 2, 6–7, 12, 18, 20, 23, 45, 107, 174
  as ecological thinker, 12, 19, 70, 99, 126, 172, 174
  and Enlightenment, 18–19, 22, 37, 45–46, 92, 93, 97, 164, 167, 171, 172, 174; Scottish Enlightenment, 45–46, 49, 7
  and Eurocentrism, 20, 46, 71, 103, 125–26, 171
  fame of, 1–5, 84, 122, 143, 171
  and French Revolution, 17–18, 150–55, 162–70, 171–73
  and India, 26, 87, 98, 100, 104–7, 111, 161, 172
  and multilingualism, 6, 18–19, 23, 26–30, 33, 37, 103, 173–74
  national identity of, 6, 24–27, 161, 174
  and pessimism, 20, 46, 80–82, 86, 127, 134–35, 172–73
  and Poland, 6, 24, 86, 93–94, 131
  as political activist, 7, 12, 17, 115, 142, 171, 174
  and publishers, 10, 25, 33, 39–42, 105, 156, 171
  and religious dogmatism, 86, 96–97, 119–21, 135, 142, 154, 165, 171, 172, 174
  as university librarian, 20, 34, 37, 84, 115, 144
  as translator, 5, 12, 19, 29–30, 32–42, 45, 51, 84, 87–88, 103, 105, 115, 150, 161, 171, 174
Forster, Georg (George), works of
  "Breadfruit Tree, The" (Der Brodbaum), 61–62
  "Cook, the Discoverer" (Cook, der Entdecker), 51–58, 73, 80, 99, 134–35, 137
  "Depiction of the Revolution in Mainz" (Darstellung der Revolution in Mainz), 163–67, 173
  "History of English Literature" (Geschichte der Englischen Litteratur), 35, 151
  "Look into Nature as a Whole, A" (Ein Blick in das Ganze der Natur), 46–51, 56–57, 60, 82, 173
  "Memories of the Year 1790" (Erinnerungen aus dem Jahr 1790), 151, 154
  "New Holland and the British Colony" (Neuholland und die brittische Colonie), 49–51, 57
  "On Delicacies" (Über Leckereyen), 99–100
  "On Local and Universal Development" (Über lokale und allgemeine Bildung), 100–104, 114–15
  "On Proselytizing" (Über Proselytenmacherei), 97, 154
  "On the Relationship of Statesmanship to Human Happiness" (Über die Beziehung der Staatskunst auf das Glück der Menschheit), 164, 167–69
  "Parisian Sketches" (Parisische Umrisse), 164, 169–70
  "Preface to Sakuntala" (Vorrede zur Sakontala), 18, 87, 106–7, 111–12, 115
  "Relationship of the Citizens of Mainz to the French" ("Verhältniß der Mainzer gegen die Franken"), 157–58, 173
  "Review of C. Meiners" (Rezension zu C. Meiners), 90
  "Revolutions and Counter-Revolutions" (Revolutionen und Gegenrevolutionen), 153–55
  "Schiller's 'Gods of Greece'" (Götter Griechenlands), 95–96
  Short Works (*Kleine Schriften*), 24, 34
  "Something More About Human Races" (Noch etwas über die Menschenraßen), 87–93
  Views of the Lower Rhine (*Ansichten vom Niederrhein*), 12, 20–21, 24, 34, 39–40, 97, 102, 113–42, 148, 150, 154, 164, 173, 183n; and climate change, 126–27, 142, 173; and Enlightened absolutism (despotism), 116–18, 135–42, 147–48, 154–55; and Enlightenment, 114–15, 119–22, 125, 130, 133–36, 142; and Eurocentrism, 125–26; and global trade, 114, 122, 124–26, 142; and pessimism, 134–35, 142; and religious dogmatism, 119–21, 135–36, 140–42
  Voyage Round the World, A (*Reise um die Welt*), 3, 19, 21, 24, 30–33, 43–46, 58–82, 84, 92, 97, 113–14, 127, 173; and civilizing mission, 19, 50–52, 58, 66–67, 71, 79, 82, 92, 114, 171–73; critique of, 18–19, 53–57, 71–80, 172–73; status of

women, 72, 74–78; and cultural pessimism, 46, 57–58, 80–82, 172; and Enlightenment optimism, 19, 46, 52–53, 55–58, 66, 77, 82, 173; and Eurocentrism, 45–46, 171; and indigenous peoples, 66–71, 69, 70, 77–80, 83–84, 172; and nature, 19, 46–50, 57–60, 62–66, 71, 81–84, 170–72; social hierarchies aboard ship (crew), 19, 43–44, 51, 59, 61, 63–64, 66, 72–75, 78, 127, 178n31
Forster, Johann Reinhold, 1, 2, 3, 6, 9, 11, 24, 30–33, 35, 39, 59, 62, 63, 73, 75, 76, 90–91, 96, 149
  Observations, 44, 49–50, 114, 179n63, 180n87
Forster-Huber (Heyne), Therese, 38, 42, 93–95, 105, 143, 160–63, 178n30
  Seldorf Family, The (Die Familie Seldorf), 143
Foucault, Michel, 7, 29
Francis II, Holy Roman Emperor, 145
Franklin, Benjamin, 1
Frederick II 'the great', king of Prussia, 13–14, 117–18, 168
Frederick William II, king of Prussia, 95–96
French Revolution, 21–22, 109, 116, 129, 131, 134, 142, 144, 147, 148–49, 155–70
  and ancient Rome, 162, 165, 169–70
  and centralization, 147, 160, 169–70
  as disease, 152–56, 166–67
  and Enlightenment, 22, 152, 156
  as force of nature, 12, 133–34, 152, 155, 163, 168
  and imperialism, 17–18, 148, 158–60, 170
  and local disturbances, 148–50, 154
  and nation-state, 16–17, 109, 146
  and public sphere, 169–70
  relation to Germany, 10–12, 104, 107–12, 152–53, 155, 159, 170
  and universal rights, 17, 154
Friedrich, Caspar David, 60
Furneaux, Tobias, 31

Gatterer, Johann Christoph, 85
George III, king of England, 1, 114, 117–18, 142, 146
Gervinus, Georg Gottfried, 2, 175n5
Goethe, Johann Wolfgang von, 1–5, 6, 20, 22, 23, 29–30, 35, 36, 41–42, 60, 84, 86, 94, 95, 98, 110–11, 117–18, 140, 143–45, 147, 155, 159, 175n5
  Egmont, 21, 116, 123, 139, 141, 147, 183n19

Faust, 47, 56–57, 135, 142, 173
Götz von Berlichingen, 4
Groß-Cophta, 182–83n19
Hermann and Dorothea, 42
Iphigenia, 120, 183n19
"Literary Sansculottism," 6
"On the Lake" (Auf dem See), 48–49
"Prometheus," 121, 164, 173
Sorrows of Young Werther, 4, 46–47, 82
Torquato Tasso, 183n19
Wilhelm Meister's Travels (Wanderjahre), 30
"Xenia," 2, 175n5
Goldstein, Jürgen, 12, 46, 73, 114, 133–34, 147, 152, 168, 178n3, 182n6, 182n18, 183n1, 184n59
Gomsu, Joseph, 181n73
Görres, Joseph, 106
Gramling, David, 176n79
Greenblatt, Stephen, 47–48
Grimm, Jacob, 28
Günderrode, Karoline von, 42

Habermas, Jürgen, 169, 182n18
Haller, Albrecht von, 48
  "Alps, The" (Die Alpen), 48
Hardenberg, Friedrich von (Novalis), 20, 106, 111
  "Christianity or Europe" (Die Christenheit oder Europa), 107, 109
Harpprecht, Klaus, 33, 72, 122, 137, 156, 176n17, 182n6
Hastings, Warren, 104, 182n76
Haug, Christine, 37
Hawkesworth, John, 31
Heine, Heinrich, 109–11
  Germany: A Winter's Tale (Deutschland. Ein Wintermärchen), 109
Heraclitus, 47
Herder, Johann Gottfried, 1, 3, 14–17, 23, 29, 51, 84, 86, 88, 94–96, 100, 102, 140, 172, 178n25, 181n44
  Another Philosophy of History (Auch eine Philosophie der Geschichte), 15
  Ideas Concerning the Philosophy of Human History, 16, 47, 95, 170
  Letters on Humanity (Briefe zur Beförderung der Menschheit), 138
  Spirit of Hebrew Poetry, The, 16
  Treatise on the Origin of Language, 28
Herzberg, Ewald Friedrich, 129
Heyne, Christian Gottlob, 25, 34–35, 85, 144–45, 149, 150

Hitler, Adolf, 94
Hoffmann, Ernst Theodor Amadeus, 42
  Golden Pot (*Der goldene Topf*), 38
Hokenson, Jan Walsch, 177n49
Hölderlin, Friedrich, 42, 86, 94–95
  Hyperion, 95
Holy Roman Empire (German Reich, old Reich), 11, 13–18, 21, 107–10, 115–18, 122, 125, 128–29, 142, 144–45, 147, 152–53, 155, 158, 165, 173
  and Austria, 13–16, 21, 117–18, 129, 135–37, 141, 144–45, 147–48, 170
  and Austrian Netherlands, 117–18, 135
  and Christian universalism, 18, 110
  and colonialism, 11, 53
  and enlightened absolutism, 13–18, 116, 118, 140, 147–48, 154–56, 158, 168, 170, 171
  and federalism, 10, 13, 104, 107–9, 115, 146–47, 158, 160, 173
  and League of Princes (Fürstenbund), 117–18
  and Prussia, 13–16, 21, 109, 117–18, 128–29, 144–47, 150, 158–59, 167–68, 170
Home, Henry, Lord Kames
  Six Sketches of the History of Man, 46, 91, 180n87
Horkheimer, Max, 7, 22
Huber, Ferdinand, 105, 143
Humboldt, Alexander von, 2, 11–12, 19, 21, 47, 60, 64–65, 84, 104, 114–15, 127–29
  Cosmos, 12
  Personal Narrative (*Relation historique*), 44, 178n2
  Views of Nature (*Ansichten der Natur*), 12, 56
Humboldt, Wilhelm von, 84, 95–97, 150

Imperialism (European)
  and cosmopolitanism, 86–87, 99–104, 107–12
  and Enlightenment, 7–10, 17–19, 171–74
  German relation to, 10–12, 53, 86, 104, 107–12, 166–67, 170

Jacobi, Friedrich Heinrich, 35, 36
Japp, Uwe, 180n91
Jones, William, 3, 104–6
Joseph II, emperor, 1, 13–15, 53, 93, 117–18, 135–40, 142, 147–48, 154–56, 158, 170, 171
  See also Holy Roman Empire: and enlightened absolutism

Kant, Immanuel, 1, 3, 20, 86, 93, 98, 102–3, 152, 167, 181n31
  "Defining the Concept of a Human Race" (Bestimmung des Begriffs einer Menschenrasse), 88–92
  "Idea for a Universal History" (Idee zu einer allgemeinen Geschichte), 55, 99
  "On the Different Human Races" (Von den verschiedenen Rassen der Menschen), 88–92
  "What is Enlightenment?," 152, 168
Kappeler, Floran, 176n49
Karl August, duke of Weimar, 3, 42, 117
Kittler, Friedrich, 38
Kleist, Heinrich von, 86
  "On the Marionette Theater," 98
Klopstock, 14
  "Lake Zurich" (Der Zürchersee), 48
Körner, Christian Gottfried, 98
Koselleck, Reinhard, 12–13, 110
  revolution, concept of, 13, 122–23, 128–29, 148
  Sattelzeit, 12–13, 21, 110, 142
Kramsch, Claire, 27
Kumar, Krishnan, 16, 109

Lamb, Jonathan, 178n31, 179n61
Lapérouse, comte de (Jean François de Galaup), 7
La Roche, Sophie von, 104
Larrimore, Mark, 180n11
Leonhardt, Jürgen, 28–29
Lessing, Gotthold Ephraim, 86
Lichtenberg, Georg Christoph, 51, 94
Linnaeus, Carl, 65
Livingstone, David, 91, 180n9, 181n36
Locke, John, 120
  Second Treatise of Government, 67
Louis XVI, king of France, 115, 155–56
Lowe, Lisa, 10, 67
Lubrich, Oliver, 178n2
Lucretius, 47, 173
  On the Nature of Things (*De rerum natura*), 47–48
Lux, Adam, 168

Magellan, Ferdinand, 7
Mainz Republic (Revolution in Mainz), 2, 7, 12, 20, 22, 26, 38, 73, 86, 115, 131, 144–45, 156–61, 164–68, 171–73
  German Jacobin Club, 22, 156–57, 159, 165

Mani, B. Venkat, 2–3, 111, 175n9
Mann, Thomas, 20, 109, 111, 140
Marchand, Suzanne, 8
Maria Theresa, empress, 117
Martin, Alison E., 177n40
Marx, Karl, 82
Maximilian III Joseph, elector of Bavaria, 117
May, Yomb, 181n31
Meiners, Christoph, 2, 20, 85, 86, 89–90, 181n31
    Outline of Human History (*Grundriß der Geschichte der Menschheit*), 89
Mereau, Sophie, 37
Mesmer, Franz, 96
Meyer, Friedrich, 178n30
Michaelis, Johann David, 85, 106
Millar, John
    Observations Concerning the Distinction of Ranks in Society, 46, 180n87
Monolingualism (mother-tongue, multilingualism), 15, 27–30, 42, 103, 176n27
Montagu, John, earl of Sandwich, 31
Montaigne, Michel de, 78
Moorehead, Alan, 83–84
Moretti, Franco, 37
Moritz, Karl Philipp, 4
Möser, Justus, 147, 183n17
Münkler, Herfried, 111
Munson, Marcella, 177n49
Muthu, Sankar, 9–10, 77–78

Napoleon Bonaparte, 4, 98
Neumann, Michael, 178n4
Noot, Heinrich von der, 135, 141
Novalis. *See* Hardenberg, Friedrich von (Novalis)
Noyes, John K., 17

Obeyesekere, Gananath, 52
Özdamar, Emine Sevgi, 27

Paine, Thomas, 26, 120
Piper, Andrew, 29–30, 37, 41
Popkin, Jeremy, 169
Pratt, Mary Louise, 111–12
Prinz, Alois, 176n10
Pugh, David, 140

Race (racism)
    biological, 66, 86
    and civilizing mission, 51, 79, 82, 92–93, 114, 173

and polygenesis, 86, 91, 181n36
and skin color, 76–77, 81, 85, 89, 91, 157
and slavery, 12, 62, 86, 90, 92
and University of Göttingen, 84–90
See also Kant, Immanuel; Meiners, Christoph
Raspe, Rudolf Erich, 32–33
    Surprising Adventures of Baron Munchausen, 32
Reed, T. J., 94
Roach, Joseph, 4
Robertson, Ritchie, 119
Rousseau, Jean-Jacques, 5, 49, 53–54, 99
    Discourse on the Origins of Inequality, 54
    Social Contract, 123
Rubens, Peter Paul, 121

Safranski, Rüdiger, 181n67
Said, Edward W., 7
Saine, Thomas P., 183n4
Sakuntala (*Sakontala*), 3, 18, 87, 98, 100, 104–7, 111–12, 115, 182n87
Sanches, Manuela Ribeiro, 180n31
Sandwich, earl of. *See* Montagu, John, earl of Sandwich
Schama, Simon, 139
Schelling, Friedrich, 49, 65
Schiller, Friedrich, 1, 20, 23, 35, 36, 84, 86, 94–95, 98, 102, 105, 110, 111, 118, 143, 155, 181n67, 182n89
    "Artists, The" (Die Künstler), 97–98
    Don Carlos, 21, 116, 139–40
    "German Greatness" (Deutsche Größe), 107–9
    "Gods of Greece (Die Götter Griechenlands), 86, 95–97, 120
    History of Revolt of the Netherlands (*Geschichte des Abfalls*), 116, 139
    On Naive and Sentimental Poetry, 98
    On the Aesthetic Education of Man, 55–56, 95
    Review of Goethe's *Egmont*, 139
    "Xenia," 2
Schlegel, Friedrich, 2, 6, 23, 106
Schleiermacher, Friedrich, 28, 177n25
Schlieffen, Martin Ernst von, 129
Schlözer, August Ludwig von, 85
Schmidt, Georg, 108–9
Sedgwick, Eve Kosofsky, 176n20
Snow, C. P., 60
Soemmerring, Samuel Thomas, 3–4, 88, 143–44, 175n, 181n37, 181n63

Spencer, Vicki A., 178n25
Spener, Johann Karl Philipp, 5, 24, 25, 33, 34, 35, 37, 39–41, 105, 181n63
Spinoza, Baruch de, 47
Steiner, Gerhard, 115
Stolberg, Friedrich Graf zu, 95–96
Suphan, Bernhard, 182n89

Tang, Chenxi, 10, 48–49, 60, 65
Tautz, Birgit, 11, 180n11
Tawada, Yoko, 27
Thomas, Nicholas, 177n45, 178n8, 179n61
Tieck, Ludwig, 42
Tischbein, Johann Heinrich Wilhelm, 23
Touaillon, Christine, 37
Tuchman, Barbara, 146

Uhlig, Ludwig, 45, 160, 176n17

Vasco da Gama, 7
Venuti, Lawrence, 177n25
Vickers, Nancy J., 5
Vollpracht, Adolf, 25
Voltaire, 14
Vonck, Jan Frans, 135, 141
Vorpahl, Frank, 72, 179n44

Voss, Christian Friedrich, 25, 35, 39–40, 156–57, 184n50

Wales, William, 32–33
Walkowitz, Rebecca, 32
Weber, Eugen, 183n15
Weimar Classicism, 84–87, 94, 174
   See also Age of Goethe
West, Hugh, 180n93
Whaley, Joachim, 17
Wieland, Christoph Martin, 1, 29, 84, 94
Wilke, Sabine, 179n45
Wilson, Jason, 178n2
Winckelmann, Johann Joachim, 86, 94, 121
Wollstonecraft, Mary, 26
Woodmansee, Martha, 36–37
World literature, 2, 3, 19, 30, 32, 45, 110–11
Wulf, Andrea, 64–65

Yildiz, Yasemin, 19, 27–28
Young, Robert, 7–8

Zaimoğlu, Feridun, 27
Zammito, John, 88
Zantop, Susanne, 53, 85–86, 104, 183n28
Zhang, Chunjie, 178n8, 179n45, 179n84, 180n93

www.ingramcontent.com/pod-product-compliance
Lightning Source LLC
Chambersburg PA
CBHW022056290426
44109CB00014B/1119